SNOB WORDS

SNOB WORDS

30 DAYS TO A MORE SOPHISTICATED VOCABULARY

TODD MORRILL

AEROPLANE PRESS

Copyright © 2019 by Todd Morrill

Published in the United States by Aeroplane Press

www.snobwords.com

ISBN: 978-0-5787-0158-5

Printed in the United States of America

10 9 8 7 6 5 4 3 2 1

First Edition

To my parents
and my children,
none of whom
thought I would ever
finish this book.

Surprise!

CONTENTS

Preface xi

PART ONE

PART TWO

PART THREE

Preface

So you want to develop a sophisticated vocabulary. Are you prepared for the blood, sweat, and tears it will take to truly *develop a sophisticated vocabulary?*

Relax—I jest.

There will be no bleeding, sweating, or crying in this course. One, because I don't want to ruin the furniture, and two, because this isn't actually a course. It's simply a series of enlightening conversations between you and me—a series of scintillating *tête-à-têtes,* if you will—at the end of which, in one month, you will have learned 250 important words and phrases that will change your life.

In other words, we're here to have fun: to be *flâneurs* of the lexical landscape.

Forget memorization.

Forget moldy-smelling classrooms.

Forget everything that you've ever learned about learning vocabulary.

We're here to develop a spirit of *bonhomie,* to chat across the cocktail table (the term our friends at *Architectural Digest* now use to refer to the piece of furniture formerly known as the coffee table), to become good friends. When you acquire a snobcabulary in the process (and you will), it will seem like a bonus.

Of course, during our conversations you *will* need to look over some definitions, and yes, we do have things called exercises and exams, but allow me to let you in on a little secret: these are actually *games*. Yes, games designed to let you know how well you're doing, and where you might need to improve.

How fun is that?

And for those of you who can't put down your novels or stop watching Netflix long enough to chat with me for an average of twenty minutes a day, we've incorporated into our visits our own irresistible melodrama/snobcom/saga—*The Expensive Escapades of Marco and Giselle, Professional Beautiful People*—that will keep you on the edge of the couch at all times. It's that good.

Finally, we're going to learn our 250 snob words while traveling the globe. Yes, you heard correctly: we're not going to chat in the same boring place every day. We'll be taking my Learjet to a different location germane to each lesson, and while there, take in sights, sounds, history, culture, and food that will aid us in truly learning that day's snob words.

Don't worry, that's all included in the price of this book. And since I happen to own *pieds-à-terre* all over the world, we won't need to stay in those ghastly five-star hotels. Who knows who bathed in that gold-plated tub before you did?

In other words, this is going to be fun, not work, and I will be your mentor—not your *tormentor*. Our daily visits will be a source of pleasure to you, rather than a fount of stress, grief, or gnashing of teeth.

So, let us go then, you and I....

Todd Morrill, the Word Snob
Founder and Editor-in-Chief
snobwords.com

PART ONE

Day 1

What are Snob Words?
AND WHY SHOULD I LEARN THEM?

LOCATION: **FIFTH AVENUE, NEW YORK CITY**

Welcome to our first lesson! It's a pleasure to meet you. I'll be your Sherpa, your mentor, your *cicerone,* your docent—in other words, your personal vocabulary trainer—on this thirty-day adventure.

Sorry to have kept you waiting. I was playing croquet in the roof garden (or should I say *on* the roof garden?) and didn't hear the bell.

Never played croquet, you say? We'll remedy that soon enough. You like the *boiserie?* Louis Quinze, taken from a Loire Valley château. Thank you, yes, I think it *does* go well with the *parquet de Versailles.*

Since the weather's nice, I thought we'd chat on the terrace, which has a lovely view of Central Park. Right this way. You're correct, this *is* a *prewar apartment.* The plasterwork is original. And yes, the *co-op* board is impossible: it took fifteen years to get permission to create this *duplex!*

Please, have a seat—wherever you'd like—on the *chaise longue,* on that *bergère,* or on one of the *fauteuils.* I want you to be comfortable.

Allow me to present Helga, my housekeeper. Helga, could you be a dear and ask Jean-Claude to prepare a tray of *foie gras, fraises des bois* (with *crème fraîche,* of course)...and perhaps some *Wagyu* tartare? Thank you.

Ah, to be *en plein air.*

OUR MISSION

Now, let's get to the point of why you're here. If I'm not mistaken, it's because you frequently come in contact with words you don't know. Am I right?

Fortunately, most of these unfamiliar words don't pose a problem. For example, if your mechanic says your car needs a new *transaxle,* and you have no idea what that is, you're not embarrassed. *Transaxle* is a term only mechanics and auto aficionados are expected to know.

Likewise, when your doctor says you have *edema* in your elbows, you're not embarrassed to ask for an explanation in plain English, since *edema* (which means 'swelling') is a term generally reserved for medical personnel.

But when the diamond-bedecked woman at your daughter's ballet benefit leans over and confides, *sotto voce,* that the academy's director is her *bête noire* (and you don't know whether to congratulate her or console her) you *are* embarrassed.

Why? Because *bête noire* is a member of a class of highborn, patrician words that educated and cultured people like you are *expected* to know, but often *don't.*

I call these *snob words.*

(Several of the italicized words in the preface, and thus far in this lesson, fit this category. Recognize any of them?)

WHERE SNOB WORDS LURK

Snob words aren't used by the general public, but they do appear frequently in all types of media (including books, magazines, newspapers, television shows, radio programs, and websites) aimed at upscale, educated audiences.

For example, have you ever thumbed through an issue of *Architectural Digest?* If so, you probably felt the immediate need for a French dictionary. The magazine is chock-full of French-based design terms, from *trompe l'oeil* and *faux marbre* to *chinoiserie* and *objet d'art.*

National newspapers, such as the *New York Times* and the *Wall Street Journal,* aren't far behind in their use of snob words. There's rarely a day when these publications fail to include elusive terms like *rara avis, couturier, gravitas,* and *de rigueur.*

And it's not just the printed news that favors fancy-pants parlance: anchors and guests on national television and radio news broadcasts also throw out their fair share of snob words.

Finally, books and websites devoted to artistic, academic, and other esoteric topics are further prime hideouts for snob words.

YOU'RE NEVER SAFE

In addition to their media presence, snob words often raise their hoity-toity heads in the white-collar workplace, where they can help determine promotions...and demotions.

CEOs, college presidents, heads of government agencies, and many others in powerful positions often use snob words, and they expect their subordinates to understand them.

If your boss gives you *carte blanche* to deal with the situation in Peoria, will you jump into action—or jump to google *carte blanche?*

Snob words are also regular interlopers in polite conversation. Say you're chatting with one of the mothers at your son's lacrosse game (the woman who always looks as if she just stepped out of the salon), and she asks your opinion on whether she should add a *loggia* or a *lanai* to her thirty-room villa on *St. Barts.*

Will you be forced to feign a coughing attack?

Or will you confidently launch into an architectural discussion involving one of the Caribbean's ritziest islands?

TYPES OF SNOB WORDS

The truth is, you can't afford to ignore snob words, which come in four flavors—I mean, varieties (I just got back from Rome and I have authentic Italian gelato on my mind):

- **foreign terms**, such as *terra firma* and *en plein air*, snobby ways of saying things that have perfectly good Anglo-Saxon equivalents ('dry land' and 'outdoors');

- **foreign terms** that lack satisfactory or succinct equivalents in English, including the German *Schadenfreude* and the Italian *pizzicato* (we'll learn these words later in the course);

- **English terms**, like *prewar apartment* and *Old Master,* which refer to snooty, artistic, or intellectual concepts largely unknown to the general population (we'll eventually get to these words, too); and finally,

- **names of people and places** that add snob value to text or conversation, including names of artists, fashion designers, exclusive shopping streets, and high-rent residential enclaves. ("I purchased the *Chanel* scarf on *l'avenue Montaigne* and wore it to Lucretia's fête in *the Hamptons.*")

CHECK YOUR SNOB QUOTIENT

More Evian? You haven't touched your pâté! Don't try to tell me you're on a *foie-gras*-free diet.

Let's put our discussion on hold for a moment and take inventory of where you currently stand on the snob-word spectrum. We'll do that by calculating your snob quotient, or SQ.

Set a timer for ten minutes and complete as many questions on the following pretest as you can.

Meanwhile, I'll be playing croquet on the roof.

I. MULTIPLE CHOICE

1. An *atelier* is:
    a. an artist's studio
    b. a painting comprised of three panels
    c. a recent trend
2. *Sfumato* is a:
    a. painting technique that uses high contrast
    b. painting technique that results in no outlines
    c. type of Italian ice cream
3. A *soigné* man:
    a. spends most of his time at the gym
    b. has an Ivy League education
    c. is elegantly dressed and groomed
4. The **opposite** of *au courant* is:
    a. 'behind the times'
    b. 'in the know'
    c. 'on the contrary'
5. Which could be considered an *objet d'art?*
    a. a full-sized replica of the *Venus de Milo*
    b. a Fabergé egg
    c. the *Mona Lisa*
6. *Chinoiserie* is:
    a. French for men's 'chino' pants
    b. a decorating style based on Chinese motifs
    c. French for 'Chinese takeout'
7. The term *dernier cri* refers to:
    a. the latest fashion
    b. the latest stock market update
    c. the most recent crisis
8. A *couturier:*
    a. runs a courier service
    b. appreciates creature comforts
    c. makes bespoke women's clothing

9. A *gourmand:*
   a. has extensive training in the culinary arts
   b. loves to eat, without regard to food quality
   c. appreciates high-quality food

10. *Locavores:*
   a. eat only food produced near their homes
   b. like to eat on trains
   c. enjoy "livin' la vida loca"

ANSWERS: (1) a; (2) b; (3) c (4) a; (5) b; (6) b; (7) a; (8) c; (9) b; (10) a

II. TRUE OR FALSE

(T/F) 11. An *aria* is an operatic composition that usually moves the story forward.

(T/F) 12. *Pizzicato* is Italian for 'cutting pizza ingredients into small pieces.'

(T/F) 13. A *scion* is likely to inherit a large fortune.

(T/F) 14. A *loggia* is a roofed area that's open to the elements on at least one side.

(T/F) 15. Members of the *beau monde* stay in cheap hotels and usually eat at fast-food restaurants.

(T/F) 16. *Enfilade* is an architectural term that refers to a series of aligned doorways.

(T/F) 17. The *glitterati* always wear shiny clothing.

(T/F) 18. If you commit a *faux pas*, you'll be arrested.

(T/F) 19. If someone tells you something *entre nous,* they expect you to share it with everyone.

(T/F) 20. An *orangerie* is a store that sells citrus fruits.

ANSWERS: all false except (13), (14), and (16).

III. DRAWING A BLANK?

Fill the blanks in the statements below using the following list of snob words. Each word is used once.

prewar apartment	the Hamptons
parterre	bel canto
aerie	intermezzo
tapis vert	St. Moritz
pied-à-terre	North Michigan Avenue

21. "We played croquet on the _____."
22. "The villa had a _____ planted with box-wood and begonias next to the swimming pool."
23. "To get the high ceilings, large rooms, and ornate details we wanted, we decided on a _____."
24. "While there's something to be said for opera singers who perform in a forceful Wagnerian style, I prefer the softer, more melodic tones of _____."
25. "Jack wants to go to Martha's Vineyard, but for top restaurants, chic boutiques, and an overall hotter social scene, I prefer a seaside trip to _____."
26. "Joe and Linda just purchased a(n) _____ that overlooks Los Angeles."
27. "There was a(n) _____, or musical interlude, about halfway through the opera.
28. "_____ is the place to buy luxury items in Chicago."
29. "Juan Carlos is looking for a _____ in Buenos Aires—just something small where he can crash after polo matches."
30. "We used to go to Courchevel 1850 for the holidays, but we got tired of the *nouveaux-riches* Russians who frequent the resort. Now we do our skiing in _____.

ANSWERS: (21) tapis vert; (22) parterre; (23) prewar apartment; (24) bel canto; (25) the Hamptons; (26) aerie; (27) intermezzo; (28) North Michigan Avenue; (29) pied-à-terre; (30) St. Moritz

IV. MATCHING

Match each snob word with its definition.

____ 31. *al fresco*   a. movie with a dark mood

____ 32. *au contraire*   b. informal French eatery

____ 33. *en famille*   c. 'in the open air'

____ 34. *dacha*   d. pleasure in others' misfortune

____ 35. *film noir*   e. 'fixed price'

____ 36. *faux marbre*   f. 'on the contrary'

____ 37. *bistro*   g. 'as a family'

____ 38. *prix fixe*   h. Russian country house

____ 39. *Schadenfreude* i. 'between the two of us'

____ 40. *entre nous*   j. painted to look like marble

ANSWERS: (31) c; (32) f; (33) g; (34) h; (35) a; (36) j; (37) b; (38) e; (39) d; (40) i

V. COMPLETE THE STORY

Getting these down?

Time to introduce you to the stars of our course-long melodrama: Giselle Van de Kamp and Marco Grimaldi. We'll get to know them quite well over the next thirty days.

Use the following words to fill the blanks in the passage below. Each word is used only once.

Enjoy!

imbroglio

pas de deux

sotto voce

rara avis

gravitas

petits pois

fraises des bois

jamón ibérico

ad hoc

foie gras

The Expensive Escapades of
MARCO & GISELLE
Professional Beautiful People

Episode One: Meaningless in Milan

Marco Grimaldi, the twenty-six-year-old polo-playing son of a rich Argentine landowner, is in Milan for a polo match.

As he sits alone—handsome and well dressed—at an over-priced sidewalk café, he spies the lovely Giselle Van de Kamp, American heiress to a frozen-food empire, also sitting alone.

MARCO: *Scusi, Signorina.* You are American?

GISELLE: Yes. Yes, I am.

MARCO: You are…alone?

GISELLE: I'm waiting for my mother, who's at the market looking for (41)_____. She takes her berries very seriously.

MARCO: I may join you, then?

GISELLE: Sure. We can share the (42)_____ I just ordered. You know, I've never understood all the hoopla about Spanish ham. I actually prefer American ham.

MARCO: *Ay, Señorita (sitting down next to Giselle)*, I can teach you to appreciate Spanish ham.

GISELLE: You can?

MARCO: Of course! Each country has its specialties. As you know, the French are crazy about (43)_____. But in my country, Argentina, we like *large* peas. We feed the small ones to the pigs.

GISELLE: *(stifling a yawn)* You don't say?

MARCO: Yes, and it is the same with ham. Americans like ham with no taste, but Spaniards like ham with a robust flavor.

GISELLE: So you're saying American ham is inferior?

MARCO: Not exactly. I would not wish to cause an international (44)_____, but I *do* prefer Spanish ham. *(He notices a well dressed woman of a certain age walking down the sidewalk toward them.)* Excuse me, but might that woman be your mother?

GISELLE: Heavens no, that's the Countess of Calabaza, who, unfortunately, is staying in the suite next to ours. She's a real (45)_____.

I'll say this (46)_____, so she won't hear me: *(whispers)* she does ballet in her sleep.

MARCO: In her sleep?

GISELLE: Yes, we hear her every morning around 3 a.m. But this morning was worse than usual. It sounded like someone was dancing with her in a (47)_____.

MARCO: *(with an air of* (48)_____ *)* Maybe it was a ghost.

GISELLE: A ghost with an unusually heavy step! It was as if cannonballs were crashing onto the parquet. We set up a(n) (49)_____ sound barrier by putting our mattresses against the wall, but if it happens again tonight, we'll ask for another suite. We didn't sleep at all on the floor.

MARCO: Speaking of tonight, there's a little French restaurant down the street that has amazing (50)_____. Would you consider joining me for dinner?

ANSWERS: (41) fraises des bois; (42) jamón ibérico; (43) petits pois; (44) imbroglio; (45) rara avis; (46) sotto voce; (47) pas de deux; (48) gravitas; (49) ad hoc; (50) foie gras

HOW'S YOUR SNOB CRED?

Was that so bad? Aren't Marco and Giselle just delightful? Tally your score and double it in order to arrive at your snob quotient. Then consult the table below for your corresponding snob status.

Brace yourself! It could be ugly.

96-100 **Word Snob** (Sorry, you wasted your money on this course. Give the book to a friend! No refunds.)

90-96 **Junior Word Snob** (You've almost got your lexical snob on—but not quite.)

80-90 **Demi-Word Snob** (We've got some work to do.)

70-80 **Word Snob Poseur** (You know just enough to be dangerous!)

60-70 **Word-Snob-in-Progress** (There's hope for you.)

50-60 **Demi-Word Slob** (Sorry—the truth hurts.)

0-50 **Certified Word Slob** (You are hereby under court order to complete this course.)

Happy with your score? If so, congratulations.

If not, congratulations on making the decision to take this thirty-day journey of vocabulary enhancement. *You have no reason to be embarrassed.* We'll eventually learn all fifty snob words included in the pretest, as well as 200 more.

If you put in the time, we'll make a word snob of you. Guaranteed.

WE NOW RETURN TO OUR
FASCINATING DISCUSSION OF SNOB WORDS,
ALREADY IN PROGRESS.

WHY SNOB WORDS PERSIST

The reason snob words *remain* snob words—and inaccessible to the general public—is that they're rarely, if ever, *taught.*

It's unlikely that you ever saw words like *louche, dernier cri,* or *Gesamtkunstwerk* on a spelling test.

And unless you grew up in a penthouse on Manhattan's Upper East Side, or had Harvard professors for parents, you probably didn't hear words like *scion* or *hoi polloi* around the dinner table.

Yes, up until now, snob words have had to be acquired, one by one, over a lifetime of listening and reading. The higher one's social class, the more advanced one's education, and the more cultured one's environment, the easier—and faster—this process has been.

NOW THERE'S A FAST TRACK

But thanks to *Snob Words: 30 Days to a More Sophisticated Vocabulary*, it no longer takes decades to acquire an extensive snobcabulary.

In fact, in just one month, this course will put you well on your way to word snobdom by teaching you the 250 snob words most vital for a cultured and educated person like you to know *now*.

How did I select these important terms? By scouring newspapers, magazines, books, websites, and broadcasts to find the most relevant snob words used most frequently today.

The words fall into a wide range of snobby categories: art, design, architecture, gardening, music, film, high-end real estate, and fashion, to name just a few. But my main criterion in choosing these words was that each one be *practical*.

NO MUSEUM WORDS HERE

This course does not include what I call *museum words,* or terms that appear in dictionaries and vocabulary books, but not in real life.

Saponaceous, meaning 'having the qualities of soap,' is one such word. Is it an interesting word? Perhaps. Is it a practical word? Not at all. Let's face it: you'll never hear, write, or say *saponaceous*. Try a comment like, "My dear, your hands are absolutely *saponaceous!*" and you'll likely get a slap in the face. Yet most vocabulary programs include dozens, if not hundreds, of useless, saponaceousesque words.

Not this one! True snob words are active, busy, in demand—they're not gathering dust in glass cases.

HOW THE COURSE WORKS

In order to most effectively teach you these supremely practical words, I've divided the course into thirty lessons.

Twenty-five of these will present you with ten unique snob words each, along with definitions, pronunciation guides, and study exercises—er, *games*—to help you thoroughly learn each word.

The other five lessons are dedicated to this introduction, two mid-course exams, a final review, and a final exam.

If you'll meet me for just one lesson a day (we'll try to keep it to around twenty minutes per lesson), you'll be the proud owner of a sophisticated snobcabulary within one month.

And don't try to tell me that you don't have twenty minutes a day to devote to this course. Come on, you already paid for it! Give up a few minutes you would normally spend on television, video games, or Facebook. You *do* have time.

Speaking of time, it's time to wrap up this discussion, but I have a few (I'll be brief!) final topics to cover.

A WORD OF WARNING

First, this course contains many words with foreign origins. Please don't assume that these words have the same meanings in their native languages that they have come to have in English, or that they even still *exist* in their native tongues.

For example, the Italian term *alfresco* (or *al fresco*), literally 'in the cool' or 'in the fresh,' was adopted into English more than two hundred years ago, and means, for Anglophones, 'in the open air.' Hence, we often dine *alfresco*.

Today's Italians, however, don't use the term in that sense. To them, to be *al fresco* is to be incarcerated. So don't ask an

Italian if he or she would like to dine *alfresco* unless you enjoy prison cafeterias.

Furthermore, some of the other foreign-based words and phrases we feature in this course have been completely phased out of their original languages.

Take the French snob phrase *je ne sais quoi,* for example, literally, 'I don't know what.' It's used in English to denote a quality—usually a positive one—that's difficult to describe. ("This *Snob Words* course has a certain *je ne sais quoi.*")

But I once made the mistake of using the phrase with a native speaker of French. "You mean 'je ne sais *pas*,' she replied, which is current French for 'I don't know.'

"No," I argued back, "I mean 'je ne sais *quoi*.' There's a difference between 'I don't *know*' and 'I don't know *what*.' "

The native Francophone insisted, however, that she'd never heard the phrase.

As it turns out, English adopted *je ne sais quoi* in the mid-17th century, and modern French no longer uses it. Oops.

My point: use these foreign words and phrases with other speakers and readers of English; do not expect native speakers of the terms' original languages to understand them.

A NOTE ON ITALICS

On a related topic, as you know, foreign terms are, at times, italicized in English. The key words are *at times.* It all depends on context.

The general rule is to italicize, on first use, any foreign term your readers may not know.

If you use the term again (in the same document, paper, book, essay, blog post, or whatever it is you're writing), you have a choice to make. If you think your readers will now recognize and understand the term, put it in regular (Roman) type. If not, keep it in italics.

In this manual, contrary to the rule, we italicize *all* of our snob words (including the ones with foreign origins) *all* of the time. We hope this will keep them fresh in your mind.

FUN WITH PHONETICS

As you're also aware, dictionaries use various (and often confusing) symbols to indicate how words should be pronounced. I've tried to avoid this practice in this course, opting, instead, for a simpler system using familiar combinations of letters from the standard English alphabet.

For example, while some dictionaries use up to three symbols in their phonetic spellings of the Latin term *deus ex machina* ('dā-əs-eks-'mä-ki-nə), I use none: day´-uhs ex MAH´-kuhn-uh.

However, for accuracy, I've been forced, on very few occasions, to use two phonetic symbols: **ō** (the long *o* sound in 'ho, ho, ho') and **ē** (the long *e* sound in 'hee, hee, hee').

STRESS TEST

In order to let you know which part of a word should be stressed, or pronounced the loudest, I've capitalized the stressed syllable and marked it with an accent (in the case of *deus ex machina,* or day´-uhs ex MAH´-kuhn-uh, the stressed syllable is MAH´).

For words that have more than one stressed syllable, such as *intelligentsia,* I've capitalized and accented the primary stress, and simply accented the secondary stress (in-tel´-uh-JENT´-see-uh).

When it comes to stressing the proper syllables of French and French-based words, there's a slight difficulty: unlike words in English, French words do *not* have permanently stressed syllables. Instead, every syllable in French receives nearly equal emphasis, and what Anglophones think of as "stress" generally comes at the end of a phrase. That means French words may seem to be stressed differently in different contexts.

For the pronunciation guides in this manual, I've usually chosen to stress a French-based word the way native speakers stress it when it appears at the end of a phrase. That's generally on the last or next-to-the-last syllable, depending on the word.

This follows the practice of most English dictionaries, but don't be surprised if you hear actual Francophones stressing these words differently at times.

GO SNOBBY OR GO HOME

Many of the snob words featured in this course have two acceptable pronunciations: one based on how a word is (or *was*) pronounced in its original language and the other based on the way the word has come to be pronounced in English.

I've generally chosen the more snobby foreign option, especially if the word has French origins. If you're going to use a snob word, why not go whole hog when pronouncing it?

There's one small problem with this philosophy, however, when it comes to the French *r*. As you're likely aware, the French pronounce the *r* similar to the way Anglophones pronounce the *h* in 'hot,' although the French make the sound a little lower in the throat.

Anglophones are often reluctant to attempt this sound (we assume it's more difficult than it actually is), so in most cases, I haven't tried to replicate it in the pronunciation guides.

However, if you can pull off a French *r*, by all means do it—it's very snobby.

FINALLY...

This introduction took longer than I hoped, but now that our housekeeping's done, let's get your lexical snob on!

Go to bed early tonight, because tomorrow morning we'll travel to Italy to study snobby art words.

Day 2

Smart about Art
PAINTING & DRAWING TERMS

LOCATION: **FLORENCE, ITALY**

B *envenuto a Firenze!* (Welcome to Florence!) I trust you enjoyed our flight on my Learjet, and that you were pleased with the attention of my staff.

Today we learn ten snob words dealing with the art world, so it's perfectly appropriate to hold our session here at my villa in **Fiesole**, a suburb on a hill overlooking historic Florence.

As you're probably aware, Florence is the birthplace of the **Italian Renaissance** (c. 1350-1600), and the artistic techniques developed here more than five hundred years ago are still widely used by contemporary artists.

As a result of its Renaissance achievements, Florence is home to many of the world's greatest works of art. We'll see a few of these while here, including Michelangelo's *David,* Botticelli's *La Primavera,* and Ghiberti's *Gates of Paradise.*

But first, let's get started on our vocabulary. We could go inside, but if it's all right with you, I'd rather stay here in the garden, where we can sniff lemon blossoms, listen to fountains gurgle, and pluck (and eat!) fresh pomegranates as we proceed with our lesson.

Why must we learn snobby art terms? Allow me to recount an experience.

I was in an art gallery one afternoon with my kids when we paused in front of some large Impressionist-style landscapes.

"Did the artist go outside to paint these?" asked Andy, who was ten at the time.

I didn't know, since I'd never heard of the artist, so I asked the stiff, sour-faced woman behind the desk if the paintings had been done outdoors.

This self-anointed High Priestess of Art paused a moment to keep us in suspense. Then she looked down her nose, sniffed, and said, "Yes, they're *plein air*."

There's nothing like art to bring out the snob in people. Whether it's snooty gallery employees, uppity collectors, smug academics, or condescending artists themselves, the art world offers enough snob words to fill a book.

In this lesson, however, we'll focus on ten terms that will prove useful when you visit galleries, read about art in periodicals, discuss art with friends, or buy art for your own collection.

I. PRONOUNCE AND DEFINE

Read over the following list of snob words related to art, paying special attention to their phonetic spellings (in parentheses). Proper pronunciation is very important!

Now say each word aloud several times until it rolls off your tongue like the amazing *pistacchio* gelato they sell down on the corner. (Don't worry, we'll take a gelato break soon.)

1. **chiaroscuro** (key-ah´-roh-SKOO´-roh)
2. **etching**
3. **gouache** (gwahsh)

4. **lithograph** (LITH´-uh-graf)
5. **Old Master**
6. **plein air** (plane-AIR´)
7. **screen print**
8. **sfumato** (sfoo-MAW´-toh)
9. **triptych** (TRIP´-tick)
10. **atelier** (ah´-tell-YAY´)

Recognize any of these terms?

Some of them have foreign origins. Others describe rather complicated processes. But anyone can learn to understand them and use them with a little time and patience.

Let's go over their definitions:

1. ATELIER: (French, 'artist's studio' or 'craftsman's workshop') not a snooty word in its native language. In fact, in France, where everyone from cobblers and mechanics to world-famous sculptors work in *ateliers*, it's a neutral term. We Anglophones have given the word its snob value.

For example, in English, no one would think of using *atelier* to describe a place where you fix cars. Instead, snobby art critics and collectors use the term to refer to the studios of certain artists, especially those who are French or who have worked in France.

One of these is **Pablo Picasso** (1881-1973), the Spanish painter who had his first Paris *atelier* on a winding street in the **Montmartre** district.

2. CHIAROSCURO: (Italian *claro*, 'light,' and *obscuro*, 'dark') the technique of juxtaposing bright and dark areas in a painting to create drama, tension, and three-dimensional effects.

Paintings in the *chiaroscuro* style generally have dark, nearly black backgrounds, while the main subjects shine as if illuminated by spotlights.

Night Watch (1642), by **Rembrandt van Rijn** (1606-69), is frequently cited as a prime example of the *chiaroscuro* technique. It looks as if a police car is shining its headlights on a group of suspects (albeit rich Dutch merchant suspects).

3. GOUACHE: a paint made by mixing watercolor with white paint or glue. You're likely familiar with poster paint, used for signs and banners, which is a form of *gouache*.

Watercolor is transparent, which makes it difficult for artists who use the medium to correct mistakes. *Gouache*, however, is opaque enough to cover underlying paint.

Many famous artists, including Picasso, have worked in *gouache*.

Look for the term on those tiny cardboard rectangles pasted on the walls next to paintings in museums and art galleries.

When you see descriptions such as "gouache on canvas" or "gouache on paper," smile and know that you're one of the few people on earth who actually know what *gouache* is.

4. OLD MASTER: refers to a group of artists, generally painters, as well as their works. The term is not exact, but roughly encompasses artists and works from the period between 1350 (the dawn of the Renaissance) and 1800 A.D.

That means that artists like **Leonardo da Vinci** (1452-1519) and **Michelangelo** (1475-1564) are considered *Old Masters*, but **Claude Monet** (1840-1926) and **Vincent van Gogh** (1853-90) are not.

Likewise, da Vinci's *Mona Lisa* (begun around 1503) is an *Old Master*, while van Gogh's *Irises* (1889) is not.

An *Old Master* designation *may* signify high quality, but not necessarily, since auction houses use the term chronologically. As a result, auctions of *Old Masters* may include masterpieces as well as works of lesser quality from the period.

5. **PLEIN AIR**: (French, 'open air') used to describe paintings executed outdoors, as well as the practice of painting or sketching outside, known as painting *en plein air*.

Artists began making outdoor sketches in the 17th century, but the invention of paint tubes in the late 19th century made it practical to bring paintings to near completion outside.

Painting *en plein air* became the norm for **Impressionists**, especially for Monet, who did most of his painting outdoors.

6. **SFUMATO**: if you've ever driven around Los Angeles, you've experienced this phenomenon. Through the smog, everything takes on a misty, ethereal quality—Golden Arches meld imperceptibly with the San Gabriel Mountains, palm fronds dissipate into the gray of the Disneyland Matterhorn.

It's all very delightful until you remember that deadly PM-10s are responsible for the effect.

Fortunately, the *sfumato* technique used in paintings won't give you lung cancer. The term, which comes from the Italian *fumo* ('smoke'), describes the process of blending colors so carefully that they merge without a visible outline, resulting in a "smoky," soft-focus look.

Leonardo da Vinci was a pioneer of the *sfumato* style, which was in stark contrast to the earlier Italian tradition of sharp outlines. You can see *sfumato* at work in the ***Mona Lisa***, especially where the subject's right cheek blends imperceptibly with her hair.

7. **TRIPTYCH**: (rhymes with *cryptic*) a painting or carving consisting of three separate canvases or panels meant to be displayed as a group.

The term comes from the Greek *triptychos*, 'having three folds,' a word both the ancient Greeks and Romans employed to refer to a hinged writing tablet made of three panels.

Medieval and Renaissance artists used this hinged, three-piece format to produce easy-to-transport altarpieces.

Modern artists like **Roy Lichtenstein** (1923-97) and **David Hockney** (b. 1937) have also used the *triptych* format.

BONUS WORD: a **diptych** (DIP'-tik) is a painting or carving consisting of *two* panels.

The final three words in this lesson are types of **prints**. A *print* is a work of art printed on paper through a mechanical process.

In contrast to original works of art, such as oil paintings or watercolors, *prints* can be mass produced, making them generally less valuable. Artists often attempt to increase the value of their *prints* by issuing them in limited editions and by signing and numbering each copy.

8. ETCHING: to make this type of print, an artist begins by drawing a design on a wax-coated metal plate using an *etching* needle. Wherever the needle touches the plate, it removes wax and exposes metal. Once the design is finished, the plate is placed in an acid bath, which "bites" indentations into the exposed metal areas.

The plate is later inked and wiped clean, leaving ink in the indentations only. When paper is pressed firmly against the plate, the ink adheres to it, creating the design.

The first dated *etching* is from 1513, but Rembrandt, who worked in the following century, is often considered the master of the genre.

9. LITHOGRAPH: a type of print created through *lithography*, a process developed in Germany around 1800. Because the process is time-consuming and technical, most artists simply produce designs for *lithographs* and hire skilled technicians to make the actual prints.

To begin the *lithographic* process, a technician transfers an artist's design to a zinc or aluminum plate using oil-based ink. (Originally, a piece of limestone was used instead of a plate—hence the name, *lithography*, from the Greek *lithos*, stone, and *graphein*, to write.)

The plate is then moistened with water and coated with additional oil-based ink. Because water and oil don't mix, the new ink adheres only to the previously-inked design.

To form a print, the plate is pressed against a piece of paper, which picks up the inked design. The process can be repeated an unlimited number of times by re-inking the plate.

Many contemporary artists produce *lithographs*, but two masters of the genre, both from 19th-century France, were **Honoré Daumier** (1808-79) and **Henri de Toulouse-Lautrec** (1864-1901).

10. SCREEN PRINT: a print made through the process of *screen printing*, in which paint is forced through a mesh screen stretched over a wooden frame.

The technique is also referred to as *silkscreen printing*, since early screens were made exclusively of silk. Today, screens are also made of cotton, nylon, and metal.

To produce a *screen print*, an artist applies varnish or wax to a screen wherever he or she does *not* want the paint to pass through (the negative).

The artist then places the screen over a piece of paper and uses a rubber blade to force paint through the unvarnished or unwaxed areas of the mesh. This creates the positive design.

Screen printing was invented around 1900, but it didn't become widely used as a fine art medium until the **Pop artists** took it up in the 1960s.

A member of that group, **Andy Warhol** (1928-87), created a series of *screen prints* of Campbell's Soup cans, one of which sold for $9 million in 2010.

II. FILL IN THE BLANKS

Bewitching as this garden is, it's time to head to the center of Florence, where we'll take a look at one of the world's most famous sculptures: Michelangelo's *David*.

As we drive through these narrow, history-oozing streets in my red Lamborghini, fill each blank below with the snob word that best matches the given definition.

plein air	screen print
Old Master	chiaroscuro
sfumato	lithograph
gouache	atelier
etching	triptych

1. _____ painting that consists of three panels or canvases
2. _____ technique of painting outdoors
3. _____ French word for artist's studio
4. _____ technique of blending colors so that few distinct outlines remain
5. _____ painter or painting from the period between 1350 and 1800 A.D.
6. _____ print made by forcing paint through a mesh screen
7. _____ technique of juxtaposing areas of light and shadow in a painting
8. _____ print made by "biting" a design into a metal plate using acid
9. _____ paint made of watercolor mixed with white paint or glue
10. _____ print made through a process that transfers a design to a piece of limestone or metal plate

ANSWERS: (1) triptych; (2) plein air; (3) atelier; (4) sfumato; (5) Old Master; (6) screen print; (7) chiaroscuro; (8) etching; (9) gouache; (10) lithograph

III. TRUE OR FALSE

We have now arrived at the **Galleria dell'Accademia,** the museum that houses the *David.*

Don't mind the line—I know the director. *Grazie!* Right this way. There it is. Larger than you thought? It's seventeen feet tall, made to be placed on a rooftop and seen from below.

As we let the majesty sink in, test your knowledge of today's snob words with the following true-or-false game:

(T/F)   1. Painters use *chiaroscuro* to add drama and tension to their works.

(T/F)   2. Monet painted *plein air* scenes of the interiors of chic Paris apartments.

(T/F)   3. The *etching* process originally made use of a piece of limestone.

(T/F)   4. *Atelier* is French for 'art gallery.'

(T/F)   5. Andy Warhol used the *sfumato* technique to create his paintings of Campbell's Soup cans.

(T/F)   6. Leonardo da Vinci painted a famous *lithograph* on the wall of a monastery.

(T/F)   7. *Gouache* is opaque enough to cover previous work.

(T/F)   8. Three separate panels or canvases meant to be displayed together form a *triptych.*

(T/F)   9. *Screen prints* are generally more valuable when produced in limited editions and signed and numbered by the artist.

(T/F) 10. If an auction house categorizes a painting as an *Old Master*, it must be of high quality.

ANSWERS: all false except (1), (7), (8), and (9).

IV. MULTIPLE CHOICE

Our next stop is the **Uffizi Gallery**, where we'll take a look at *La Primavera* (*Spring*, c. 1480). This important Renaissance painting, by **Sandro Botticelli** (1445-1510), features nine elegant figures in a lavish garden (google the image).

Zephyrus, the west wind, is seen breathing life into the goddess Flora, who represents spring. The other figures include Venus, Mercury, and the Three Graces, all dressed in elaborate costumes and surrounded by jewel-toned fruits and flowers.

I could spend all day here, but I imagine you'd like that gelato break I promised you. Don't like pistachio? No worries, try the *cioccolato* (chocolate), *stracciatella* (vanilla with chocolate flakes), or the *frambola* (strawberry). Or try them all!

Meanwhile, let's play a multiple-choice game:

1. Monet's *atelier* in Giverny contained:
    a. olive oil
    b. oil paint
    c. motor oil
2. Who used the *screen print* technique?
    a. Pop artists
    b. Impressionists
    c. Byzantine monks
3. The etching process includes placing a metal plate in:
    a. an offset press
    b. etching solution
    c. acid
4. If you're not sure of your painting's composition, and plan to experiment, you'd be wise to use:
    a. watercolor
    b. India ink
    c. gouache

5. The *chiaroscuro* technique uses contrasting areas of:
   a. light and shadow
   b. red and green
   c. matte and gloss
6. Artists who paint *en plein air* complete all, or at least most, of a painting:
   a. on the plains
   b. outdoors
   c. in a helicopter
7. The term *Old Master* refers to the period between:
   a. 1800 B.C. and 1350 B.C.
   b. the dawn of the Renaissance and 1800 A.D.
   c. 1800 A.D. and the present
8. Limestone was originally used in the process of:
   a. lithography
   b. etching
   c. screen printing
9. *Sfumato* comes from the Italian word for:
   a. fumes
   b. smoke
   c. tomato
10. A painting consisting of three separate panels is a:
    a. triptych
    b. polyptych
    c. diptych

ANSWERS: (1) b; (2) a; (3) c; (4) c; (5) a; (6) b; (7) b; (8) a; (9) b; (10) a

V. WHAT WOULD YOU SAY?

Did you enjoy your gelato? Next time try *albicocca,* which is apricot. Amazing.

Now let's walk to the **Piazza del Duomo**. Here, next to the Cathedral of Florence, or **Duomo**, we'll find the **Baptistery**, which features a pair of seventeen-foot gilt-bronze doors that Michelangelo described as "worthy to be the doors of paradise."

Now known as the *Gates of Paradise,* the doors, completed in 1452 by **Lorenzo Ghiberti** (1378-1455), are composed of ten panels that depict scenes from the Old Testament.

The doors revolutionized the art world the moment they were set in place because of their use of the newly discovered technique of linear perspective, as well as their highly realistic depictions of the human form.

As we gaze on these masterpieces (actually very good copies, since the real doors are in a nearby museum), let's get to the whole point of this unit—making these art terms your own.

Below you'll find ten real-life art scenarios in which you could easily find yourself. Fill each blank with a snob word from this lesson. Each word will be used only once; make words plural where necessary.

(en) plein air	**screen print**
Old Master	**chiaroscuro**
sfumato	**lithograph**
gouache	**atelier**
etching	**triptych**

1. You're in the Metropolitan Museum of Art with your significant other. You come across the *Merode Altarpiece* by Robert Campin, which consists of three separate panels. "Look at that amazing _____!" you shout.

2. You're outside in a park when you notice a woman behind an easel working on an oil painting. "How charming," you say, "she's painting _____."

3. You're in the Louvre with your mother-in-law, who adores the paintings of Leonardo, Rembrandt, and Canaletto. After two hours of looking at Renaissance, 17th-, and 18th-century paintings, you say, "Let's go see something more recent—I've seen enough _____."

4. You're in the Musée Toulouse-Lautrec, in Albi, France, which has a collection of advertising posters designed by Henri Toulouse-Lautrec. Your daughter says the posters are *etchings*, but since they were printed using a piece of limestone, you insist they're _____.

5. During a visit to the Hermitage Museum in St. Petersburg, Russia, you discover Leonardo da Vinci's *Madonna with a Flower*. A business acquaintance points out that the Virgin's fingers seem to meld imperceptibly with the Christ Child's chest. "Yes," you say, "that's a superb example of _____."

6. You're surfing the internet for vacation rentals in France when you come across an ad for a charming apartment, which the owner claims was Picasso's first studio in Paris. You quickly call to book the place. Since the owner speaks no English, and you don't speak much French, you simply say, "Rent…Picasso's… _____."

7. As you tour the National Gallery in Washington, D.C., your guide points out a work she says was done by "biting" an image onto a metal plate. "That must be a(n) _____!" you say to yourself.

8. At the National Gallery in London, you admire Leonardo da Vinci's *Virgin of the Rocks*. A stranger approaches and says, "I studied art history in college, but I can't remember what it's called when an artist uses dramatic juxtapositions of light and dark." "Simple," you say, "that's _____."

9. You're in an art supply store, looking for a present for your daughter—something that will encourage her to be artistic. First you consider a set of watercolors, but then you remember what a perfectionist she is. You decide that _____ might be a better option.

10. Your decorator has found exactly what your dining room needs: a rare Andy Warhol work on paper called *Beware of Dog*. When you see the price, you say, "Surely you jest! Twenty-thousand dollars for a(n) _____?"

ANSWERS: (1) triptych; (2) en plein air; (3) Old Masters; (4) lithographs; (5) sfumato; (6) atelier; (7) etching; (8) chiaroscuro; (9) gouache; (10) screen print

How did you do on this last exercise?

Ready to face the cold, cruel art world on your own?

Congratulations are in order because you've now learned your first ten snob words. Was that so bad? Now you can visit art galleries and museums with confidence, and you can discuss art with friends and acquaintances without embarrassment.

Rest up for tomorrow! We'll be traveling to Paris to tackle snob adjectives with French origins.

Day 3

Excuse My French
FRANCOPHONE ADJECTIVES

LOCATION: **PARIS, FRANCE**

Where better to study French snob words than in Paris? Welcome to my *hôtel particulier,* the French term for a large and elegant townhouse (we'll learn the term in depth on Day 13 when we study real estate snob words).

My townhouse is located in the **Triangle d'Or** (Golden Triangle), the premier luxury district of the city. It's a short walk to the famed **Champs-Elysées**, as well as to **Avenue Montaigne**, the snootiest shopping street in Paris.

We'll eventually see these places, but let's begin today's discussion on my second-story terrace, which has a wonderful view of the *parterres* (see Day 12) in the formal garden.

This is just the first of several days we'll devote to French snob words, so let's start off with a little history. French words have had snob appeal in English since at least 1066. That's the year **William, Duke of Normandy** (William the Conqueror), invaded England, proclaimed himself king, seized the estates of the native Anglo-Saxon nobles, and granted them to his Norman warriors.

As a result, Anglo-French, based on 11th-century Norman French, became the language of the English aristocracy, as well as the language of English government and culture.

French remained the official language of the island's bureaucracy and courts for the next three hundred years, until Parliament passed a statute in 1362 requiring all government proceedings to take place in English.

But by that time, there was no turning back, because English had adopted thousands of French words. For example, thanks to the Norman conquerors, words dealing with *meat* became Frenchified: Anglophones now eat *pork* instead of *pig, beef* instead of *cow,* and *mutton* instead of *sheep.* (Imagine sitting down to *pig chops* rather than *pork chops,* or *cow stew* rather than *beef stew.* Just doesn't sound as appetizing.)

The French invasion applied to more than food, however. In this lesson we present ten French-based adjectives that describe people, places, and things in a snobby way.

But before we begin to pronounce these words, let's take a quick look at the French *accent aigu* (´), or acute accent, used on two of our snob words. When placed over an **é**, this accent gives the letter an 'ay,' sound, as in *consommé.*

Dictionaries vary on which adopted French words retain their accents and which do not, but play it safe and use them. These little foreign marks make snob words even snobbier.

I. PRONOUNCE & DEFINE

Say each of the following words aloud several times, paying close attention to their phonetic spellings. As we've already mentioned, pronunciation is very important.

In fact, if you're not confident about pronouncing a certain snob word, don't pronounce it at all. A mispronounced snob word will lose all snob value and leave you sounding like a fool.

Likewise, pay close attention to the *spelling* of these words. A misspelled snob word will also backfire on you.

    1. **chic** (sheek)
    2. **chichi** (SHEE´-shee)
    3. **soigné** (swahn-YAY´)
    4. **de trop** (duh-TROH´)
    5. **par excellence** (pahr´-ek-suh-LAWNS´)

Now consider these words in sentences that hint at their meanings.

1. Carol has a natural *chic* that comes with being French: she could accessorize a burlap bag and come off looking stunning.
2. Amy's wedding dress is covered in hundreds of tiny Swarovski crystals, yards of Portuguese lace, and dozens of fine satin bows, but the effect of this unrestrained finery is *chichi,* not stylish.
3. Once Jessica had set the table, she realized one centerpiece was enough—the other four were *de trop.*
4. The wedding bouquets, the most beautiful we had ever seen, were obviously the work of a florist *par excellence.*
5. Kyle, whom Daniela had met at the surf competition, looked surprisingly *soigné* after he cut his hair and put on a tuxedo.

NOTE: when *soigné* describes a woman, it's spelled **soignée**.

II. FILL IN THE BLANKS

As we continue our chat, let's stroll down **Avenue Montaigne** (we'll explore it in depth on Day 23), home to some of luxury shopping's biggest names, including Chanel, Prada, Dolce & Gabbana, Louis Vuitton, and Gucci.

While we window-shop, match the following snob words with their definitions:

chichi   chic
soigné   de trop
par excellence

1. _____ elegantly dressed and well groomed
2. _____ supreme; the best of its kind
3. _____ fashionable; stylish; assertiveness
                    and confidence in dress
4. _____ unwelcome; too much; in the way
5. _____ pretentious; fussy or frilly; trying to
                    be stylish, but falling short

ANSWERS: (1) soigné; (2) par excellence; (3) chic; (4) de trop; (5) chichi

NOTES:

Be careful with the term *chichi.* While occasionally used as a synonym for *chic,* it's more often used in the negative sense described above. If someone says your outfit is *chichi,* it's probably not a compliment.

Also, *chic* is both an adjective and a noun: you can *be* chic and *have* chic. Remember that *chic* is used more frequently to describe women than men (*chic* woman = *dapper* man).

Finally, *soigné(e)* and *chic* are sometimes used as synonyms, but there's a distinction: *soigné* means well groomed and appropriately dressed. It also means sleek and elegant.

Chic, on the other hand, refers to a clever stylishness and confidence in dress. A *chic* woman is not a slave to fashion, but rather adapts current styles to her own personality.

Chic can also mean 'fashionable' and 'stylish' in regard to things other than fashion, e.g., a *chic* apartment.

III. PRONOUNCE & DEFINE

As we proceed with our promenade, here are five more descriptive snob words from French for you to pronounce.

> 6. **gauche** (gōsh)
> 7. **comme il faut** (kuh´-meal-FOE´)
> 8. **de rigueur** (duh´-ree-GRR´)
> 9. **au courant** (oh´-coo-RAWN´)
> 10. **outré** (ooh-TRAY´)

Again, try to guess at the definitions of these words from their use in the following sentences:

1. Would it be *gauche* to ask the countess her age?
2. When Patricia's fifteen-year-old son began jumping on the sofa, Sarah realized things were not *comme il faut* in that household.
3. For a male lifeguard on the Jersey Shore, a tattoo is *de rigueur.*
4. Denise's father is *au courant* when it comes to national politics and the NFL, but in the case of fashion, he's decades behind.
5. The art in Eleanor's living room—including a nine-foot sculpture made entirely of chewing gum—is decidedly *outré.*

IV. FILL IN THE BLANKS

Now match these snob words with their definitions:

gauche	**au courant**
outré	**de rigueur**
comme il faut	

1. _____ outrageous; unusual; startling
2. _____ required by fashion or etiquette
3. _____ aware of the latest news and
   trends; up to date
4. _____ socially inappropriate
5. _____ as things should be; proper

ANSWERS: (1) outré; (2) de rigueur; (3) au courant; (4) gauche; (5) comme il faut

V. TRUE OR FALSE

We're coming up on the **Hôtel Plaza Athénée**, where we'll have lunch at **Alain Ducasse**, a Michelin three-star restaurant that pairs midcentury-modern furnishings with Corinthian columns and elaborate plaster ceilings.

As we wait—under the massive chandelier—for our Breton lobster and white asparagus to arrive, let's play this game:

(T/F) 1. A *gauche* person lacks social awareness.
(T/F) 2. A naturally *chic* woman relies on her friends for fashion guidance.
(T/F) 3. Paying income tax is *de rigueur* in the U.S.
(T/F) 4. If something is *de trop*, you want more of it.
(T/F) 5. An *au courant* person is uninformed.
(T/F) 6. In order to look *soigné*, a man should at least comb his hair and put on a clean shirt.
(T/F) 7. *Chic* people usually dine at *chichi* restaurants.
(T/F) 8. If something is *comme il faut*, it is illegal.
(T/F) 9. An *outré* idea is appropriate and conventional.
(T/F) 10. Top restaurants employ chefs *par excellence*.

ANSWERS: all false except (1), (3), (6), and (10).

VI. OPPOSITES

Before we return to my *hôtel particulier,* let's wander over to the Champs-Elysées, the wide boulevard that links two of the city's most impressive traffic circles: **Place Charles de Gaulle** (home to the **Arc de Triomphe**) and **Place de la Concorde.**

This was once the most elegant street in Paris, but its snob cred has suffered with the appearance of chain stores and fast food outlets. As we take a quick stroll, match each snob word below with the definition most **opposite** its actual meaning.

_____	1. *outré*	a.	optional; not necessary
_____	2. *chic*	b.	unkempt; poorly dressed
_____	3. *de rigueur*	c.	behind the times
_____	4. *comme il faut*	d.	improper; not the norm
_____	5. *par excellence*	e.	welcome; desired
_____	6. *de trop*	f.	elegant; tastefully in style
_____	7. *au courant*	g.	socially adept; graceful
_____	8. *soigné*	h.	conservative; usual; expected
_____	9. *chichi*	i.	of the lowest quality
_____	10. *gauche*	j.	lacking fashion confidence

ANSWERS: (1) h; (2) j; (3) a; (4) d; (5) i; (6) e; (7) c; (8) b; (9) f; (10) g

VII. SNOB APPEAL

How did those opposites turn out for you? A little tricky? Time for a little more practice.

Fill the blanks in the following statements with snob words from this lesson. Each word is used only once.

chic	gauche
chichi	comme il faut
soigné	de rigueur
de trop	au courant
par excellence	outré

1. "Susan and I have made an effort to include Diane in our activities all these years, but to tell the truth, she's always been _____."

2. "Lily asked how much I paid for the Aston Martin. I've never known anyone so _____ !"

3. "Sheila, you are always stuck in last season! Why can't you be _____, like me?"

4. "Yes, Mary was in charge of the charity banquet. What an _____ event! The waiters, dressed as hula dancers, served dessert first and ended with soup."

5. "Peggy tries, bless her heart, but she doesn't know when to stop. Two chocolate fountains would have been classy, but six made the wedding look _____."

6. "Baker, the CFO, says that Miller will be axed before next quarter. He says Miller's division has problems—it's not exactly _____."

7. "A black leather tote is absolutely _____ this season! Both Catherine Deneuve and Anna Wintour carried them at the Paris collections."

8. "I've never seen anyone look as _____ as our Danny did at the rehearsal dinner. He's always been handsome, of course, but his Hugo Boss suit was such a change from his usual jeans and T-shirts."

9. "Jean-Michel, I absolutely love it! It looks just like me!" (Three kisses on alternating cheeks.) "You truly are a sculptor _____ !"

10. "Louise always looks _____, and she does it all herself: no stylists, no makeup artists, no designers on call."

ANSWERS: (1) de trop; (2) gauche; (3) au courant; (4) outré; (5) chichi; (6) comme il faut; (7) de rigueur; (8) soigné; (9) par excellence; (10) chic

VIII. COMPLETE THE STORY

Felicitations! (That's 'congratulations' in French.)

You now have ten French terms in your snobbery arsenal that you can use to describe everything from breakfast cereal to caviar.

As we return to my *hôtel particulier,* let's relax in the garden—which is so shady and cool this time of day—as we complete our final activity.

Surprise! Marco and Giselle are here to help you review today's terms.

Fill the blanks in the following passage with snob words from this lesson. Each word is used once.

chic	gauche
chichi	comme il faut
soigné	de rigueur
de trop	au courant
par excellence	outré

The Expensive Escapades of
MARCO & GISELLE
Professional Beautiful People

Episode Two: Soigné Lake

As you'll remember from *Episode One,* Marco Grimaldi is the handsome and (1)_____ son of a rich Argentine landowner.

Marco is also a polo player (2)_____ who flies to matches around the world in his private jet. Of course, for someone who travels so frequently, a private plane is (3)_____.

Taking commercial flights—even first class—would not be (4)_____.

Giselle Van de Camp, heiress to a food-processing fortune, grew up on the Upper East Side, a (5)_____ section of Manhattan. The twenty-three-year-old natural blonde tries to stay (6)_____ with fashion, although her mother finds her taste more (7)_____ than stylish. Giselle's father finds her outfits—in the style of early Lady Gaga—"decidedly (8)_____."

One weekend in late May, Marco and Giselle have a second chance encounter, this time at Italy's Lake Como.

The following thoughts pass through their lovely heads the moment they see each other:

MARCO'S THOUGHTS: I would like to speak to her again, but the insect antennae protruding from her coiffure—quite (9)_____, in my opinion—are making me nervous.

GISELLE'S THOUGHTS: I can't ignore him, because he knows I saw him. But why is he wearing that gaucho-style poncho with Gucci loafers? Can you say (10)_____?

ANSWERS: (1) soigné; (2) par excellence; (3) de rigueur; (4) comme il faut; (5) chic; (6) au courant; (7) chichi; (8) outré; (9) de trop; (10) gauche

You're making progress! You've now mastered twenty of the 250 snob words in this course.

Give yourself a pat on the back.

We'll stay here in Paris tonight, and tomorrow we'll take on a new set of snob words—ten terms from interior design.

Day 4

Parlez-vous Interior Decorating?
DESIGN FRENCH

LOCATION: **PARIS, FRANCE**

Shelter magazines, those glossy monthlies that focus on home décor, should carry this warning: **You must be fluent in Design French to fully understand this publication.**

Do these slick journals pay their writers according to the number of Gallic terms they can work into each article? It certainly seems so, because from the moment you open their pages, you're bombarded with words like *objet d'art, trompe l'oeil, boiserie,* and *chinoiserie,* to name just a few.

But don't despair. By the end of this lesson, you'll know how to pronounce these supercilious-sounding words, you'll understand what they mean, and you'll be confident enough to use them in your own writing, conversation, and decorating.

For today's discussion, we'll move over to my *pied-à-terre* (a temporary or second lodging, see Day 13) on the **Place des Vosges**, a stunning 17th-century square in the **Marais** district. (Yes, I maintain two homes in Paris. Don't judge me.)

Actually, compared to my townhouse in the Triangle D'Or, my place in the Marais isn't much—a simple *duplex* (two-level apartment, see Day 13) on the fifth and sixth floors of one of the grand brick and stone buildings surrounding the square.

Speaking of the square, a lovely spot furnished with lime trees, fountains, and an equestrian statue of Louis XIII, let's begin our lesson here.

I. PRONOUNCE & DEFINE

1. **boiserie** (BWAHZ´-ree)
2. **étagère** (ay-tah-ZHAIR´)
3. **objet d'art** (ōb-zhay DAHR´)
4. **bergère** (bear-ZHAIR´)
5. **fauteuil** (foh-TAY´-yuh)
6. **chaise longue** (shez LOAN´-guh)
7. **chinoiserie** (sheen-WAHZ´-ree)
8. **passementerie** (poss-MAHN´-tree)
9. **trompe l'oeil** (trohmp LAY´)
10. **ancien régime** (ahn-syahn ray-ZHEEM´)

NOTE: the 'yuh' at the end of *fauteuil* and the 'guh' at the end of *chaise longue* are pronounced quickly and softly.

Now take a look at the following definitions:

1. BOISERIE: (French for 'wood paneling' in general) when used in English, the term usually refers to the various styles of elaborate paneling used to adorn the 17th- and 18th-century palaces and noble residences of Europe.

Boiserie of this type consists of large panels of fine wood, such as oak or mahogany, painted or stained in various colors and carved with decoration in shallow relief.

In the **Rococo** style (18th century), for example, *boiserie* was often painted white with decoration picked out in gold.

2. ÉTAGÈRE: a piece of furniture consisting of a number of open shelves.

Etagères are used to display small precious objects such as ceramics, curios, and other *objets d'art* (see below).

3. OBJET D'ART: (French for 'art object') a small decorative object that one might place in an *étagère*. (Be careful with the plural: it's *objets d'art*, not *objet d'arts*.)

To qualify as an *objet d'art*, a piece must possess a certain degree of artistic merit. Examples include jeweled items meant for display (such as Fabergé eggs), fine glassware, porcelain figurines, small vases, and miniature paintings.

In addition to finding homes in *étagères*, *objets d'art* are often displayed on coffee (cocktail?) tables, desks, and side tables.

4. FAUTEUIL: (French for 'armchair') a chair with a partially exposed wooden frame, meaning it has open spaces between its arms and its seat (google some images).

Fauteuils generally have upholstered seats, while their backs may or may not be upholstered.

The word *fauteuil* came into French from an Old German word for 'folding chair'—*faltistuol*.

While *fauteuils* aren't foldable, they're light enough to pull up to the fire or to move across the room to join a conversation.

5. BERGÈRE: an armchair with closed arms, meaning it has upholstery in the area between the arms and the seat.

Most antique *bergères* have rounded backs and wide seats designed to accommodate the large dresses worn by society women in the 18th century.

6. CHAISE LONGUE: (plural, *chaises longues*) a long upholstered chair designed to allow a single person to recline. (We're not talking about La-Z-Boys—*chaises longues* have no moving parts.)

Chaises longues exist in many styles, from the 18th-century carved wooden versions made for Marie Antoinette to stark modern styles with metal frames that resemble black leather beach chairs. While modern *chaises longues* don't always have arms, most antique versions have an armrest on at least one side.

Chaises longues are often mistakenly referred to as *chaise* (mispronounced "chase") *lounges*. Please don't do this or you'll be *chased* right out of the country club.

7. **CHINOISERIE**: a decorative style in which Chinese motifs, authentic or dreamed up by Westerners, are applied to furniture, wallpaper, porcelain, and other decorative accessories. The style was especially popular in the 18th century.

Some antique *chinoiserie* was actually made in China (often with designs tailored specifically to the Western market), but much of it was produced in the West.

For example, renowned English furniture maker **Thomas Chippendale** (1718-79) designed many pieces in what he called the "Chinese style." These included chairs and bookcases with elaborate fretwork, beds shaped like pagodas, and mirrors in the form of Chinese lanterns.

Chinoiserie is still popular today, often as part of the eclectic **English country house** style.

8. **PASSEMENTERIE**: remember the tassels and fringe on your grandmother's curtains?

Those decorative elements—including braiding and other types of trim used on bed canopies, upholstered furniture, and throw pillows—are collectively called *passementerie.*

Not as popular today as in centuries past, *passementerie* still adds the final touch of elegance to formal and period rooms.

High quality *passementerie* is expensive, since much of it must be made by hand. That's why your parents made you stay away from grandma's drapes.

9. **TROMPE L'OEIL**: (French, 'deceives the eye') a visual illusion that tricks the viewer into seeing flat, painted detail as three-dimensional.

While the technique appears in fine art from time to time (figures crawling out of frames, insects that seem to be camped out on the canvas), the term generally refers to decorative painting such as murals and faux finishes.

For example, *trompe l'oeil* techniques can be used to make an indoor room seem surrounded by garden trellises or to make wooden surfaces look like stone.

10. **ANCIEN RÉGIME**: (French for 'old rule') the sociopolitical system in France prior to the **French Revolution** (1789-99).

In a design sense, the term refers to the pre-revolutionary decorative styles used by French royals and aristocrats, most notably during the reigns of Louis XIV (Baroque), Louis XV (Rococo), and Louis XVI (neoclassical).

While each of these styles was unique, they all made use of the finest materials and craftsmanship.

II. MATCHING

Any questions? As we discuss these snob terms, let's take a five-minute stroll to **Le Village Saint-Paul**, one of the city's most important art and antiques markets.

As we walk, take five of our new words and match them with their definitions:

____ 1. *boiserie*   a. small object with artistic merit

____ 2. *étagère*   b. light armchair with exposed arms

____ 3. *objet d'art*   c. armchair with closed arms

____ 4. *bergère*   d. fine wood paneling

____ 5. *fauteuil*   e. set of open shelves

ANSWERS: (1) d; (2) e; (3) a; (4) c; (5) b

Now do the same with the remaining five words:

___ 6. *chaise longue*   a. 'long chair'
___ 7. *chinoiserie*   b. 'old rule'
___ 8. *passementerie*   c. decorative fringe and tassels
___ 9. *trompe l'oeil*   d. Chinese-style furnishings
___ 10. *ancien régime*   e. 'trick the eye'

ANSWERS: (6) a; (7) d; (8) c; (9) e (10) b

III. MULTIPLE CHOICE

We've now entered Le Village Saint-Paul, where a delightful *mélange* of furniture, art, and housewares spills out of crowded shops into cobbled squares and alleys.

Here we'll see our decorating snob words in action. As we gawk at *objets d'art* while looking for *bergères* from the *ancien régime*, I'll quiz you on this lesson's snob words.

1. Tom came home from work and spread out on a long chair in front of the fire. Tom lay down on a:
   a. *chaise longue*
   b. *chaise lounge*
   c. *bergère*

2. The dining room walls are painted to give the impression that one is inside a pagoda. This technique is called:
   a. *fauteuil*
   b. *chinoiserie*
   c. *trompe l'oeil*

3. Mr. Watteau's shop specializes in antiques from the Louis XIV, Louis XV, and Louis XVI periods. The shop is dedicated to furniture from the:
   a. *ancient regime*
   b. *ancien regimen*
   c. *ancien régime*

4. Martine wishes to repair the fringe on her living room curtains. She would be wise to consult a specialist in:
    a. *passementerie*
    b. *chinoiserie*
    c. *fringerie*

5. Carlotta's dining room features hand-blocked Chinese wallpaper, Chinese Chippendale chairs, and vases from the Qing period. In short, the room is loaded with:
    a. *boiserie*
    b. *boulangerie*
    c. *chinoiserie*

6. The day after she moved into the Governor's Mansion, the new First Lady began to fill every spare space with glass figurines, porcelain eggs, and other:
    a. *objets d'art*
    b. *art d'objets*
    c. *objet d'arts*

7. Nothing adds more to the character of a room than well-chosen wood paneling, or:
    a. *chinoiserie*
    b. *trompe l'oeil*
    c. *boiserie*

8. Upper-class women of the 18th century wore large gowns that made sitting in regular armchairs difficult. As a result, the French invented the wider:
    a. *bergère*
    b. *fauteuil*
    c. *chaise longue*

9. Genevieve's breakfast room has a tall ebony stand with shelves used to display *objets d'art*. A piece of furniture of this type is called a(n):
    a. *ancien régime*
    b. *étagère*
    c. *passementerie*

10. David is searching for a pair of lightweight armchairs
    that can be easily moved to form different conversa-
    tion groups. He is looking for:
    a. *étagères*
    b. *bergères*
    c. *fauteuils*

ANSWERS: (1) a; (2) c; (3) c; (4) a; (5) c; (6) a; (7) c; (8) a; (9) b; (10) c

IV. SNOB APPEAL

Aren't these shops fantastic? Now that you've seen some
actual *bergères* and *fauteuils*, and held examples of *chinoiserie*
in your own two hands, it's time to incorporate these and our
other interior design terms into your daily life.

Use snob words from this lesson to fill the following blanks.
Each word is used once; make words plural where necessary.

boiserie	chinoiserie
étagère	passementerie
objet d'art	trompe l'oeil
fauteuil	ancien régime
chaise longue	bergère

1. We have three maids. One of them spends all of her time
   polishing the _____ on the dining room
   walls.
2. Yesterday I found the perfect _____ to
   put on the _____ in the living room.
3. Have you seen the _____ on Charlotte's
   new canopy bed? It's absolutely divine!
4. We just installed a massive _____ mural
   in our board room. Now I feel as if I'm inside a gazebo
   every time we meet.
5. Coco has two main seating groups in her Paris living room.

One has a sofa and two _____, which are easily drawn up to the fireplace in the evening. The other has an 18th-century _____ and a _____, where Coco often lies down with a book.

6. Ivana and I were at Sotheby's yesterday, where she insisted we bid on a Chinese Chippendale settee. You know how Ivana loves _____.

7. Doris and I collect 18th-century French furniture. None of that modern stuff for us. If it isn't _____, we won't look twice at it.

ANSWERS: (1) boiserie; (2) objet d'art, étagère; (3) passementerie; (4) trompe l'oeil; (5) fauteuils, bergère, chaise longue; (6) chinoiserie; (7) ancien régime

V. TRUE OR FALSE

Let's have a seat outside my favorite *pâtisserie* (pastry shop) for hot chocolate and a piece of **gâteau Saint-Honoré**.

This elaborate and delicious confection, named for the patron saint of bakers, is made of puff pastry topped with pastry cream, whipped cream, and tiny cream puffs dipped in caramelized sugar. As we indulge, decide if the following definitions are true or false:

(T/F) 1. *passementerie:* French for 'pastime'
(T/F) 2. *bergère:* armchair with wide seat and closed arms
(T/F) 3. *trompe l'oeil:* visual trick
(T/F) 4. *chaise longue:* long carriage
(T/F) 5. *ancien régime:* pre-revolutionary France
(T/F) 6. *fauteuil:* light armchair with open arms
(T/F) 7. *boiserie:* French lumber yard
(T/F) 8. *chinoiserie:* furnishings with Chinese motifs
(T/F) 9. *étagère:* sideboard or buffet
(T/F) 10. *objet d'art:* painting or large sculpture

ANSWERS: all true except (1), (4), (7), (9), and (10).

VI. WORDS IN CONTEXT

Let's stay right here, *alfresco* ('outdoors,' Day 19), watching Parisian life flow by as we finish our cake and complete our final activity.

We've taken the following passages from newspapers, magazines, and websites.

Fill each blank with the most appropriate snob word from this lesson.

Each word is used once; make words plural where necessary.

boiserie	chinoiserie
étagère	passementerie
objet d'art	trompe l'oeil
fauteuil	ancien régime
chaise longue	bergère

1. "The First Empire was a virile moment in French decor, when the froufrou and pastels of the _____ surrendered to the martial style of an age whose hunger for grandeur coexisted with a penchant for severity." (*Architectural Digest*, Sept. 2011)

2. "'As much as we try to edit down our lives, we all still have things that are dear to us,' says interior designer Natasha Baradaran. '_____ are a perfect way to showcase those ceramics and photos without cluttering up a space.'" (elledecor.com, Oct. 2016)

3. "With digital competition, hardcover books are being judged by their covers more than ever before, some earning their keep in the home and heart by doubling as _____." (*Chicago Tribune*, Dec. 2011)

4. "I would have to move, leaving behind a large duplex with a ballroom, magnificent _____, a fireplace

of marble and lustrous carved wood, and, most memorably, two floor-to-ceiling paintings...." (*Architectural Digest*, Jan. 2012)

5. "In the living room, two Louis XVI botanical-needlepoint-upholstered chairs, found at a Paris shop...keep company with a deep _____, a flea market find, covered in embossed black velvet." (*Architectural Digest*, Aug. 2002)

6. "Spina specializes in high-end, handmade _____.... Needless to say, all this froufrou does not come cheap. The satin-ribbon curtain tieback has strands of Swarovski crystal beads and costs about $550." (*New York Times*, Mar. 2003)

7. "The cover photograph of Tracy Tynan's captivating memoir *Wear and Tear: The Threads of My Life* is a portrait of her parents dressed in twin faux-leopard-skin pants, sitting on a faux-zebra-skin _____...." (*Wall Street Journal*, July 2016)

8. "When Elsa Schiaparelli launched her first fashion craze in 1927—sweaters with whimsical _____ bows— she hadn't had any training in clothing design." (*Departures*, Sept. 2003)

9. "From her mother, Hogg inherited a love of faded Oriental carpets, _____ lacquer and the chintz-like colors found in 18th-century porcelain." (*New York Times*, Feb. 2017)

10. "Classic French decor is integral to Penny Drue Baird's design philosophy, even when her interiors don't feature a single bergère or _____: Baird's Manhattan firm...employs the logic, proportion, and panache associated with French masters of days gone by." (*Architectural Digest*, Jan. 2012)

ANSWERS: (1) ancien régime; (2) étagères; (3) objets d'art; (4) boiserie; (5) bergère (6) passementerie; (7) chaise longue; (8) trompe l'oeil; (9) chinoiserie; (10) fauteuil

Well done! Now that you've successfully completed this lesson, you may proceed with plans to re-do your dining room.

But before you start knocking down walls, keep in mind that this course includes two more lessons on snobby interior design words. You may want to postpone major renovations until your quiver of high-handed decorating terms is full.

Meanwhile, let's get some rest, because tomorrow we travel to Milan for our lesson on fashion snob words.

Day 5

Fashionismo 101
THE LOWDOWN ON HIGH FASHION

LOCATION: **MILAN, ITALY**

Do you consider yourself a *fashionista?* If so, skip to the next lesson because this will be a cakewalk—er, *catwalk*—for you. But if fashion's not your forte, and you live in constant fear of the style police, this lesson will open your eyes.

You say you *do* want the fashion lesson?

Good choice. During our visit we'll focus on women's fashion, since it's more snobworthy than men's, although many of these terms apply to fashion in general.

Most of this lesson's snob words are French based, but since we've been in Paris the past two days, I've decided to present them here in Milan, Italy's fashion capital.

So, without further ado, welcome to the roof garden of my penthouse (yes, I do have a thing for roof gardens). What a view! The leafy square below is Piazza Sant'Erasmo, and we're just a five-minute walk from **Via Monte Napoleone**, the most fashionable shopping street in the city's fashion district, known as the **Quadrilatero della Moda.**

Relax in the shade of the *pergola* (a shaded walkway, see Day 12) and help yourself to *antipasti* (Italian appetizers, see Day 25) as we go over the following words:

I. PRONOUNCE

1. **haute couture** (oht´ kwi-TYUR´)
2. **couturier** (coo-CHUR´-yay)
3. **dernier cri** (dehr´-nyay CREE´)
4. **prêt-à-porter** (pwhay´-tap-oh-TAY´)
5. **bon chic, bon genre** (bōng SHEEK´ bōng ZHANG´-hruh)
6. *Women's Wear Daily*
7. **Coco Chanel** (COH´-coh shuh-NELL´)
8. **fashion's Big Four**
9. **fashion week**
10. **fashionista** (fash´-uhn-EEST´-uh)

II. DEFINE

1. HAUTE COUTURE: (literally 'high cutting' or 'high dressmaking' in French) custom-made women's clothing by top fashion designers, as well as the system that creates such clothing. This includes designers, their workshops, and specialists in embroidery, leather, and other disciplines.

While the term *haute couture* generally refers to the French high-fashion industry, based in Paris, it can also be applied to custom work by top designers in the U.S., Italy, England, Japan, and other countries.

Made of pricey materials and constructed with great attention to detail, *haute couture* is staggeringly expensive, with evening gowns commonly priced at $50,000 and above.

Because *haute couture* is a protected term in France, French producers of these high-end garments must be approved each year by the **Chambre Syndicale de la Haute Couture**, the body that regulates the industry.

2. COUTURIER: at its most basic level, the French term for male dressmaker, though it's often applied to designers, manufacturers, and merchants of women's clothing in general, male or female.

At a higher level, however, the term *couturier* refers specifically to Paris-based designers and fashion houses approved to produce *haute couture*.

BONUS WORD: just so you know, the proper French term for a *female* dressmaker is **couturière** (coo-choo-YEHR').

3. DERNIER CRI: (literal French, 'last cry') the newest fashion, whether in the field of fashion itself or in another discipline.

For example, "gauchos" for women were the *dernier cri* in women's fashion in the early 1970s, but the stark **International Style** was the *dernier cri* in architecture during the same period.

It's acceptable to say **the** *dernier cri*, but it's more snobby to use the French article, **le** (pronounced like *look*, without the *k*), as in *le dernier cri*.

4. PRÊT-À-PORTER: (French, 'ready to wear') clothing purchased off the rack, as opposed to custom-made *haute couture* items.

While most *prêt-à-porter* is moderately priced and sold in malls and mainstream department stores, many *haute couture* houses also offer pricey *prêt-à-porter* lines sold in their own boutiques and in special sections of upscale department stores.

5. BON CHIC, BON GENRE: (French, 'good style, good type') a French fashion adjective similar to 'preppy.' The term also applies to a lifestyle.

As applied to a person or outfit, *bon chic, bon genre*, often abbreviated **BCBG**, means elegant, classic, and understated.

As a lifestyle, *BCBG* refers to the privileged culture of a certain segment of the French upper class that focuses on old money, the best schools, and impeccable manners.

6. ***Women's Wear Daily:*** you're at least vaguely familiar with *Vogue, Elle,* and *Harper's Bazaar,* but have you heard of *Women's Wear Daily?*

Considered the bible of the women's fashion industry, the trade journal, often referred to as **WWD**, covers breaking news and trends in fashion, beauty, and retail.

WWD's readership consists mainly of designers, marketers, manufacturers, and financiers of women's clothing, accessories, and beauty products.

Women's Wear Daily produced a daily print edition for more than a hundred years, but in 2015 it switched to a daily digital version and a weekly print edition.

7. **Coco Chanel** (1883-1971): if you know the name of only one fashion designer, let it be this one. Though she passed away half a century ago, her name still packs a powerful fashion punch when written or when dropped into conversation.

One of the world's most influential *couturières*, Chanel is credited with liberating women from corsets and initiating a sporty and casual feminine style following World War I.

Born Gabrielle Bonheur Chanel, "Coco" popularized the **little black dress**, short hair for women, and the suntan, previously thought to be a mark of the working class. She also produced jewelry, handbags, and perfume, **Chanel No. 5** being her signature scent.

Chanel's name and design philosophy live on in the company she founded, which now has boutiques spanning the globe from Buenos Aires to Dubai.

8. **fashion's Big Four**: also known as simply the **Big Four**, the world's major fashion capitals: New York, Paris, London,

and Milan. Several other cities have a significant impact on global fashion, including Rome, Berlin, Los Angeles, Tokyo, Barcelona, and São Paulo, but these cities—at least at present—lack the fame and prestige of the *Big Four*.

World fashion capitals are not static. Berlin was considered a major fashion center in the 1920s, and Milan was not recognized for fashion until the 1970s.

9. FASHION WEEK: the truth is, there's not just one—there are at least ten official *fashion weeks* held around the globe each year.

Each of the *Big Four* fashion capitals holds at least two annual *prêt-à-porter* fashion weeks: one in February or early March (to showcase upcoming fall/winter collections), and another in September or early October (to highlight the following year's spring/summer designs).

During each fashion week, designers based in the host city present runway shows for the press, merchants, celebrities, and prospective clients.

Big Four fashion weeks are always held in order, with New York taking the first week, followed by London, Milan, and Paris.

Paris holds two additional fashion weeks each year—in January and July—to showcase *haute couture* collections.

NOTE: capitalize *fashion week* when it's used with a city, e.g., Paris Fashion Week, New York Fashion Week.

10. FASHIONISTA: a person obsessed with fashion, be it a designer, promoter, journalist, or simple follower of the latest sartorial trends. The term was coined in the 1990s by combining 'fashion' with the suffix '-ista,' meaning 'follower of' in several Romance languages.

And that's it for definitions. What do you think so far? Stick with us and you'll have them down in no time.

III. TRUE OR FALSE

You like the pickled artichokes? I have an extra jar to send home with you.

Meanwhile, take a deep breath while we review what you've learned so far.

Decide whether the following definitions are **true** or **false**.

(T/F) 1. *dernier cri:* latest bad news
(T/F) 2. *bon chic, bon genre:* privileged French lifestyle
(T/F) 3. *Coco Chanel:* made suntans fashionable
(T/F) 4. *Women's Wear Daily:* fashion industry bible
(T/F) 5. *fashion's Big Four:* global fashion capitals
(T/F) 6. *fashion week:* week designated by Congress to honor fashion
(T/F) 7. *couturier:* pricey custom women's clothing
(T/F) 8. *haute couture:* famous male dressmaker
(T/F) 9. *fashionista:* militant protester against fashion
(T/F) 10. *prêt-à-porter:* ready-to-wear clothing

ANSWERS: all true except (1), (6), (7), (8), and (9).

Now let's walk down to Via Monte Napoleone to see examples of the fashion terms we're learning. Careful—it's more of an alley than a street, and it's full of teens on scooters.

Here we'll browse the wares of top Italian designers, including Armani, Gucci, Dolce & Gabbana, Prada, and Ferragamo, as well as the creations of top international designers.

As we survey the scene, play the following game:

IV. MULTIPLE CHOICE

1. *Women's Wear Daily* is:
      a. issued in print weekly, with daily online updates
      b. the most influential publication in women's fashion
      c. both of the above

2. At its most basic level, *couturier* refers to a(n):
   a. *haute couture* sample used for photo shoots
   b. male dressmaker or designer of women's clothing
   c. fashion critic

3. *Prêt-à-porter* clothing is:
   a. made to order
   b. ready to wear
   c. ready to order

4. *Coco Chanel* was:
   a. a famous style icon
   b. a famous *couturière*
   c. both of the above

5. Which is **not** a member of *fashion's Big Four*?
   a. Milan
   b. Berlin
   c. London

6. The term *fashionista* refers to:
   a. fascists who like fashion
   b. designers, promoters, journalists, and anyone else who is really into fashion
   c. Latin American fashion designers

7. Another term for 'latest fashion' is:
   a. *dernier cri*
   b. *demi crie*
   c. *haute couture*

8. High-priced women's clothing made to order by top designers is called:
   a. *haute cuisine*
   b. *haute couture*
   c. *haute couturier*

9. The best way to describe an ensemble that is stylish, yet classic and understated, is:
   a. *prêt-à-porter*
   b. *bon chic, bon genre*
   c. *dernier cri*

10. *Fashion week* is not just one week, but rather:
   a. at least ten official "Fashion Weeks" held each year in *Big Four* cities
   b. two weeks: one in New York and one in Paris
   c. five weeks: one each in New York, Paris, London, Milan, and Tokyo

ANSWERS: (1) c; (2) b; (3) b; (4) c; (5) b; (6) b; (7) a; (8) b; (9) b; (10) a

Did I hear you ask for a gelato break?

No? I guess it was my imagination.

At any rate, would you like a gelato break? I thought you would. There's an excellent *gelateria* right across the street.

The *nocciola?* Of course I recommend it, along with the *lampone, gianduja, castagna, mandarino....*

Let's sit down a moment to savor our frozen ambrosia as we begin our next activity, which will take us into the very bowels of New York City fashion.

V. FASHION INTERNSHIP

You're an intern for a certain devil who wears Prada at a certain top fashion magazine in Manhattan.

Reply to each of your boss's demands with the proper snob word from this lesson...or you're dismissed!

Each fashion snob word is used only once.

haute couture	*Women's Wear Daily*
Coco Chanel	fashionista
fashion's Big Four	fashion week
couturier	dernier cri
prêt-à-porter	bon chic, bon genre

1. Darling, get thee to a tanning bed! You're looking absolutely pre-_____.

2. Take Giorgio's _____ samples and drop them down the garbage chute! They don't even compare with his *haute couture* work.
3. Look at this dress! Jean-Paul promised it would be *fabulous*. He's a miserable excuse for a _____!
4. Don't let anyone at _____ know we're doing the Gaultier feature. They'll try to scoop us!
5. *Never* wear those shoes again! Can't you dress a little more elegantly, a little more _____?
6. If *Elle* is calling this the _____, then we want to stay away from it—light years away from it.
7. What were you thinking? We don't cover fashion shows in Berlin. It's not one of _____!
8. Call and confirm my reservation at the Paris Ritz. I'll be there for _____, of course.
9. We'll cover the Paris _____ collections in in the February issue, but we'll also feature plenty of *prêt-à-porter.*
10. We caught her wearing a dress from Versace's summer collection after labor day. And she has the nerve to call herself a _____!

ANSWERS: (1) Coco Chanel; (2) prêt-à-porter; (3) couturier; (4) *Women's Wear Daily*; (5) bon chic, bon genre; (6) dernier cri; (7) fashion's Big Four; (8) fashion week; (9) haute couture; (10) fashionista

Excuse me, but you have a little speck of gelato on your cheek. That's right, right there—you got it.

How about that last exercise? Glad you're not working in the fashion industry?

For our final activity, we'll check in with Giselle and Marco.

VI. COMPLETE THE STORY

In the last episode, Marco and Giselle each had issues with the other's fashion choices during a chance encounter at Lake

Como, Italy. Can they survive this sartorial scrape? Or is their budding relationship doomed?

Let's find out.

Use snob words from this lesson to fill the blanks below. Each term is used once.

haute couture	*Women's Wear Daily*
Coco Chanel	fashionista
fashion's Big Four	fashion week
couturier	dernier cri
prêt-à-porter	bon chic, bon genre

The Expensive Escapades of
MARCO & GISELLE
Professional Beautiful People

Episode Three: Perplexed in Paris

It's July, and Giselle's mother has brought her to Paris to see the ultra-expensive (1)_____ collections during (2)_____. She's hoping to make Giselle a little less Gaga and a little more Givenchy.

As they make their way through the lobby of the Hôtel Plaza Athénée on *Avenue Montaigne* (the city's prime fashion thoroughfare, remember), they happen to bump into Marco Grimaldi—literally.

MARCO: *(struggling to pick up the dozens of bags and boxes of designer clothing he has just knocked out of Giselle's arms)* Please forgive my clumsiness! I do beg your pardon.

GISELLE: Marco! What are you doing in Paris?

MARCO: I have a polo match. What are *you* doing in Paris?

GISELLE: *(rolling her eyes)* Someone—I won't mention her name—is trying to turn me into a (3)_____. Marco, please meet my mother, Amelia Van de Kamp. Mother, Marco Grimaldi, an acquaintance from Buenos Aires.

MARCO: It is a pleasure. *(He takes Mrs. Van de Kamp's hand and kisses it lightly.)*

MRS. VAN DE KAMP: Charmed, I am sure. You know, your last name rings a bell. Is your mother, by chance, Alessandra Grimaldi, whom (4)_____ calls the best-dressed woman in your country?

MARCO: I am not sure if she is the best dressed woman in Argentina, but yes, Alessandra Grimaldi is my mother.

MRS. VAN DE KAMP: She is a fashion icon! *J'adore* her style! Tell me, who is her favorite (5)_____?

MARCO: Forgive me, I do not usually discuss fashion with my mother, but I would guess that her favorite designer is a woman, the late (6)_____. My mother prefers designers who have a classic and elegant style, who take a (7)_____ approach to *haute couture* as well as to (8)_____.

MRS. VAN DE KAMP: I admire a woman with classic style. There is no need to constantly chase after the (9)_____ or to attend every fashion show in (10)_____.

Meanwhile, the bored Giselle is left wondering whether her mother and Marco will ever finish their conversation.

ANSWERS: (1) haute couture; (2) fashion week; (3) fashionista; (4) *Women's Wear Daily;* (5) couturier; (6) Coco Chanel; (7) bon chic, bon genre; (8) prêt-à-porter; (9) dernier cri; (10) fashion's Big Four

Ready to launch your own collection?

Ready to trash everything in your closet and start over?

Get some beauty sleep, but save your appetite, because tomorrow we travel to Napa Valley, California, where we'll delve into the topic of snob food.

Day 6

Foodie University
REMEDIAL CLASS

LOCATION: **NAPA VALLEY, CALIFORNIA**

There was a time, in the not-too-distant past, when most Americans were content to sit down to meat and potatoes. Every night. Not anymore!

Now it seems everyone's into food. We insist on organic this and steel-cut that, celebrity chefs have taken over the airwaves, and food is a more popular topic for conversation than sports or politics.

If you're not yet part of this culinary revolution, we'll quickly get you on board with the ten culinary snob terms in this lesson.

We'll meet at my estate in California's **Napa Valley**, one of the most food-conscious areas of the U.S. An easy drive from San Francisco, this valley, dotted with majestic oaks and fragrant eucalyptus trees, has some of the country's best produce, best artisanal food products, and best restaurants.

It's also home to the California campus of the **Culinary Institute of America**, one of the premier cooking schools in the United States.

We'll begin our lesson here on my terrace, with its view of the quaint town of **Yountville**, as we enjoy fresh figs from my orchard and *chèvre* (goat cheese) made here on the estate.

I. PRONOUNCE AND DEFINE

1. **haute cuisine** (oat´ kwee-ZEEN´)
2. **cuisine classique** (kwee-ZEEN´ claw-SEEK´)
3. **nouvelle cuisine** (new-vell´ kwee-ZEEN´)
4. **locavore** (LOW´-cuh-vor´)
5. **bon appétit** (bohng´ ap-pay-TEE´)
6. **forage** (FOR´-udge)
7. **epicure** (EP´-uh-kyur´)
8. **gourmet** (gor-MAY´)
9. **gastronome** (GAS´-truh-nohm)
10. **gourmand** (GOR´-mawnd)

1. HAUTE CUISINE: (French for 'high cooking') cooking at a high level. Most often applied to French cooking, but the phrase can refer to any type of elaborate cuisine, especially that of upscale hotels and restaurants.

French *haute cuisine* has two sub-categories: *cuisine classique* and *nouvelle cuisine,* each explained below.

2. CUISINE CLASSIQUE: the classic branch of French *haute cuisine,* known for its heavy use of cream and butter, developed over centuries in royal and aristocratic households. Chef and culinary writer **Auguste Escoffier** (1846-1935) standardized and codified the system in the early twentieth century.

Cuisine classique emphasizes rich ingredients and balanced flavors in elegant presentations. At its base are five "mother" sauces that can be endlessly varied to fit individual recipes.

The large repertoire of *cuisine classique,* which includes dishes such as *tournedos Rossini, truite meunière,* and *homard à l'americaine,* is served in restaurants all over the world.

3. NOUVELLE CUISINE: (French, 'new cooking') a late 1960s reaction to the perceived excesses of *cuisine classique.*

Nouvelle cuisine, as a healthier version of French *haute cuisine,* shuns sauces and butter, promotes fresh ingredients and natural flavors, and *(zut alors!)* even makes use of the microwave oven.

The practice of overcooking is strictly avoided in *nouvelle cuisine:* vegetables are often served with a bit of crunch.

4. LOCAVORE: a person who attempts to eat nothing but locally grown and locally raised food. "Locally" usually means within one's state (or country, if it's a small one) or within a hundred-mile radius of one's residence.

5. BON APPÉTIT: (French, 'good appetite') a phrase uttered at the beginning of a meal *(Bon appétit!)* to wish other diners an enjoyable repast.

Careful—French snobs, who consider it a term for waiters and the lower classes, don't use it.

6. FORAGE: to search for and gather edible items, such as mushrooms and pine nuts, in the wild. Some extreme *foragers* even search vacant lots in urban areas for weeds, varmints, and other treats they can cook up.

The next four words are often used as synonyms, but they have subtle differences. Pay attention!

7. EPICURE: a person who seeks out and values the pleasures of good food and drink (emphasis here on *pleasure*).

Epicures aren't necessarily interested in preparing food or knowing its history. They just show up and enjoy it.

8. **GOURMET**: a person who enjoys good food, knows a great deal about its preparation, *and* who enjoys cooking and presenting elaborate meals. The term is also used as an adjective meaning 'elaborate', 'special,' or 'high-quality,' as in *gourmet* take-out, *gourmet* oatmeal, etc.

9. **GASTRONOME**: a person who is knowledgeable about food and its preparation, enjoys good food, but does not necessarily like (or want) to cook. Food historians and restaurant critics often fall into this category.

10. **GOURMAND**: a male who lives to eat, primarily to fill his stomach; the quality of the food is secondary. A female who fits this description is a **gourmande**.

BONUS WORD: **al dente** (all DEN´-tay), 'to the tooth' in Italian, cooked to the point at which there is still some "bite" left in pasta and vegetables. The opposite of 'soggy' or 'mushy.'

• I'll have the *fettuccine al pomodoro,* prepared *al dente,* please.

Are you getting these down? Take one more look at each definition before moving on to our next activity.

II. MATCHING

Match each food-related snob word with its definition:

____ 1. *forage*   a. classic French cooking at a high level
____ 2. *bon appétit*   b. one who takes pleasure in high-quality food and drink
____ 3. *gastronome*   c. one who eats only locally produced food
____ 4. *gourmet*   d. to search for food in the wild
____ 5. *gourmand*   e. a food expert, but not necessarily a good cook

___	6. *al dente*	f. a phrase shunned by French snobs
___	7. *locavore*	g. a healthier version of *cuisine classique*
___	8. *haute cuisine*	h. a man who loves to eat a lot of almost anything
___	9. *epicure*	i. cooked to a 'still chewy' point
___	10. *nouvelle cuisine*	j. a person who knows about food, is a good cook, and likes to cook
___	11. *cuisine classique*	k. elaborate cooking at a high level

ANSWERS: (1) d; (2) f; (3) e; (4) j; (5) h; (6) i; (7) c; (8) k; (9) b; (10) g; (11) a

III. RESTAURANT LIFE

You're making good progress, but now it's time for some hands-on training.

Let's pretend you're in college (or maybe you actually *are* in college), and to make ends meet, you take a part-time job as a prep cook in a fancy French restaurant.

Below is a transcript of some typical conversation that takes place in the kitchen.

Fill the blanks with snob words from this lesson. Each word is used just once. Make words plural as necessary.

haute cuisine	forage
cuisine classique	epicure
nouvelle cuisine	gourmet
locavore	gastronome
bon appétit	gourmand
al dente	

CHEF: I told you to steam those green beans until they were (1)_____, not *à la soggy!*

YOU: I beg your pardon, but I'm a college student—not a trained (2)_____ chef.

71

RESTAURANT OWNER: *(samples a bean)* These are still crunchy! *(to chef)* I've had enough of your crazy (3)_____! *(to you)* Go ahead and steam them for at least another three minutes. And let's get some sauce on them!

CHEF: But sauces in the style of (4)_____ will make our patrons fat!

RESTAURANT OWNER: I don't care, as long as they keep coming! I know we promote our fare as (5)_____, but I need customers who are (6)_____, not finicky (7)_____, to pay my overhead!

WAITER: Special request for chanterelle mushrooms at table eight! The gentleman says they must be sourced locally because he's a(n) (8)_____.

CHEF: Chanterelle mushrooms! Tell him we can't get chanterelles *anywhere* this time of year, let alone locally.

WAITER: I already did, but he keeps insisting. He seems to be a restaurant critic or some other type of (9)_____. He's writing things in a notebook.

RESTAURANT OWNER: Tell him to go (10)_____ for his precious chanterelles in the hills outside of town and bring them in! We'll cook them for him.

And—on another note—did I hear you wish some customers (11) "_____" a few minutes ago?

WAITER: Yes. Is that a problem?

RESTAURANT OWNER: Of course it's a problem! That phrase is for lower-class French households... and for waiters in disreputable bistros in the Paris suburbs. Don't use it here!

ANSWERS: (1) al dente; (2) gourmet; (3) nouvelle cuisine; (4) cuisine classique; (5) haute cuisine (6) gourmands; (7) epicures; (8) locavore; (9) gastronome; (10) forage; (11) bon appétit

IV. SENSE—OR NONSENSE?

Now that you've had experience in the kitchen, it's time to turn the tables and have lunch in Yountville at **The French**

Laundry. This Michelin three-star temple to Franco-American cuisine, run by celebrity chef **Thomas Keller** (b. 1955), won't disappoint you: it's often cited as the best restaurant in the United States.

We'll dine in the courtyard and select the nine-course chef's tasting menu, which begins at $400 per person. (Don't worry, it's included in the price of this book.)

As we sample specialties such as *Pekin duck with caramelized cauliflower tapenade* and *charcoal-grilled Wagyu* (Japanese beef, see Day 17) *with Sicilian pistachio purée,* read over the following sentences and check each one that makes sense.

____ 1. As an exchange student in Paris, my host famly always wished me *"bon appétit!"* before going to bed.

____ 2. As an *epicure,* I take great pleasure in well prepared food.

____ 3. My mother's a *locavore,* since she'll only eat food produced in the United States and Canada.

____ 4. I have to admit my dislike for *cuisine classique.* Aside from being fattening, it wreaks havoc with my lactose-intolerant stomach.

____ 5. I consider myself a *gastronome:* I'll eat anything.

____ 6. Some days, when I have no food in the house, I *forage* in the botanical gardens down the street.

____ 7. You know, *nouvelle cuisine* really isn't new anymore, since it was developed in the 1960s.

____ 8. I love vegetables when they're cooked *al dente.*

____ 9. I'm thinking of opening a *gourmand* restaurant for people with highly discriminating palates.

____ 10. My wife is a true *gourmet:* she loves to cook, loves to eat, and knows everything about food and its preparation.

ANSWERS: numbers (2), (4), (6), (7), (8) and (10) should be checked.

73

V. SNOB STATEMENTS

As we give our palates a rest before jumping into dessert, let's look at the following hypothetical situation.

Despite the fact you have minimum culinary training, you decide to go out on a limb and hold a dinner party for ten of your snobby foodie friends and their spouses. Listed below are some of the statements they make while you're in the kitchen.

Fill the blanks with snob words from this lesson. Each word is used only once. Change verb tenses (and make words plural) where necessary.

haute cuisine	forage
cuisine classique	epicure
nouvelle cuisine	gourmet
locavore	gastronome
bon appétit	gourmand
al dente	

1. "It's certainly not _____, but it's edible."
2. "I'm not sure about that. He has very few cooking skills, and little knowledge about food in general. In othe words, he's not a _____. He should have tried something a little less experimental."
3. "This pasta is five minutes short of _____. It's actually crunchy!"
4. "We have to eat at least some of it. _____!"
5. "I thought he was a _____! The only local producer of chanterelles went bankrupt a year ago.
6. "Maybe he _____ for them."
7. "I'm sorry, but only a _____ could eat this."
8. "I'm not much of a _____ compared to the rest of you, since I don't know much about food or

its preparation, so I'm confused at our host's use of raw mushrooms, raw pasta, and simple tomato purée."

9. "It's simple, healthy, and crunchy. Maybe he's going for an Italian _____ sort of thing."

10. "I'm a(n) _____. I just can't take pleasure in this!"

11. "After we finish here, I suggest we all go to Chez Pierre to redeem our palates with _____!"

ANSWERS: (1) haute cuisine; (2) gourmet; (3) al dente; (4) bon appétit; (5) locavore; (6) foraged; (7) gourmand; (8) gastronome (9) nouvelle cuisine; (10) epicure; (11) cuisine classique

How are you feeling about these culinary snob words at this point?

Will you be able to hold your own when a group of snobby foodies actually *does* invade your house? (It happens.)

Time to get some rest! Tomorrow we'll travel to Salzburg, Austria, to study terms related to classical music.

Day 7

Do, Re, Mi, Fa, Sol...
THE SOUNDS OF CLASSICAL MUSIC

LOCATION: **SALZBURG, AUSTRIA**

As you know, today's electronic gadgets make it possible to listen to any type of music—anywhere in the world—at any time of day or night.

Unfortunately, much of this "music" is of dubious quality.

Luckily, classical music still exists, and you'll do yourself a favor by learning a few of its basic terms.

Maybe you'll never prefer Beethoven to the Beach Boys, but these ten musical snob words will help you hold your own at the symphony, choral performances, and piano recitals.

Most of these terms have Italian origins, but since we were so recently in Italy, let's have this lesson in Salzburg, Austria, one of the most music-loving cities in the world. This lovely town is the birthplace of composer **Wolfgang Amadeus Mozart** (1756-91), and home to the annual Mozart Festival.

Salzburg is also the setting for the 1965 film *The Sound of Music*, which was filmed largely on location in the city.

I happen to own a little place here in the **Altstadt**, the historic town center. From my balcony we can see the **Festungsberg**, a large hill topped with the massive **Hohensalzburg Fortress**. This towering castle, which has intimidated Salzburg's enemies for centuries, dates to the year 1077.

Before we begin our lesson, can I interest you in a piece of **Sacher torte**? One of Austria's many gastronomic gifts to the world, it consists of layers of rich chocolate cake (filled with tangy apricot jam) covered in decadent chocolate ganache.

Enjoy a piece as we explore our new snob words.

I. PRONOUNCE

You know the drill. Say the following words aloud, several times, until they flow from your mouth like a Mozart *aria* (we'll get to that definition in a minute).

1. **chamber music**
2. **aria** (AHR´-ee-uh)
3. **sonata** (suh-NAW´-tuh)
4. **cantata** (kun-TAH´-tuh)
5. **oratorio** (or-uh-TOR´-ee-oh)
6. **concerto** (kun-CHAIR´-toh)
7. **opus** (OH´-puhs)
8. **tessitura** (tess´-uh-TUR´-uh)
9. **pizzicato** (pits´-uh-CAW´-toh)
10. **staccato** (stuh-CAW´-toh)

II. DEFINITIONS

Now take a look at these definitions:

1. CHAMBER MUSIC: music specifically composed to be played by a small number of musicians in a private room or other small venue.

While compositions written as *chamber music* are often performed in large concert halls nowadays, the number of musicians remains small. The **string quartet** (two violins, a viola, and a cello) is one of the most popular chamber configurations.

2. ARIA: (traditionally 'air' in French and English) a short piece for solo voice, with or without accompaniment. *Arias* are usually light, melodic, and designed to display vocal agility.

In Italian opera, *aria* refers to the parts of a work that are actual songs, and which reflect on the action, as opposed to **recitatives** (reh´-suh-tuh-TEEVES´), or musical passages meant to imitate speech and move the story forward.

Arias also appear in *oratorios* and *cantatas*, defined below.

3. SONATA: (Italian, 'sounded' or 'played') a piece of music written for one or two instruments.

Sonatas are generally divided into three or four sections, or movements, which differ in mood, rhythm, form, or key.

4. CANTATA: (Italian, 'sung') a narrative piece of music, for one or more voices, usually sung to an instrumental accompaniment. *Cantatas*, which can be sacred or secular, usually have several movements. These distinct sections may consist of solos, duets, *arias,* recitatives, or choruses.

The *cantata* was a popular form in the 17th and 18th centuries, during which period **Johann Sebastian Bach** (1685-1750), considered the master of the form, composed two hundred surviving sacred *cantatas*.

5. ORATORIO: a large-scale *cantata* with a sacred theme. As such, it's generally a narrative work (based on scripture) for voices and orchestra, similar to an opera in length, but performed without costumes, scenery, or action.

The world's most famous oratorio is *Messiah* (1741), composed by **George Frideric Handel** (1685-1759). You've surely heard the "Hallelujah Chorus" from this work, often performed at Christmas.

6. CONCERTO: a work composed for one or more instrumental soloists and a full orchestra.

Concerti (the proper plural), which have three contrasting movements, have been written for most instruments, including piano, trumpet, violin, cello, and flute.

Italian composer **Antonio Vivaldi** (1678-1741) set the standard for the classical *concerto* using one soloist and a fast-slow-fast pattern of movements.

7. OPUS: (Latin, 'work') a term used in numbering a composer's works. For example, Mozart's *Opus 50* is theoretically his fiftieth published composition.

Opus numbers are not always accurate in that sense, however, since the composers and publishers who've done the numbering have often purposely left certain compositions out.

While the term *opus* is generally reserved for music, the term **magnum opus** may refer to a large and important work in any discipline, as well as to *the* most important work of a composer, artist, or writer.

For example, some critics consider the opera ***Don Giovanni*** to be Mozart's *magnum opus*.

PLURAL: *opuses*

8. TESSITURA: (Italian, 'texture') the range, from lowest to highest note, of a melody, vocal part, or vocal role.

For a successful performance, a vocalist's range must cover the *tessitura* of the song or role being performed.

9. PIZZICATO: (Italian, 'pinched') a technique in which performers of stringed instruments *pluck* strings, instead of playing them with a bow, in order to produce particular notes.

The term is used with string instruments of the standard orchestra (violin, viola, cello, bass), as well as with those of the lute family, including the guitar, mandolin, and banjo.

10. STACCATO: (Italian, 'detached') a musical technique in which performers play a note, or series of notes, in a quick and choppy manner.

Staccato is the opposite of **legato**, which means to "tie" a note to the preceding and following notes in a smooth manner.

NOTE: while similar, the terms *staccato* and *pizzicato* cannot be used interchangeably.

Pizzicato (plucking a string) is a form of *staccato* (playing a note in a quick, choppy manner), but *staccato* is not always achieved through *pizzicato*. Many instruments (woodwind, brass, percussion) can produce *staccato* notes without strings.

III. SENTENCES

Let's take a break and walk through the Aldstadt, beginning with its main street—the narrow, pedestrian **Getreidegasse**.

As you can see, this historic thoroughfare, which dates to medieval times, is lined with tall, slender houses that host shops at street level. Many of these are marked with antique iron guild signs: a large boot identifies the shoemaker; a mortar and pestle points out the apothecary.

Near the midpoint of the street we encounter house number 9, home to the apartment where Mozart was born and lived for the first seventeen years of his life.

As we continue to explore, read over the following sentences, which will help cement the definitions of our new snob words in your mind.

1. Margene's piano teacher reprimanded her for playing the passage in a smooth, legato manner rather than in the choppy, *staccato* style indicated on the score.

2. Rather than hire a full orchestra to play in the garden, Jessica opted to have a string quartet play *chamber music* in the dining room.
3. The orchestra performed Mozart's *Opus 40,* which was published directly after his *Opus 39.*
4. The *tessitura* of the part was just too high for Lily's voice: there were several notes she couldn't reach.
5. The piano *concerto* was performed by a piano soloist accompanied by a full orchestra.

IV. FILL IN THE BLANKS

Ready to burst out in song at this point? Fill each blank below with one of the words we've just reviewed: **chamber music, tessitura, staccato, opus,** or **concerto.** Each is used once.

1. _____ range of a piece of music or operatic role, from lowest note to highest
2. _____ composition for one or more solo instruments accompanied by full orchestra
3. _____ term used to number compositions
4. _____ music written to be performed in private rooms by a small number of musicians
5. _____ musical direction to play a note in a detached, choppy manner

ANSWERS: (1) tessitura; (2) concerto; (3) opus; (4) chamber music; (5) staccato

V. MORE SENTENCES

Let's pause for a moment in **Mozartplatz,** a picturesque square named (obviously) after the city's favorite composer, a statue of whom stands at the center.

We'll have a seat at this outdoor café and order another amazing pastry of Austrian origin: **apfelstrudel**, a delight made of apples, raisins, sugar, and cinnamon baked in tender, flaky pastry. I've requested it served with a rich vanilla custard.

Ahhhhhhhhh.

As we enjoy this heavenly confection, often considered Austria's national dessert, let's take a look at the other five snob words from this lesson in context.

1. I didn't care much for the piece. It was called "Lullaby," but it was all cymbals, tympani, and violin *pizzicato*. Who could sleep through that?

2. I liked the opera in general, but I wish it had featured more *arias*—those beautiful lyrical solos—and fewer *recitatives,* those long, speech-like passages.

3. Our church is planning to perform an Easter *cantata*, but with three movements, multiple soloists, a full chorus, and a full orchestra, it will be difficult to do it well.

4. The *sonata* Lorraine will play at the recital has three movements: the first is slow and sad; the second, fast and happy; the third, slow and mysterious.

5. Georges just completed his latest *oratorio*, an obscure format, I know. Think of it as the soundtrack of an opera (*arias* and recitatives interspersed with choral segments), without sets, costumes, or movement.

NOTE: confused on the difference between *cantatas* and *oratorios?* Let's have a quick review.

An *oratorio* is a specialized type of *cantata.* Therefore, all *oratorios* are *cantatas,* but not all *cantatas* are *oratorios.*

And while a *cantata* may be secular or sacred, an *oratorio* is always sacred.

Finally, while a *cantata* may be long or short, and may vary considerably as to the number of voices and instruments involved (there must be at least one singer and at least one instrument), an *oratorio* must be fairly long, and must have a large number of performers.

VI. FILL IN MORE BLANKS

Again, fill each blank below with one of the musical snob words we've just reviewed: **aria, cantata, pizzicato, sonata,** or **oratorio.** Each word is used only once.

6. _____ long narrative musical work for soloists, chorus, and orchestra, usually based on the Bible

7. _____ composition (with three or four distinct sections) written for one or more musical instruments

8. _____ sacred or secular multi-movement work for one or more voices and accompaniment

9. _____ melodic composition for single voice, with or without accompaniment

10. _____ technique of plucking a stringed instrument

ANSWERS: (1) oratorio; (2) sonata; (3) cantata; (4) aria; (5) pizzicato

VII. TRUE OR FALSE

It's time for some chamber music at the imposing **Residenz Palace**, now a museum, but previously home to Salzburg's ruling prince-archbishops for half a millennium. (From the 13th through the 18th centuries, Salzburg was a prince-archbishopric of the Holy Roman Empire.)

Tonight's program features *Eine kleine Nachtmusik* (1787), one of Mozart's best known serenades.

As we revel in celestial melodies, surrounded by ornate plaster ceilings and gleaming parquet floors, let's play the following true-or-false game:

(T/F)   1. The *tessitura* of a piece of music is its range, from lowest to highest note.

(T/F)   2. A *staccato* note must also be a *pizzicato* note.

(T/F)   3. An *oratorio* is a light composition designed to display vocal agility.

(T/F)   4. *Chamber music* was originally meant to be performed in homes and other small venues.

(T/F)   5. *Arias* appear in operas, *cantatas,* and *oratorios.*

(T/F)   6. A *sonata* may be played, sung, or both.

(T/F)   7. A *magnum opus* is an artist's or composer's greatest work.

(T/F)   8. A *cantata* must be based on a biblical text.

(T/F)   9. A *concerto* always features at least one soloist accompanied by a full orchestra.

(T/F) 10. *Staccato* is the technique of playing notes so that they run smoothly together.

ANSWERS: numbers (1), (4), (5), (7), and (9) are true. The rest are false.

VIII. SENSE...OR NONSENSE?

Here's another game for you as the chamber music continues. Check each of the following statements that makes sense:

_____ 1. I had a broccoli and cheddar *cantata* and a glass of orange juice for breakfast.

_____ 2. I don't generally like *oratorios*, but I make an exception each year for Handel's *Messiah*.

_____ 3. The punk rock group's most recent *aria* is all about doom, gloom, and the end of the world.

_____ 4. I have to admit my dislike for *chamber music*—I prefer music written for large venues.

_____ 5. My friend, a novelist, hopes to finish his *Opus 32* by January.

_____ 6. Roger performed the *staccato* passage perfectly: it was crisp and detached.

_____ 7. Blanche sang a *sonata* at the Christmas social.

_____ 8. The choir performed an elaborate *tessitura*.

_____ 9. As usual, the *concerto* featured no soloists.

_____ 10. Guacamole can be made from ripe *pizzicatos*.

ANSWERS: (2), (4), and (6) should be checked—the others are nonsense.

IX. SNOB APPEAL

Finally, let's finish our lesson on musical snob words in the gardens of **Mirabell Palace**, another grand residence built for Salzburg's former rulers.

Here we'll find the Baroque extravaganza of flowers, trees, statues, and fountains that features prominently in *The Sound of Music*. (Maria, played by Julie Andrews, and her charges dance around the **Pegasus Fountain** as part of the "Do-Re-Mi" number.)

It sounds as if an outdoor concert is beginning (the works of Mozart, of course). As we listen, fill the blanks below with the most appropriate snob words from this lesson.

Each word is used only once, so find the **best choice** for each blank. Make words plural as necessary.

sonata	oratorio
cantata	opus
aria	tessitura
concerto	pizzicato
chamber music	staccato

1. "Last night's piano _____ featured Jacques Leblanc as soloist."

2. "I'm afraid Taylor's voice just doesn't match the role's _____."

3. "Don't get me wrong—I *do* enjoy Brahms' *Intermezzo in A,* but I much prefer his _____ *116.*"

4. "Yes, a symphony performed by a full orchestra would be a grand gesture, but I think _____ is more appropriate for an at-home wedding."

5. "Madge has a smooth and melodious voice, but her husband speaks in a clipped, _____ manner."

6. "We'd like to perform the _____ at Easter because of its religious message, but we don't have the large number of performers needed."

7. "A _____ is a good choice for a piano recital because if audience members don't like one movement, they may like another."

8. "I'm familiar with Bach's sacred vocal work, but I didn't realize he'd also written secular _____."

9. "The singer who performed the _____ in the opera's first act was divine!"

10. "I hate these _____ passages—they hurt my fingers!"

ANSWERS: (1) concerto; (2) tessitura; (3) opus; (4) chamber music; (5) staccato; (6) oratorio; (7) sonata; (8) cantatas; (9) aria; (10) pizzicato

Congratulations on finishing another lesson.

Ready to purchase season tickets to the symphony? Does your playlist now contain more tunes from the Three Tenors than from Maroon 5?

Be that as it may, you now have ten new musical terms in your snob words quiver. Use them or lose them!

Alas, we must bid *auf Wiedersehen* to Salzburg as we head to Greece, where tomorrow we'll study architectural snob words.

Day 8

More is Definitely More
ARCHITECTURAL SNOB TERMS

LOCATION: **SANTORINI, GREECE**

We're surrounded by structures, though few of us understand the language of architecture.

Why is it important to be familiar with building terms? So we can show off, of course.

Why build your dream house if you can't brag about its outstanding features?

Or why spend the summer in a *Tuscan villa* (see Day 13) if you don't have the snobcabulary to tell the world how fabulous it is through social media?

The ten terms in this chapter will raise your architectural snob cred higher than the Empire State Building.

But since ancient Greece is where Western architecture got its start, we'll have our lesson in Athens. We'll stay at my villa on the exclusive Greek island of **Santorini,** a short and spectacular helicopter ride from the capital.

Strap yourself in, and let's go!

I. POP QUIZ

As we settle into my villa—a lovely composition of white-washed cubes and blue domes that hangs off the cliffs outside the town of **Oia**—let's take a quick quiz to see what you already know about architecture.

In honor of **Ludwig Mies van der Rohe** (1886-1969), the German-American architect who popularized the term "less is more," we'll keep it short.

Good luck!

1. An *enfilade* is a:
    a. French dance step
    b. series of rooms with aligned doorways
    c. room open to the outside air on at least one side
2. A *Palladian window* consists of:
    a. large panes overlooking a palladio
    b. three sections, the middle one arched
    c. two equal parts connected by a cornice
3. In French, *porte-cochère* literally means:
    a. 'coach door'
    b. 'porthole in a coach'
    c. 'porter who attends to coaches'
4. A *portico* is a:
    a. porch on a veranda
    b. porch with a roof supported by columns
    c. series of columns supported by a porch
5. A *loggia* is a:
    a. private area inside a chapel
    b. room open to the outside air on at least one side
    c. large closet
6. *Pilasters* can best be described as:
    a. plaster columns
    b. square columns attached to walls
    c. workers who apply plaster

7. A *colonnade* is made up of a series of:
   a. columns
   b. enfilades
   c. pilasters
8. A *veranda* is a(n):
   a. covered, open-air sitting area, usually at ground level
   b. wide entrance for cars and carriages
   c. Hawaiian porch
9. The *entablature* of a classical building is found at its:
   a. bottom
   b. top
   c. midpoint
10. A Hawaiian term for 'porch' is:
   a. *lanai*
   b. *kauai*
   c. *molokai*

ANSWERS: (1) b; (2) b; (3) a; (4) b; (5) b; (6) b; (7) a; (8) a; (9) b; (10) a

II. PRONOUNCE AND DEFINE

How'd you do on the quiz? Don't worry if your score wasn't exactly *skycraping*. You'll get there.

As we take a quick dip in the infinity pool, which is the same cobalt blue as the bay below, say the following snob words aloud several times. Then look at their definitions.

1. **porte-cochère** (PORT´-coh-SHAIR´)
2. **pilaster** (pih-LAS´-ter)
3. **entablature** (en-TAB´-luh-chur)
4. **colonnade** (cawl-uhn-ADE´)
5. **portico** (POR´-tuh-coh)
6. **Palladian window** (puh-LAY´-dee-uhn)
7. **enfilade** (EN´-fuh-layd)
8. **loggia** (LOW´-juh)

9. **veranda** (vuh-RAN´-duh)
10. **lanai** (luh-NIGH´)

1. PORTE-COCHÈRE: (French for 'coach door') an entrance, wide enough to accommodate cars and carriages, that leads from the street to a courtyard. If the courtyard is located in front of the house or building in question, the *porte-cochère* simply passes through a wall. But if the courtyard is located behind the edifice, the *porte-cochère* includes a tunnel-like structure that leads beside, or through, the building.

True *portes-cochères* (the proper plural, pronounced the same as the singular) are seldom found in the U.S., but are common in France and other European countries, where they allow access to grand townhouses and certain other structures.

Portes-cochères are usually faced with large double doors that are often arched.

The term *porte-cochère* is also used to refer to a covered area formed by a roof that extends from a building's entrance over an adjacent driveway. This arrangement, found at many hotels and apartment buildings, is meant to shield passengers from the elements as they enter and exit vehicles.

While there is no other good way to describe such structures, true word snobs will avoid using *porte-cochère* in this sense.

2. PILASTER: a rectangular column attached to a wall. *Pilasters* project into a room in a shallow manner, usually by less than one-third of their width.

Pilasters may be structural, and actually support a building, or they may be simply decorative. They're generally topped with a classical *entablature* (see below).

3. ENTABLATURE: in classical Greek and Roman architecture, a three-part structure resting atop a series of columns or pilasters.

Traditionally, *entablatures* were made of stone, but they can also be constructed of masonry or wood.

The lowest part of an *entablature* is the **architrave**, the beam that sits directly atop the columns or pilasters.

Above the *architrave* is the **frieze**, a horizontal band that's often decorated with carvings.

The topmost element of the *entablature* is the **cornice**, a decorative, horizontal molding (or series of moldings) that crowns a structure. A cornice often extends outwards from a building, several inches or more, in order to protect its façade from rain.

While *entablatures* are generally exterior features, the *entablature* form may also be applied to furniture, mantels, and other interior projects.

4. COLONNADE: a series of columns spaced at regular intervals. For example, all four sides of a classical Greek temple have *colonnades,* which support the roof of the building.

Colonnades are also used in an arrangement called a *portico* (see below).

Finally, *colonnades* can be freestanding, supporting a simple series of stone or wooden beams, as in the case of a *pergola* (see Day 12).

Two of the most impressive *colonnades* in the United States are on the front and back façades of the **U.S. Capitol**.

5. PORTICO: a covered porch, usually at the front of a building, formed by a *colonnade* supporting an extended roof.

Think of the **White House**, which has *porticos* (or *porticoes*) on its north and south sides. These classical *porticos* are topped with triangular shapes called **pediments**.

6. **PALLADIAN WINDOW**: a large, composite window made of three vertical sections. The middle section, which is wider than the side sections, has an arched top.

Palladian windows, also referred to as **Venetian windows**, are named for **Andrea Palladio** (1508-80), the 16th-century Italian architect who often used them in his designs.

The windows are a common feature of architectural styles based on Palladio's works, including **Georgian** (c. 1714-1830), popular in Britain and its colonies, and **Federal** (1785-1820), unique to the post-revolutionary United States.

7. ENFILADE: a series of aligned internal doorways that forms a long vista when the doors are open.

Enfilades were an important feature of palace architecture in the **Baroque** period (17th century), when they were often used instead of corridors, even in bedroom wings.

This arrangement meant residents and visitors often had to traipse through occupied salons and bedchambers to reach particular parts of a palace.

To minimize interruptions, the aligned doorways were generally placed to the front of rooms, near window walls, and beds were equipped with draperies for privacy.

Versailles Palace, outside Paris, and **Catherine Palace**, outside St. Petersburg, have especially fine *enfilades*.

8. LOGGIA: a roofed porch, gallery, or hall open to the outside air on one or more sides.

Loggias evolved in the Mediterranean region as open sitting rooms that offered protection from the sun. During the **Italian Renaissance** (roughly 1350-1600), a *loggia* was considered an essential element of a proper villa.

While *loggias* may be constructed on the ground level of a structure, they're usually found on upper stories.

9. VERANDA (also **verandah**): a platform, usually roofed, and usually level with the ground floor, attached to the side of a building.

The name comes from Hindi (*varandā*) through Portuguese (*varanda*), meaning 'railing' or 'balustrade.'

Verandas are used as porches as well as informal sitting and dining rooms.

10. LANAI: the Hawaiian term for 'porch,' 'veranda,' or 'terrace.' *Lanais*, which can be on any level of a house, are generally associated with dwellings in tropical areas, and can take nearly any form a porch or terrace can take.

III. FILL IN THE BLANKS

Is your mind spinning with architectural elements at this point? Are visions of pilasters, porticos, and Palladian windows dancing in your head? We hope so.

Now it's time to report to the helipad. As we fly to Athens, please play the following game.

Pretend you're a writer for an architectural review magazine. Fill each blank in your article below with the most appropriate snob word from this lesson. Make words plural where necessary. Each word is used only once.

enfilade	Palladian window
porte cochère	portico
loggia	pilaster
colonnade	veranda
entablature	lanai

Say 'Hello' to Heavenly House

Heavenly House sits on a hill overlooking the Pacific, and its grand façade, which features a long (1)_____ forming a(n) (2)_____ at its center (where the family sits to admire amazing sunsets), can be seen for miles. Atop the columns is an elaborate (3)_____ that rivals that of any Greek temple.

To enter the residence, one must pass through a grand (4)_____ that leads to a gravel entrance court. Above the imposing front doors is a(n) (5)_____ that lets copious amounts of light into the entrance hall.

From this hall, which is surrounded by a series of decorative (6)_____, a(n) (7)_____ composed of stately rooms proceeds in both directions. This arrangement allows the visitor to see through the entire house to a(n) (8)_____ on one end, where the family is known to take the ocean breeze in the evenings, and a covered area on the other end that the lady of the house, raised in Hawaii, refers to as the (9)_____.

Obviously, much of the "living" in this house takes place outdoors, and this theme continues with the second-story (10) _____, a popular place for *alfresco* meals.

ANSWERS: (1) colonnade; (2) portico; (3) entablature; (4) porte-cochère; (5) Palladian window; (6) pilasters; (7) enfilade; (8) veranda; (9) lanai; (10) loggia

Great job! I give you an A+ on your article. You have a fabulous career in journalism ahead of you!

As you can see, we've now reached the sprawling metropolis that is Athens. We'll head straight to the **Acropolis**, the rocky outcropping at the center of the city that's home to the remains of the **Parthenon** (c. 430 B.C.)—the most famous Greek temple—and several other classical Greek structures.

As we admire these masterpieces, let's play another game.

IV. SENSE...OR NONSENSE?

Check each of the following sentences that makes sense:

_____ 1. This morning I had breakfast on the *colonnade* while I admired the sunrise.
_____ 2. My architect told me I can't remove the *pilasters* because they're structural.
_____ 3. We drove through the *portico* to get to the courtyard.
_____ 4. I refuse to approve plans for the *entablature* until I've had time to study some authentic Greek models.

_____ 5. When I heard the gunman was loose, I quickly locked the *porte-cochère*.

_____ 6. Having dinner on the *loggia* was a nice idea, but the cold November rain made it a miserable experience.

_____ 7. We need a small, inconspicuous opening to let light into the bathroom—perhaps a *Palladian window*.

_____ 8. I wish you'd stop calling the *veranda* a *lanai*. You do realize we live in Siberia.

_____ 9. The effect of the *enfilade* was ruined because Andrew refused to leave the doors open.

_____ 10. I'd like to put some plants on my *veranda*, but I'm too lazy to carry them up to the second floor.

ANSWERS: numbers (2), (4), (5), (6), (8), and (9) should be checked—the others are nonsense.

V. BUILD YOUR DREAM HOUSE

You're no architect—yet—but by now you should have a good idea of what you want in the house of your dreams.

To make that a reality, we've arranged for you to meet with a celebrity architect, or *starchitect* (star + architect).

Fill each of the blanks in your conversation below with the most appropriate snob word from this lesson. Make words plural where necessary.

enfilade	Palladian window
porte cochère	portico
loggia	pilaster
colonnade	veranda
entablature	lanai

YOU: One thing we'd like is a covered, outdoor room for dining, sitting, and relaxing.

STARCHITECT: You have several good options. If you'd like this room to be on the ground floor, we could build you a

(1)_____. If you'd like a more formal space, we could construct a classical (2)_____ (with a triangular pediment) at the front of the house.

If you'd like an outdoor space off the second floor, we could design a (3)_____. And if you decide to build in a tropical setting, we'd call this outdoor, covered room—whatever form it should take—a (4)_____.

YOU: I'd also like a covered entrance that will keep guests out of the elements as they enter and exit their vehicles.

STARCHITECT: You're referring to what is often, though incorrectly, called a (5)_____.

YOU: Yes—that's what we want, call it what you will—the more grand the better.

STARCHITECT: Certainly. We could dress it up with a row of columns, which is called a (6)_____, and top it with an impressive (7)_____.

YOU: As for the interior of the house, I'd like it to be very formal. In fact, I'd like it to look like a museum, but it must have lots of light.

STARCHITECT: One way to achieve formality would be to surround the great hall with a series of (8)_____. Then we could add several (9)_____ to let the sunshine in.

We could also align the doorways of all the principal rooms to form a(n) (10)_____, which would add even more light and formality to the house.

ANSWERS: (1) veranda; (2) portico; (3) loggia; (4) lanai; (5) porte-cochère; (6) colonnade; (7) entablature; (8) pilasters; (9) Palladian windows; (10) enfilade

VI. COMPLETE THE STORY

It sounds as if your dream house is coming along swimmingly! Please invite me to visit once it's finished.

Meanwhile, let's head back to Santorini, where we'll have a long, relaxed dinner at an outdoor restaurant in the village.

You'll love the fresh fish, the *moussaka* (a casserole made of eggplant, cheese, and béchamel sauce), and the *tzatziki* (a dip made of yogurt, cucumbers, and garlic), which is served with pita bread.

As we eat, let's check in with Marco and Giselle.

Use snob words from this lesson to fill the blanks in the passage below.

You know the drill: use each word only once, and make words plural where necessary.

enfilade	Palladian window
porte cochère	portico
loggia	pilaster
colonnade	veranda
entablature	lanai

The Expensive Escapades of
MARCO & GISELLE
Professional Beautiful People

Episode Four: Vacuous in the Veneto

It's now August, and once again, Giselle and Marco meet by chance. This time it's in **Vicenza**, Italy, the town west of Venice that's home to a collection of impressive **Palladian villas**, or grand houses designed by architect Andrea Palladio.

Our hero and heroine come face to face at **Villa La Rotonda** (c. 1590), Palladio's most famous work.

MARCO: Giselle! You are a vision of loveliness on this porch, which is technically a (1)_____, since it is formed by a (2)_____ supporting an extended roof. What are you doing here?

GISELLE: I'm meeting my mother in Venice tonight, and I had some time to kill. The question is, what are *you* doing here? You're the last person I expected to be interested in columns and square columns—aren't they called (3)_____?— and that kind of thing.

MARCO: *Au contraire, ma chére.* I love architecture.

GISELLE: Then maybe you can answer a question. You say this place where we're standing is a *portico* because it has columns supporting an extended roof. But how does a *portico* differ from a *veranda*...or a *lanai*...or a *loggia?*

MARCO: Those are excellent questions. First, a *portico* is generally classical in nature, like this one, which has Ionic columns supporting a pedimented roof. Then there is the less formal (4)_____, a roofed, open-air living room on a ground floor. Next we have the (5)_____, a Hawaiian term that can be used to describe any type of porch or terrace, roofed or not, especially in a tropical setting. Finally, a (6)_____ is a room with Italian origins that is open to the elements on at least one side, and which may exist on any level of a building.

GISELLE: *(looking confused)* Well, you *do* seem to know your architectural terminology. But do you actually *like* these types of buildings? Would you actually want to *live* in a place like this?

MARCO: Absolutely! I would give up all my polo ponies to live in a place like this! I adore the (7)_____ atop the colonnades, as well as the (8)_____, which run the length of the house in each direction and allow light to penetrate the building. Sheer perfection! It's odd, however, that Palladio's most famous villa does not have a single (9)_____.

GISELLE: I don't know what you're talking about, but if I owned this place, I'd extend one of these *porticos* outward to form a (10)_____. That way, guests wouldn't get rained on as they entered and exited their vehicles.

MARCO: I understand what you mean, but I'm afraid your use of the term is incorrect.

ANSWERS: (1) portico; (2) colonnade; (3) pilasters; (4) veranda; (5) lanai; (6) loggia; (7) entablatures; (8) enfilades; (9) Palladian window; (10) porte-cochère

Who said architecture can't be romantic?

If you got at least nine questions correct on this last section, I'll order *baklava* for dessert.

Meanwhile, are you ready for a career in architecture?

No? Well, at least you've gained the tools to admire and describe great buildings.

Now let's get ready for tomorrow, when we'll say goodbye to Greece and head to the French **Cote d'Azur**. There we'll study snob words to describe the rich and famous.

Day 9

Lifestyles of the Rich and Famous
TERMS FOR WEALTH & RENOWN

LOCATION: **CÔTE D'AZUR, FRANCE**

Today's lesson covers snob words describing the wealthy, the famous, and the glamorous. And no place on earth attracts more people who encompass all three of these qualities than the **Côte d'Azur,** the French term for the area we Anglophones generally call the **French Riviera**.

The Côte d'Azur, or Azure Coast, has no official boundaries, but it roughly corresponds with the eastern half of France's Mediterranean coast.

The snobbiest segment of this vacation paradise—which will be our focus—begins at the ultra-swank **Saint-Tropez** and runs east to the Italian border, encompassing the independent (and very arrogant) principality of **Monaco**.

The area now known as the Côte d'Azur was a backwater of poor fishing villages until the late 1700s, when English and Russian nobles began to "winter" in the region to escape the harsher climates of their own countries.

A century later, when rail service reached the area, luxury trains brought even more aristocrats, as well as royals, to the Côte d'Azur, including Russia's Tsar Alexander II and England's Queen Victoria.

In the 20th century, writers, artists and film stars joined the blue bloods, and today the French Riviera is arguably the snobbiest stretch of coastline on earth.

During our visit here, we'll be staying on my yacht, currently docked in the über-exclusive **Cap d'Antibes**, but we'll visit various spots on the Côte d'Azur in the course of our lesson.

To begin, let's take a look at our first five words.

I. PRONOUNCE AND DEFINE

1. **beau monde** (boh-MOANED´)
2. **jet set**
3. **carriage trade**
4. **scion** (SIGH´-uhn)
5. **noblesse oblige** (no-BLESS´ oh-BLEEZH´)

As you let these terms roll around on your tongue, let's step off the yacht and explore our current surroundings, home to some of the planet's priciest real estate.

While we walk, notice the immense villas, gleaming white with red-tile roofs, that are half-hidden behind impenetrable gates.

These belong to the multibillionaires of the world, and they overlook the best beaches on the Cote d'Azur. Palm trees, umbrella pines, and bougainvillea complete the scene.

As we continue to explore the area, consider our snob words in sentences that hint at their definitions.

1. Members of Miami's *beau monde* showed up for the new art museum opening wearing Versace and Prada.

2. Acapulco was once a favorite destination of the *jet set*, but now that the Mexican resort is plagued with drug violence, well-heeled travelers have largely moved on.

3. The little bakery on Market Street currently caters to the *carriage trade*, but before the area became gentrified, it served the working class.

4. Twenty-eight-year-old Juan Carlos is a *scion* of the Montalba family, which owns several large banks in Colombia.

5. Duchess Dorothea wanted to fire the governess for starting a fire in the nursery, but she let the poor woman stay on out of a sense of *noblesse oblige*.

II. FILL IN THE BLANKS

Did you get the general drift of these snob words' meanings? Now see if you can match each word with its actual definition.

1. _____ French for 'nobility obligates,' the concept that high birth or rank obligates one to behave generously and honorably

2. _____ a person, generally young, born into a rich and influential family

3. _____ the wealthy clientele of a business; the well-to-do

4. _____ the international group of wealthy and fashionable people who travel widely for pleasure and congregate at chic resorts

5. _____ the world of fashion and high society

ANSWERS: (1) noblesse oblige; (2) scion; (3) carriage trade; (4) jet set; (5) beau monde

III. PRONOUNCE & DEFINE

Our next stop is **Saint-Tropez**, the one-time fishing village that became an international hot spot after it appeared in the 1956 film *And God Created Woman,* starring French actress **Brigitte Bardot** (b. 1934).

As we browse the boutiques of the tony **Rue de la Miséri-corde,** in the town's historic center, let's pronounce the remaining five snob words on today's agenda:

6. **haute bourgeoisie** (oat´ burr-zhwah-ZEE´)
7. **arriviste** (ah-ree-VEEST´)
8. **beautiful people**
9. **glitterati** (gli´-der-AH´-dee)
10. **nouveau riche** (new´-voh REESH´)

NOTE: the plural of *nouveau riche* is *nouveaux riches,* pronounced the same as the singular.

Let's pause at this sidewalk café for a lunch of **steak-frites** (panfried rib-eye steaks served with mountains of crisp fries, or *pommes frites*). As we eat, we'll watch a game of **pétanques.**

Not familiar with the sport? It's played by two players or two teams (usually older men), on flat, gravelled courts. The first player (selected by coin toss) throws a small wooden target ball, called the *cochonnet,* onto the gravel.

He or she then throws a metal, baseball-sized ball *(boule)* onto the court, attempting to get it as close to the cochonnet as possible. The other players follow suit, until all the boules have been thrown (depending on the number of competitors, each participant is allowed either two or three boules). The player (or team) whose boules land closest to the cochonnet wins.

Too tame for you? Give it a chance!

We'll finish our meal with a **tarte Tropézienne** (spongecake filled with orange-blossom-flavored custard), a local specialty, while we consider our last batch of words in context.

1. John, one of the richest men in New York, had made a fortune from internet businesses, but Manhattan's established families wanted nothing to do with him—they dismissed him as a *nouveau riche.*

2. Jean-Claude lacked a noble title, but as a fifth-generation member of a prominent banking family, no one doubted his place in the *haute bourgeoisie.*

3. Although Giselle was not known for her physical beauty, she was one of the *beautiful people:* she was rich, she wore nothing but *haute couture,* and she was constantly featured in the gossip magazines.

4. At Café Vogue, a favorite haunt of the fashion *glitterati,* you can always find supermodels, high-powered editors, and top designers nibbling at salads.

5. The first lady wowed the country with her flashy jewelry and designer gowns, but Washington society saw her as a vulgar *arriviste.*

IV. FILL IN THE BLANKS

Match the snob words from the previous section with their definitions below.

1. _____ the group of wealthy, famous people who lead expensive and highly publicized lifestyles; physical beauty not required

2. _____ a 1950s word that combines 'glitter' and 'literati;' refers to the group of stylish people involved in show business and other activities perceived as glamorous, such as art and fashion

3. _____ the upper-middle class, especially in France

4. _____ a person who is newly rich and who flaunts his or her money in conspicuous and tasteless ways

5. _____ a person who is just beginning to arrive on a social or artistic scene, and who may be viewed as either lacking credentials or as being unscrupulous in his or her climb to the top

ANSWERS: (1) beautiful people; (2) glitterati; (3) haute bourgeoisie; (4) nouveau riche; (5) arriviste

V. DEFINITIONS

How are you doing with these words so far? Confused?

Five of our terms—*carriage trade, jet set, beau monde, beautiful people,* and *glitterati*—are synonyms to some degree, but they can't be used interchangeably.

Let's look more closely at their subtle differences.

CARRIAGE TRADE: a term that originally referred to business transacted with rich clients, but with time, has also come to describe the group of rich clients themselves.

As a general term for the well-to do, *carriage trade* doesn't necessarily carry the connotation of 'fashionable,' but it does imply a certain degree of polite behavior.

Nouveaux-riches rock stars and ill-mannered sports celebrities need not apply.

carriage trade = well-mannered rich people

BEAU MONDE: (French, 'beautiful world') the world of high society and fashion. Members of the *beau monde* meet the requirements for membership in the *carriage trade* (they're rich and well behaved), but they have the additional qualities of high social status and style.

beau monde = stylish, high-born, well-bred rich people

JET SET: the international group of rich people who congregate at the world's most fashionable resorts.

Members of the *jet set* are also members of the *carriage trade,* due to their high net worth, but they may or may not have the social status necessary to belong to the *beau monde.*

In short, to belong to the *jet set,* you need money, fashion sense, and sufficient leisure time to travel frequently to ultra-ritzy locales.

jet set = fashionable rich people who travel

BEAUTIFUL PEOPLE: wealthy, famous people whose expensive and glamorous lifestyles are well publicized.

There's no requirement to be physically beautiful. Nor is it required to be aristocratic or well behaved.

Some fashion sense is usually expected, however.

Therefore, Hollywood divas, NFL stars, and top recording artists can all be *beautiful people,* regardless of their behavior, backgrounds, or physical characteristics.

These are the folks who fill the pages of *People* magazine.

beautiful people = famous, rich, well-publicized people

GLITTERATI: fashionable people involved in activities perceived as glamorous, such as show business, fashion, and art.

There's no requirement to be rich, although most members of the *glitterati* are successful in their fields, and are, therefore, at least comfortably well off.

glitterati = fashionable people in glamorous occupations

Did that help?
Give these terms some time.
Meanwhile, let's move on to our next activity.

VI. TRUE OR FALSE

Not far from here is **Ramatuelle**, a *village perché,* or hilltop village, whose enchanting medieval streets have been taken over by movie types, *fashionistas,* artists, and wealthy travelers in general.

In other words, the place is teeming with *glitterati* and *beautiful people,* with some *jet-setters* thrown in.

As we wander this gem of a town, and rub shoulders with the rich and famous, let's play the following true-or-false game:

(T/F) 1. A fashionable rich person with high social connections belongs to the *beau monde.*

(T/F) 2. A *nouveau riche* comes from generations of family money.

(T/F) 3. Members of the *glitterati* must wear shiny, showy clothing.

(T/F) 4. An *arriviste* is someone who has 'arrived,' or made it to the top.

(T/F) 5. Members of the *haute bourgeoisie* are just below the upper class on the social scale.

(T/F) 6. Businesses that cater to the *carriage trade* sell wheels, axles, hay, and oats.

(T/F) 7. You can find the *jet set* at the world's most luxurious resorts.

(T/F) 8. To be counted among the *beautiful people,* one must be a movie star or a model.

(T/F) 9. The daughter of a village baker would usually be considered a *scion.*

(T/F) 10. A count could demonstrate *noblesse oblige* by turning his estate into a public park.

ANSWERS: All false except (1), (5), (7), and (10).

VII. SNOB APPEAL

Let's get back on the yacht and head over to **Cannes**, the alluring Riviera resort famous for the annual film festival that attracts movie stars and directors from around the globe.

As we stroll **La Croisette**, the town's palm-lined, see-and-be-seen promenade (there's Angelina Jolie!), fill each blank in the following snob statements with the most appropriate snob word from this lesson.

Each word is used only once.

beau monde	haute bourgeoisie
jet set	arriviste
carriage trade	beautiful people
scion	glitterati
noblesse oblige	nouveau riche

1. "Ginger had money and style, but she lacked the aristocratic family pedigree necessary to be a true member of the
_____."

2. "I've chaired the Easter Cotillion for the past decade! I can't believe the board chose that _____
Natasha to take my place this year!"

3. "Tom's new house, which has two indoor pools, a bowling alley, an indoor tennis court, and a twenty-car garage, absolutely screams _____."

4. "Strangely enough, you don't have to be beautiful to be one of the _____."

5. "My fiancé, Roger, is a _____ of the McIntosh applesauce family."

6. "The CEO lacked any sense of _____: he treated workers as if they were indentured servants."

7. "The guest list for the opening of Clyde's show includes _____ from the art world.

8. "We started out selling cheap cars to the working class. Now we sell high-end European imports to members of the_____."

9. "No, she's not noble, but she *does* descend from prominent members of the _____."

10. "We just renovated our Bora Bora resort, which we hope will become a favorite of the _____."

ANSWERS: (1) beau monde; (2) arriviste; (3) nouveau riche; (4) beautiful people; (5) scion; (6) noblesse oblige; (7) glitterati; (8) carriage trade; (9) haute bourgeoisie; (10) jet set

VIII. MULTIPLE CHOICE

Our last stop for this lesson is **Menton**, the easternmost town on the French Riviera, positioned directly on the Franco-Italian border.

Billed as the sunniest spot in France, this former fishing village is now known for its vacation villas and citrus groves, which rarely see frost due to the town's balmy microclimate.

The climate is also amenable to exotic botanical gardens. We'll visit one, the **Jardin Val Rahmeh**, a paradise of tropical and subtropical plants from all over the world.

As we walk through this assemblage of palms, citrus trees, bamboo, and lily pads, let's review this lesson's snob words with these questions:

1. A person who belongs to the *haute bourgeoisie* is:
   a. working class
   b. upper middle class
   c. of noble descent

2. Membership in the *beau monde* requires:
   - a. fame, money, and travel
   - b. social status, money, and style
   - c. fame, money, and style

3. A person born into a rich and powerful family may be called a(n):
   - a. *scion*
   - b. *arriviste*
   - c. *noblesse oblige*

4. Which of the following is **not** an example of *noblesse oblige?*
   - a. a duchess donates her fortune to an orphanage
   - b. a parish priest volunteers at a soup kitchen
   - c. a famous actress does a free public service announcement for homeless children

5. The plural of *nouveau riche* is:
   - a. *nouveau riches*
   - b. *nouveaus riches*
   - c. *nouveaux riches*

6. If your business caters to the *carriage trade,* you offer:
   - a. cheap products to the masses
   - b. exclusive products to rich customers
   - c. mid-range products over the internet

7. Where would you **least likely** encounter members of the *jet set?*
   - a. Akron, Ohio
   - b. Palm Beach, Florida
   - c. Aspen, Colorado

8. Which group does **not** belong to the *glitterati?*
   - a. prominent Hollywood actors
   - b. top fashion designers
   - c. highly paid CEOs in the medical field

9. The requirements to belong to the group known as the *beautiful people* are:
   a. fame, intelligence, and money
   b. fashion sense, fame, and beauty
   c. money, some fashion sense, and fame
10. To call a person an *arriviste* is:
    a. an insult
    b. a compliment
    c. a neutral statement

ANSWERS: (1) b; (2) b; (3) a; (4) b; (5) c; (6) b; (7) a; (8) c; (9) c; (10) a

Alas, it's time to bid *adieu* to Menton, but we're not yet leaving the Cote d'Azur.

Tonight we'll take the yacht to **Monaco**, a Lilliputian country whose snob factor greatly outweighs its size and population.

There, in the morning, we'll take our first midterm, which covers all the snob words in the first third of this course.

Study up!

Day 10

First Midterm Exam
GOT YOUR SNOB ON?

LOCATION: **MONTE CARLO, MONACO**

Phew! You've now mastered eighty snob words. Or have you? We're about to find out here in **Monte Carlo**, the one and only city in the tiny principality of Monaco.

This charming and very snobby locale is mainly composed of luxury high-rise apartment buildings squeezed onto a steep, narrow strip of land that runs between the mountains (dominated by the rocky **Mont Agel**) and the Mediterranean Sea.

Why take our first midterm—I mean, *comprehension assessment game*—here? Because there's a high snob vibe. Snobbism is in the air, you could say, which should put you into the snob zone and help improve your score.

I also just happen to own a penthouse here, so why not take advantage of it? Exam with a view!

The test covers the first nine lessons of this course, and if you score ninety percent or higher, we'll promptly present you with your bachelor of arts degree in snobcabulary.

It's important to get an accurate measure of your progress, so while we urge you to review our past snob words *before* beginning the game, we beg you to resist the urge to look back at previous lessons once you've begun. (Besides, we have cameras mounted in this book. We'll catch you!)

The midterm contains eighty questions in true-or-false, fill-in-the-blank, multiple-choice, matching, and story formats.

Once you're ready, set a timer for twenty minutes, and go! (Take a few extra minutes if you need to.)

I. MULTIPLE CHOICE

1. A business that caters to the *carriage trade:*
   a. offers carriage rides
   b. sells automobiles
   c. targets wealthy clients
2. If you're having lunch on the *veranda,* you're:
   a. eating on the run
   b. eating in an outdoor, covered area
   c. eating next to a pool
3. An evening of *chamber music* might consist of:
   a. a string quartet in a private home
   b. a Dixieland band in a judge's chambers
   c. a large orchestra performing a full symphony
4. A *gourmand:*
   a. primarily wants to fill his stomach
   b. is knowledgeable about food and its preparation
   c. has a culinary degree
5. *Women's Wear Daily* is known as:
   a. the best place to find *haute couture* coupons
   b. the bible of the women's fashion industry
   c. a gossipy rag full of yellow journalism
6. *Ancien régime* furniture was produced:
   a. prior to the French Revolution
   b. before Castro took over Cuba
   c. during the days of ancient Greece

7. A person who is 'up to date' is:
    a. *au jus*
    b. *au contraire*
    c. *au courant*

8. A *triptych* is:
    a. an artwork consisting of two panels
    b. an artwork consisting of three panels
    c. an artwork safely packed for a journey

9. *Chichi* means:
    a. chic sushi
    b. being naturally and confidently stylish
    c. showy, but lacking true style

10. A *screen print* is an artwork made by:
    a. forcing paint through a screen onto paper
    b. printing a design from a computer screen
    c. screening a print of a movie

ANSWERS: (1) c; (2) b; (3) a; (4) a; (5) b; (6) a; (7) c; (8) b; (9) c; (10) a

II. TRUE OR FALSE

(T/F)   1. The proper way to pronounce *chaise longue* is chase LOAN-gyoo.

(T/F)   2. *Haute couture* is French for 'ready to wear.'

(T/F)   3. A *locavore* eats only what is produced locally.

(T/F)   4. A *loggia* is a room that's open to the outdoors on at least one side.

(T/F)   5. In *pizzicato*, strings are played with a bow, rather than being plucked.

(T/F)   6. *Old Master* always signifies high quality.

(T/F)   7. A chef *par excellence* is a very good chef.

(T/F)   8. It's possible to put a life-size statue in an *étagère*.

(T/F)   9. The *dernier cri* is the latest fashion.

(T/F)   10. *Nouvelle cuisine* uses lots of butter.

ANSWERS: all false except (3), (4), (7), and (9).

III. SNOB STATEMENTS

Fill the blanks in the statements below using the following list of snob words.

Each word is used only once.

scion	de trop
fashion's Big Four	chiaroscuro
enfilade	concerto
gastronome	chinoiserie
sonata	soigné

1. "Eli played *Tropical* _____ for the recital."
2. "The mansion has a(n) _____ that allows one to see through all the principal rooms to a view of Lake Como."
3. "The resort was quite amazing, with five swimming pools, sixteen tennis courts, and twelve restaurants, but the gold-plated toilets seemed _____."
4. "My best friend is a _____ of the rich and powerful Walton family."
5. "It was a _____, since the solo pianist was backed up by a full orchestra."
6. "Felipe loves to eat. Since he has a discriminating palate and an extensive knowledge of food, however, he's not a gourmand, but a _____."
7. "Tokyo is *not* included in _____."
8. "The portrait artist used _____ to make our faces stand out against the dark background."
9. "He's a _____ kind of guy who has a different briefcase to match each of his Armani suits."
10. "I have nothing against _____ in general, but too much makes a room look like a restaurant."

ANSWERS: (1) sonata; (2) enfilade; (3) de trop; (4) scion; (5) concerto; (6) gastronome; (7) fashion's Big Four; (8) chiaroscuro; (9) soigné; (10) chinoiserie

IV. MATCHING

Match each snob word with its definition.

____ 1. *atelier*   a. to search for food in the wild
____ 2. *gauche*   b. newly rich; displaying expensive, but bad, taste
____ 3. *boiserie*   c. term used to number musical compositions
____ 4. *Coco Chanel*   d. artist's studio
____ 5. *forage*   e. socially inappropriate
____ 6. *opus*   f. decorative wood paneling
____ 7. *lanai*   g. covered porch or terrace, especially in Hawaii
____ 8. *nouveau riche*   h. influential fashion designer
____ 9. *entablature*   i. upper middle class
____ 10. *haute bourgeoisie* j. topmost portion of a building in classical style

ANSWERS: (1) d; (2) e; (3) f; (4) h; (5) a; (6) c; (7) g; (8) b; (9) j; (10) i

V. SENSE…OR NONSENSE?

Check each of the following sentences that makes sense.

____ 1. The painting over the Steinway in the living room was done *en plein air.*
____ 2. *Chic* women always buy their clothing at thrift shops.
____ 3. One of my favorite *objets d'art* is a full-size copy of Michelangelo's *David.*
____ 4. I'm not much of a *fashionista*—I spend most of my time at fashion shows and in expensive boutiques.
____ 5. Jason's *gourmet* meals usually take less than ten minutes to prepare.
____ 6. If you adjust the *tessitura,* the car will run better.

___ 7. The mansion had a graceful *colonnade* across its front.

___ 8. Modeling agencies are the best places to find the *beautiful people*.

___ 9. Sharon works as an *arriviste* at JFK Airport.

___ 10. The musical, entitled *Choppy Waters*, features a great deal of *staccato*.

ANSWERS: numbers (1), (7), and (10) should be checked—the others are nonsense.

VI. MORE MATCHING

Again, match each snob word with its definition.

___ 1. *Palladian window*	a.	composition for voices and instruments
___ 2. *jet set*	b.	male dressmaker
___ 3. *cantata*	c.	outrageous; improper
___ 4. *epicure*	d.	wide chair with closed arms
___ 5. *passementerie*	e.	as things should be; proper
___ 6. *outré*	f.	fringe and tassels
___ 7. *etching*	g.	has three sections and a center arch
___ 8. *comme il faut*	h.	made by scratching a metal plate
___ 9. *bergère*	i.	one who takes pleasure in food
___ 10. *couturier*	j.	group of rich people who frequent fashionable resorts

ANSWERS: (1) g; (2) j; (3) a; (4) i; (5) f; (6) c; (7) h; (8) e; (9) d; (10) b

VII. TRUE OR FALSE

(T/F) 1. A *fauteuil* can be easily moved.

(T/F) 2. If a piece of clothing is *bon chic, bon genre,* it's outlandish and calls attention to itself.

(T/F) 3. *Haute cuisine* refers to expensive, custom-made clothing by top designers.

(T/F) 4. An *aria* is a speech-like song that moves the story forward in opera.

(T/F) 5. A *pilaster* can be described as a square column.

(T/F) 6. *Noblesse oblige* means 'nobility obligates.'

(T/F) 7. A true *porte-cochère* is a door wide enough to allow carriages and autos to enter a property.

(T/F) 8. An *oratorio* is a long work, with a religious theme, performed by vocalists and orchestra.

(T/F) 9. Pasta cooked *al dente* is mushy.

(T/F) 10. Fashion's *Big Four* are New York, Paris, London, and Tokyo.

ANSWERS: (1), (5), (6), (7), and (8) are true; the others are false.

VIII. COMPLETE THE STORY

Fill the blanks with the following words, each used once.

de rigueur	fashion week
prêt-à-porter	portico
bon appétit	glitterati
de trop	lithograph
sfumato	faux marbre

The Expensive Escapades of
MARCO & GISELLE
Professional Beautiful People

Episode Five: Lollygagging in London

It's now mid-September, and Giselle and her mother are in London for (1)_____. Having ordered several dozen *haute couture* designs while they were in Paris in July, they're now here to see what the Brits will offer next season in the way of less expensive (2)_____.

While the two have afternoon tea in the **Palm Court** of the **London Ritz**, Giselle notices a familiar gentleman seated at the next table.

GISELLE: *(covering her face with a napkin)* Excuse me, I think we met recently on a (3)_____ in Vicenza.

MARCO: Giselle? Can that possibly be you?

MRS. VAN DE KAMP: *(turning to face the young man)* Marco! What are you doing in London?

MARCO: Hello, Mrs. Van de Kamp. I am here for another polo match.

MRS. VAN DE KAMP: What a delightful surprise! Do come and sit at our table.

MARCO: Thank you, and (4)_____! *(He sits down next to Giselle.)*

GISELLE: You do know that the "good sort" of French people consider that phrase vulgar.

MARCO: I do realize that, since my mother is originally from France. But since the English use the phrase frequently, I feel obligated to play along when I'm in London.

MRS. VAN DE KAMP: There's nothing wrong with the phrase, especially here in London, as you have noted, Marco. You'll have to excuse Giselle. Ever since she returned from her Swiss finishing school, she's felt the need to correct the entire world.

GISELLE: Not the entire world, mother *(something catches her eye)*. Look! Look over there! This place is literally *crawling* with fashion (5)_____. There's Ralph Lauren.

MARCO: *(staring at a green marble column to one side of the table)* You don't say?

MRS. VAN DE KAMP: Is something wrong, Marco?

MARCO: No—not at all. I was just wondering whether this column was real or (6)_____.

MRS. VAN DE KAMP: I should hope *real* marble would be (7)_____ in an establishment such as this.

GISELLE: Actually, this place is so fussy that I find the marble columns (8)_____. If I had my way, I'd tear all this froufrou out and replace it with something sleek, modern, and less challenging to the eye.

MARCO: With all due respect, I think that would be a crime.

MRS. VAN DE KAMP: So do I! How could you throw away all this richness—this beauty?

GISELLE: I guess I just enjoy simplicity. It's like when we're in the art museums, mother. You love the Leonardos and the Rembrandts, with their *chiaroscuro* and (9)_____, while I gravitate to the modern works like Toulouse-Lautrec's (10)_____."

ANSWERS: (1) fashion week; (2) prêt-à-porter; (3) portico; (4) bon appétit; (5) glitterati; (6) faux marbre; (7) de rigueur; (8) de trop; (9) sfumato; (10) lithographs

IX. HOW DID YOU DO?

Was that so difficult?

Take a deep breath and add up your scores. Then check to see what degree you've earned according to the following grading scale:

75-80   **Bachelor of Arts in Snobcabulary,** *cum laude*
70-75   **Bachelor of Arts in Snobcabulary**
60-70   **Associate of Arts in Snobcabulary,** *cum laude*
50-60   **Associate of Arts in Snobcabulary**
40-50   **40 credits** toward your snobcabulary degree
  0-40   **Sorry, you failed**—go back and try again.

Congratulations! I'm going to assume you did well.

But no matter how you did, let's celebrate your completion of the first third of this course with dinner at **Le Louis XV,** another **Alain Ducasse** restaurant with three Michelin stars (if you remember, we dined at Ducasse's namesake restaurant in Paris on Day 3).

This gastronomic Valhalla, located in the fanciful **Hotel de Paris**—one of Monte Carlo's most exclusive hotels—has a dining room straight out of the Palace of Versailles.

After dinner, we'll spend another night on the yacht as the crew guides us to the port of Marseilles. My chauffeur, Jean-

Claude, will meet us there tomorrow morning and drive us to the **Luberon**, a magical area of **Provence**.

There we'll begin PART TWO of this course, which covers more French, more food, and more interior design, as well as snob words from Italian, Latin, and the worlds of gardening, sports, real estate, and the performing arts.

PART TWO

Day 11

Taking French Leave
GALLICISMS FOR MANNERS & BEHAVIOR

LOCATION: **PROVENCE, FRANCE**

Yes, another chapter on French words. Why? Because the French practically invented manners and etiquette. While Americans were taming the wilderness and burning witches, the civilized Sun King, **Louis XIV** (1638-1715), and his cohorts filled their days with playful *repartee* (see below) in the **Palace of Versailles**, and their nights with sophisticated *soirées* (evening parties, see Day 28) in the surrounding gardens.

The **French Revolution** (1789-99) eventually brought an end to the fun, but Gallic words still reign supreme in describing polite (and sometimes not-so-polite) behavior.

Since we've already had two lessons in Paris, we'll present this lesson's snob words here in **Provence**, the historic region in the **South of France** known for its brilliant light, hearty food, and fields of sunflowers and lavender.

We'll stay at my *bastide* (a Provençal manor house, see Day 13), which is about a mile outside **Rousillon**, just one of dozens of medieval hilltop towns here in the rocky, picturesque area known as the **Luberon**.

As we take a first look at our new words, have some crusty bread with the local cheese, **Banon**, a creamy white disk made of goat's milk.

I. PRONOUNCE AND DEFINE

1. **faux pas** (foe PAW´)
2. **badinage** (bad-uh-NAHZH´)
3. **repartee** (rep-er-TEE´)
4. **savoir faire** (sav-wah FAIR´)
5. **bonhomie** (bahn-ah-MEE´)
6. **entre nous** (ahn-truh NEW´)
7. **joie de vivre** (zhwah duh VEE´-vruh)
8. **bon vivant** (bone´ vee-VAHN´)
9. **mauvais quart d'heure** (moh´-vay kat DUR´)
10. **flâneur** (flaw-NUR´)

1. FAUX PAS: (French, 'false step') an embarrassing social mistake; a breach of manners or good conduct.

Using the wrong fork at a formal dinner is a *faux pas*, as is asking a woman her age.

PLURAL: written and pronounced the same as the singular (foe PAW´)—one *faux pas*, two *faux pas*, etc.

2. BADINAGE: good-natured verbal sparring; teasing that fails to cross the line into actual insult, though it may come close. Synonyms include ribbing, joshing, banter, and raillery.

3. REPARTEE: quick and witty conversation between two or more people.

Like *badinage*, *repartee* is a form of verbal sparring, but it lacks the teasing (and semi-insulting nature) of *badinage*.

4. **SAVOIR FAIRE**: (French, 'know-how') the ability to act correctly and confidently in any social situation. Those who possess *savoir faire* have worldly experience and a polished confidence in their behavior.

Most English dictionaries spell *savoir faire* as two separate words, but for a little added snobbery, spell it the French way, with a hyphen *(savoir-faire)*.

5. **BONHOMIE**: (from the French *bonhomme*, 'good fellow') geniality or easy friendliness. Chatting with strangers in an elevator is an example of *bonhomie*.

6. **ENTRE NOUS**: (French, 'between ourselves') phrase meaning 'just between the two of us,' used when a speaker wishes to keep a matter private.

- Let's keep this information strictly *entre nous*.
- *Entre nous*, I think this company's days are numbered.

7. **JOIE DE VIVRE**: (French, 'joy of living') an extreme enjoyment of life or feeling of happiness about life.

8. **BON VIVANT**: a person who has cultivated and refined tastes, who has an appreciation for good food, and who likes parties and other social events.

PLURAL: *bons vivants*, pronounced the same as the singular (bone´ vee-VAHN´).

9. **MAUVAIS QUART D'HEURE**: (French, 'bad quarter of an hour') a brief experience that is unpleasant, embarrassing, or both. Running into one's bitter ex-spouse in the post office, for example, could constitute a *mauvais quart d'heure*.

10. **FLÂNEUR**: a man who strolls about town, often observing society; an idler or dawdler.

The term dates to the late 19th century, soon after Paris had been redesigned with wide, leafy boulevards lined with elegant mansions and apartment buildings.

At that time, a *flâneur* was a man, usually of independent means, who wandered these new boulevards in search of amusement, adventure, and enlightenment.

Today the term refers to strollers, saunterers, and men-about-town of any city.

PLURAL: *flâneurs* (flaw-NUR'), pronounced the same as the singular.

BONUS WORDS: what *flâneurs* do is called **flânerie** (flawn-REE'); a female *flâneur* is a **flâneuse** (flaw-NOOCE').

II. MATCHING

As you can see, my *bastide* is a two-story stone manor with the typical Provençal accoutrements of turquoise shutters and geranium-filled window boxes. It was built in the early 17th century, and we've tried to keep it as authentic as possible.

Of course, we added the pool, the tennis court, central heating, and indoor plumbing, but other than that, the original owners would feel right at home.

We have eight bedrooms—choose whichever one you like! As you settle in, match five of our new snob words with their definitions.

____	1. *flâneur*	a. 'between the two of us'
____	2. *entre nous*	b. person of refined taste who enjoys parties and good food
____	3. *bon vivant*	c. zest for life
____	4. *joie de vivre*	d. brief, but embarrassing, situation
____	5. *mauvais quart d'heure*	e. man who wanders about town

ANSWERS: (1) e; (2) a; (3) b; (4) c; (5) d

Now do the same with the remaining five snob words.

___	6. *bonhomie*	a.	false step; social mistake
___	7. *savoir faire*	b.	exchange of good-natured insults
___	8. *repartee*	c.	clever conversation
___	9. *badinage*	d.	knowledge of what to do in any social situation
___	10. *faux pas*	e.	friendliness; geniality

ANSWERS: (6) e; (7) d; (8) c; (9) b (10) a

III. MULTIPLE CHOICE

I'm ready for lunch, are you? And I know the perfect little place in the village.

As we walk there, first through fields of sunflowers, and then through vineyards and a bit of pine forest, let's play the following multiple-choice game:

1. If you have *savoir faire*, you:
   a. behave appropriately in all social situations
   b. enjoy parties and good food
   c. savor the good things in life
2. If a person has *joie de vivre*, he/she:
   a. has broad social skills
   b. loves life
   c. displays an easy friendliness
3. A brief, but painful experience is a:
   a. *quart heure d'mauvais*
   b. *mauvais heure d'quart*
   c. *mauvais quart d'heure*
4. A *bon vivant* is a person who:
   a. loves life
   b. loves social situations and good food
   c. wants to be left alone

5. Fast-paced, scintillating conversation is:
   a. *repartee*
   b. *badinage*
   c. *bonhomie*
6. A social gaffe is a:
   a. *fox paw*
   b. *faux paw*
   c. *faux pas*
7. *Bonhomie* is:
   a. French for 'best friend'
   b. general amiability
   c. the art of creating a beautiful home
8. A French word for mild taunting and teasing:
   a. *badinage*
   b. *buddynodge*
   c. *budinage*
9. A *flâneur* is:
   a. considered an idler
   b. always male
   c. both of the above
10. If someone tells you something *entre nous:*
   a. you should share it with the world
   b. you should keep it to yourself
   c. you should tell three friends, but no more

ANSWERS: (1) a; (2) b; (3) c; (4) b; (5) a; (6) c; (7) b; (8) a; (9) c; (10) b

IV. JOURNAL TIME

Yes, it was a bit of a hike to reach Rousillon, but wasn't it worth it? Look at these views of the countryside!

We'll pass through three or four of these narrow medieval alleys to get to the restaurant. Here it is!

Let's take a table on the sidewalk. I suggest the white asparagus (which just happens to be in season) and Provençal pizza—called **pissaladière**—topped with grilled eggplant and fennel. *C'est délicieux!*

As we dine, take time to study the locals and jot down your observations in a journal (you never know when you'll need material for your next novel or screenplay). Fill the blanks below with snob words from this lesson.

faux pas	bonhomie
badinage	entre nous
repartee	bon vivant
savoir faire	mauvais quart d'heure
joie de vivre	flâneur

People-Watching Journal

The first person to walk by is a tall woman, dressed in a pink Chanel suit, leading two impeccably groomed poodles. I smile at her, and then realize, from her stony glance in reply, that I have committed a (1)_____.

I act as if nothing has happened, but (2)_____, I secretly pass through a (3)_____.

Next I notice a group of teen boys in school uniforms who are pushing and shoving each other as they make their way down the street.

These boys are shouting things in French—good-natured (4)_____, I assume. It's refreshing to see young people with so much energy and (5)_____.

Then a young mother comes by pushing two toddlers in a double stroller. In contrast to the Chanel-wearing older lady, this woman smiles, and then, in a spirit of (6)_____, greets me with a French phrase that I don't understand. I nod and smile.

Finally, a dapper older gentleman, oozing sophistication and (7)_____, walks by with a bouquet of roses.

Is he a (8)_____, I wonder, off to provide sparkling (9)_____ at a swank lunch party?

Or is he simply a loafer, wandering the streets as a small-town (10)_____?

ANSWERS: (1) faux pas; (2) entre nous; (3) mauvais quart d'heure; (4) badinage; (5) joie de vivre (6) bonhomie; (7) savoir faire; (8) bon vivant; (9) repartee; (10) flâneur

V. TRUE OR FALSE

Did you get some good material? Isn't this asparagus divine?

As we finish our meal, indicate whether the following definitions are true or false.

(T/F) 1. *joie de vivre:* 'joy of living'
(T/F) 2. *bon vivant:* a man who wanders the boulevards
(T/F) 3. *mauvais quart d'heure:* 'a bad fifteen minutes'
(T/F) 4. *bonhomie:* good-natured teasing or taunting
(T/F) 5. *entre nous:* 'between us'
(T/F) 6. *faux pas:* an embarrassing social error
(T/F) 7. *badinage:* easy friendliness
(T/F) 8. *savoir faire:* confidence in any social situation
(T/F) 9. *flâneur:* a cultivated person who loves parties
(T/F) 10. *repartee:* witty and fast-paced conversation

ANSWERS: all true except (2), (4), (7), and (9).

VI. WORDS IN PRINT

It's almost time to leave this lovely corner of France, but before we do, let's watch the sun set from my terrace as we look at how these French terms are used in the media.

Fill each blank with one of this lesson's snob words. Each word is used once; make words plural or possessive where necessary. *Bonne chance!*

faux pas	bonhomie
badinage	entre nous
repartee	bon vivant
savoir faire	mauvais quart d'heure
joie de vivre	flâneur

1. *Esquire,* "A Century of Style," 18 Sept. 2017:

   But his _____ approach to life and style is best embodied on the back of his favorite vest. It's an old French phrase: *Je ne consulte que mon plaisir.* Translation: "I only consult my pleasure."

2. *New York Times,* "Why Trump's Budding Bromance With Xi Is Doomed," 3 May 2017:

   Beneath the _____, experts say, are differences of strategic interest that may keep President Trump from getting the results he wants on North Korea.

3. *Boston Globe,* "A Dull villain imperils 'Justice League,'" 15 Nov. 2017:

   "Wonder Woman," from earlier this year, is the only film in the current cycle that feels light on its feet—that has the excitement and fun and _____ you want from a movie in which people can fly....

4. *Architectural Digest,* "Uncommon Areas," 31 Mar. 2015:

   A fashion designer turned president of the Scalamandré fabric house turned globe-trotting author and _____, Steven Stolman certainly knows chic.

5. *New Yorker,* "Permission to Enter,' 30 July 2012:

   Keisha Blake, whose celebrated will and focus did not leave her much room for angst, watched her friend ascend to the top deck

in her new panda-eyed makeup and had a _____,
wondering whether she herself had any personality at all or was
in truth only the accumulation and reflection of all the things
she had read in books and seen on television.

6. *cntraveller.com,* "Travel Guide to Martinique," 11 Nov.
2009:

The pretty Caribbean island of Martinique is sophisticated and
well developed, an island outpost with _____,
a French département that shares with the 'mainland' a proper
appreciation of the finer things in life: namely food and romance.

7. *vogue.com,* "Tory Burch Fall 2017 Ready-to-Wear Collection," 14 Feb. 2017:

The times demand an outspoken muse. Tory Burch looked to
Tracy Lord, Katharine Hepburn's character in *The Philadelphia
Story,* a blue blood of sharp-witted _____ and a
glamorous Adrian-designed wardrobe.

8. *New York Times,* "The Secret to a Long Life Is Bocce," 17
Nov. 2017:

These men are talented chop-busters engaged in a ceaseless
_____ of brotherhood: "Don't listen to that guy,
he don't know bocce;" "That guy's trouble, stay away from that
one...."

9. *Wall Street Journal,* "What Not to Do in a Wine Store...
Ever," 7 Sept. 2017:

Dogs set loose in the aisles, excessive perfume, phony French
accents—wine store owners have seen (and hated) it all. Here's a
retailer's-eye view of _____ to avoid.

10. *Vanity Fair,* "Tour de Gall," April 2011:

> But still, it's undeniable that L'Ami Louis really is special and apart. It has earned an epic accolade. It is, all things considered, _____, the worst restaurant in the world.

ANSWERS: (1) flâneur's; (2) bonhomie; (3) joie de vivre; (4) bon vivant; (5) mauvais quart d'heure; (6) savoir faire; (7) repartee; (8) badinage; (9) faux pas; (10) entre nous

Congratulations on completing yet another lesson!

You say your brain is fried?

I guess you could say it's *French fried.*

Bad puns aside, your task now is to work these French snob words into your everyday conversation and writing.

Get some rest, because tomorrow we head to England to examine my garden.

Day 12

How Does Your Garden Grow?
HELLO HAUTE HORTICULTURE

LOCATION: **KENT, ENGLAND**

You don't need a green thumb to enjoy fine gardening. After all, the gardeners do all the dirty work—we snobs just show up and savor their efforts.

But to properly appreciate fine gardens and landscapes, and to talk (and brag) about them, you must know the lingo.

What if someone invites you to meet her (or him) in the *pergola*, and you don't know where or what that is? What if your hostess tells you lunch will be served on the *tapis vert* in front of the *orangerie?*

Will you arrive on time? Or at all?

These frightful scenarios will be avoided if you commit these horticultural snob words to memory.

Today we'll be meeting in Kent, known as the garden county of England, where I own an estate with a traditional English garden that includes French and Italian elements.

Welcome! Let's first appreciate the garden from the second-story windows of the Georgian manor house as we get acquainted with our new snob words.

I. PRONOUNCE & DEFINE

1. **parterre** (par-TEHR´)
2. **belvedere** (BELL´-vuh-deer)
3. **pergola** (PER´-gol-uh)
4. **folly** (FALL´-ee)
5. **orangerie** (OR´-uhn-jree)
6. **treillage** (tray-YAHZH´)
7. **allée** (al-LAY´)
8. **espalier** (es-PAL´-yer)
9. **grotto** (GRAW´-doh)
10. **tapis vert** (TAW´-pee VEHR´)

1. **PARTERRE:** a flat garden terrace composed of various elements (which may include paths, fountains, shrubs, and flower beds) that form a symmetrical design.

A *parterre* is best appreciated from the upper floors of a house.

2. **BELVEDERE:** a garden structure, often in the form of a Greek temple, that provides a pleasant view.

3. **PERGOLA:** a tunnel-like framework, often consisting of two parallel rows of columns connected by overhead beams, on which climbing plants are trained.

Pergolas can be long or short, and are often used as a shady way to get from point A to point B in a garden.

4. **FOLLY:** a decorative and often extravagant garden structure. *Follies,* which are meant to catch the eye and accentuate

the landscape, are often built to resemble historic or exotic structures, such as ruined castles or Chinese pagodas.

5. **ORANGERIE**: a garden building, independent or attached to another structure, designed for wintering tropical and subtropical plants (such as palm, orange, and lemon trees) in harsh climates.

Often architecturally elaborate, *orangeries* usually have tall windows on their south sides.

Orangeries are frequently used to host events, especially in inclement weather.

6. **TREILLAGE**: a generic term for latticework, often in the form of arbors, trellises, and *pergolas*, used to support vines and other climbing plants.

7. **ALLÉE**: a walkway or driveway lined with tall shrubs or trees that produce a tunnel effect. *Allées* often lead to dramatic views.

8. **ESPALIER**: as a noun, a tree or shrub whose branches have been trained to grow against a wall, usually supported by wires or a lattice framework *(treillage)*.

Espaliers are most often employed in courtyards and walled gardens, where limited space makes full-size trees impractical.

As a verb, *espalier* means to train a tree or shrub to grow flat against a wall.

9. **GROTTO**: a small, picturesque cave, usually man-made, set in a garden or park.

PLURAL: *grottos* or *grottoes*.

10. **TAPIS VERT**: ('green carpet' in French) a large, flat, unbroken expanse of lawn used as a landscape element.

Tapis verts (the plural, pronounced the same as the singular) are usually highly manicured and often bordered by gravel walks or flower beds. They're a common feature of French Baroque gardens, such as those at the **Palace of Versailles**.

II. FILL THE BLANKS

Are you thoroughly confused? Relax, these terms will be yours before you know it.

But before we actually enter the garden, let's review our new words by using them to fill the blanks below.

parterre	tapis vert
belvedere	grotto
pergola	treillage
espalier	allée
orangerie	folly

1. _____ large expanse of grass resembling a rug
2. _____ garden feature best viewed from above
3. _____ large and elegant greenhouse
4. _____ picturesque garden structure
5. _____ garden structure with a view
6. _____ cave set in a garden
7. _____ lattice used to support plants
8. _____ tree-lined drive or walkway
9. _____ fruit tree growing against a garden wall
10. _____ vine-covered structure over a walkway

ANSWERS: (1) tapis vert; (2) parterre; (3) orangerie; (4) folly; (5) belvedere; (6) grotto; (7) treillage; (8) allée; (9) espalier; (10) pergola

III. MULTIPLE CHOICE

1. If you wish to grow fruit in limited garden space, you'd be wise to consider:
   a. *pergolas*
   b. *espaliers*
   c. *parterres*

2. A dark place where garden visitors can take refuge from summer heat:
   a. *allée*
   b. *espalier*
   c. *grotto*

3. A garden structure that provides a pleasant view is a:
   a. *belvedere*
   b. *folly*
   c. *pergola*

4. A manicured piece of grass in the form of a green carpet is a(n):
   a. *espalier*
   b. *parterre*
   c. *tapis vert*

5. A *parterre* may be composed of:
   a. shrubs, flower beds, fountains, and paths
   b. trees trained to grow against a wall
   c. a tunnel-like framework covered in vines

6. If you want a shady way to get from the house to the *orangerie,* you may consider installing a:
   a. *folly*
   b. *parterre*
   c. *pergola*

7. A driveway lined with tall trees or shrubs is a(n):
   a. *allée*
   b. *treillage*
   c. *parterre*

8. *Espaliers* are often trained on a framework of:
   a. *treillage*
   b. *tapis vert*
   c. *parterre*

9. A miniature Chinese pagoda, set to the side of a lake in a garden, could be considered a:
   a. *pergola*
   b. *folly*
   c. *treillage*

10. If you're hosting an outdoor wedding, and it starts to rain, you may want to move the event to the:
    a. *treillage*
    b. *parterre*
    c. *orangerie*

ANSWERS: (1) b; (2) c; (3) a; (4) c; (5) a; (6) c; (7) a; (8) a; (9) b; (10) c

IV. GARDEN TOUR

Now let's head into the garden itself for a complete tour. Despite what I said earlier, we might actually get our feet a bit dirty. (Feel free to leave your Jimmy Choos here at the house and go barefoot.)

Fill each blank below with one of our snob words, each of which is used once. Alter words as needed to fit context.

parterre	tapis vert
belvedere	grotto
pergola	treillage
folly	allée
orangerie	espalier

We enter the garden through a(n) (1)_____ of cypress trees that leads to a manicured (2)_____ as smooth as a carpet.

Beyond that, we pass by a(n) (3)_____ composed of flower beds and fountains surrounded by clipped boxwood hedges.

It's beautiful from the ground, but its symmetrical layout was even more impressive when we saw it from the second floor of the house.

Next, we enter the secret garden. This charming space has apple and pear (4)_____ growing on the (5)_____ that covers the brick walls.

We move on to a(n) (6)_____ covered in grape vines, which shields us from the sun and leads us to the (7)_____. This is where the potted citrus trees are kept during the winter.

Then we enter the wilder side of the garden, where we stumble upon a(n) (8)_____, dark and covered in moss. We cool off here for a few moments.

As we exit, we notice what looks like a ruined castle across the lake. We head to this (9)_____, not knowing exactly what to expect.

When we arrive, however, we find that it is not just decorative: it also functions as a(n) (10)_____, affording a beautiful view across the lake to the house.

ANSWERS: (1) allée; (2) tapis vert; (3) parterre; (4) espaliers; (5) treillage; (6) pergola; (7) orangerie; (8) grotto; (9) folly; (10) belvedere

V. SENSE...OR NONSENSE?

Isn't my garden lovely?

Let's pause here a moment in the *belvedere* as we continue to review the proper use of each of our gardening snob words.

Put a check beside each sentence below that makes sense.

_____ 1. The reception will include dancing in the *treillage*.

_____ 2. I picked lemons from the *espaliers* this morning.

_____ 3. The *pergola* has a great view of the stars.

_____ 4. Ellen keeps her orchid collection in the *orangerie*.

_____ 5. Installing the *folly* (a miniature Greek temple) cost me a fortune!

_____ 6. I love the *grotto*—it's full of light and fresh air.

_____ 7. The *tapis vert* needs water. It's looking dry.

_____ 8. You enter the estate through an *allée* of flowers.

_____ 9. You can't call it a *belvedere:* there's no view!

_____ 10. It took about ten minutes to drive up the *parterre*.

ANSWERS: numbers (2), (4), (5), (7), and (9) should be checked.

VI. COMPLETE THE STORY

Look at your thumbs. Are they turning green? Maybe a little turquoise…or chartreuse?

Give them time!

To finish this lesson, we present yet another episode of your favorite snob opera. Today's installment takes place in Italy, another country enamored of its gardens.

Fill the blanks below with snob words from this lesson, each of which is used once. Alter words to fit context.

The Expensive Escapades of
MARCO & GISELLE
Professional Beautiful People

Episode Six: The Tiger of Tivoli

parterre	tapis vert
belvedere	grotto
pergola	treillage
folly	allée
orangerie	espalier

It's a warm afternoon in late October, and Giselle is visiting one of the fantastic Renaissance gardens in Tivoli, Italy. Suddenly she hears a series of moans coming from a deep, dark (1)_____.

Our heroine bravely throws aside her phobia of confined, eerie places and rushes inside. There, on the ground, lies a young man wearing riding boots and a gaucho-style poncho.

GISELLE: Marco! Why are you in Tivoli? And why are you writhing in pain?

MARCO: Giselle—you have come to save me! I am afraid I have broken my ankle.

GISELLE: Well, in the spirit of full disclosure, I didn't purposely come here to save you, but now that I'm here, I'll gladly try to get you to a place that's soft and level—perhaps the (2)_____—where you can lie down in comfort.

Or would you prefer a bench in the (3)_____, which has a lovely view of the fish pond?

MARCO: I would be happy to crawl through a thorn-covered (4) _____ filled with killer mosquitos if it meant getting out of this cave.

GISELLE: You poor dear! *(She takes Marco's arm and helps him stand up. Marco winces in pain.)* How did this happen?

MARCO: Well, I was walking through the secret garden, examining some of the (5)_____ growing on the (6)_____, when a tiger showed up out of nowhere and started to chase me.

GISELLE: A tiger?

MARCO: Yes, a tiger. Don't ask me how it got to Tivoli, or why it was in such a bad mood, but it chased me out of the secret garden, down the (7)_____ of cypress trees that leads to the lower garden, and onto the (8)_____.
I tried to take refuge in a bed of daisies surrounded by a hedge, but the tiger jumped in with me.

Next, I ran to the (9)_____, hoping to take shelter inside with the citrus trees, but the door was locked. So I headed to that (10)_____ by the side of the lake—you know, the decorative Chinese pagoda that cost a hundred thousand lire when it was installed in 1785—but as it turns out, it has doorways, but no doors. I ran right through it with the tiger on my heels.

Finally, when the tiger wasn't looking, I slipped into this grotto, tripping on the cobblestone floor and breaking my ankle in the process.

ANSWERS: (1) grotto; (2) tapis vert; (3) belvedere; (4) pergola; (5) espaliers; (6) treillage; (7) allée; (8) parterre; (9) orangerie; (10) folly

Once you've dried your eyes, allow me to congratulate you. You're now horticulturally snob-certified! Feel free to redesign your grounds.

Meanwhile, wash up and get ready for tomorrow, when we'll return to Manhattan to learn snobby real estate words.

Day 13

Location, Location, Location!
EXCLUSIVE REAL ESTATE TERMS

LOCATION: **MANHATTAN, NEW YORK CITY**

Chances are, you're not a realtor, much less a vendor of über-high-end real estate. It's also unlikely that you're currently looking to buy a multi-million-dollar dwelling. But that doesn't mean you can afford to ignore the terminology of outrageously pricey residential property.

You may never be in the market for an *hôtel particulier,* but you could be invited to stay at one. You may never live in a *brownstone,* but they're mentioned frequently in books, magazines, and movies. And you may never see the inside of a *bastide,* but when your boss boasts about renting one for the entire month of July, you'll impress her by knowing what she's talking about.

For today's lesson, we return to Manhattan, home to some of the world's most expensive and exclusive residential real estate. You've already visited my apartment, at the beginning of the course, but please make yourself at home again. As you'll remember, it's a *duplex* in an exclusive *prewar co-op.* Let's sit down in the double-height sitting room as we take a look at today's words.

I. PRONOUNCE & DEFINE

1. **duplex** (DOO´-plecks)
2. **prewar apartment**
3. **co-op** (COH´-ahp)
4. **hôtel particulier** (oh-tell paw-teak-oo-LYAY´)
5. **brownstone**
6. **aerie** (AIR´-ee)
7. **pied-à-terre** (pyay´-duh-TEHR´)
8. **loft**
9. **Tuscan villa** (TUS´-kuhn VILL´-uh)
10. **bastide** (bah-STEED´)

1. DUPLEX: in flyover country, a *duplex* is a two-family home, usually divided down the center, and often rather downscale. But in larger cities, especially New York, a *duplex* is an apartment made of up two stories (or parts of two stories) of a highrise building.

Because space is at such a premium in Manhattan, and in certain areas of other large cities, a *duplex* apartment—depending on its size, location, and amenities—is often considered an extreme luxury.

BONUS WORD: a **triplex** is an apartment composed of *three* stories.

2. PREWAR APARTMENT: a unit in a type of elegant apartment building constructed in New York City prior to 1941, the year the U.S. entered World War II.

Prewar apartments were built with large rooms, high ceilings, crown moldings, hardwood floors, thick (soundproof) walls, and elaborate plaster ornamentation. These qualities, in high demand today, bring premium prices.

Realtors often divide the term *prewar apartment* into three subcategories. In this system, true *prewar apartments* date from the beginning of World War I to the beginning of World War II (or from 1914-41); *pre-prewar apartments* date from the Spanish-American War to the beginning of World War I (1898-1914); and anything built prior to 1898 is a *pre-pre-prewar apartment.*

Thoroughly con-con-confusing?

At any rate, the **Upper West Side**, the area west of Central Park, has Manhattan's greatest concentration of *prewar apartments,* but the city's most pricey and coveted *prewars* are on Fifth and Park avenues on the **Upper East Side** (area east of park).

At the very top of Manhattan's *prewar apartment* hierarchy are the elegant and spacious units in buildings designed by architect **Rosario Candela** (1890-1953). Candela apartments are known for oversized windows, abundant fireplaces, libraries, terraces, and grand foyers with curved staircases.

3. **CO-OP**: short for *cooperative,* a building owned by shareholders, each of whom has the right to the use of an apartment within the building.

Co-ops differ from condominiums in that condominium owners actually *own* their individual condos as real property, while *co-op* members are investors in a building.

Co-op boards set their own standards for approving new members, and they can be notoriously picky about whom they select.

Most of New York City's *prewar* apartment buildings are run as *co-ops.*

4. **HÔTEL PARTICULIER**: a large French townhouse, usually freestanding, set between an entrance court and a garden.

Hôtels particuliers typically have at least three stories, with steep Mansard roofs and tall, narrow windows that give them an elegant and sophisticated look.

Historic *hôtels particuliers* often have perpendicular wings, which originally housed kitchens and stables, extending from the main house along the sides of the entrance court.

Most large French cities are home to *hôtels particuliers*, but those featured in design publications are usually in Paris.

5. **BROWNSTONE**: a multistory residential building—usually a row house in the Eastern United States—faced with red-brown sandstone carved in elaborate designs.

In general, *brownstones* have a ground floor, a parlor floor (reached by a stairway from the sidewalk), and additional stories that house bedrooms.

Most brownstones were built in the 19th century, and those that retain their elegant details, such as fireplaces with carved mantles, hardwood floors, pocket doors, and ornate moldings, command the highest prices.

The majority of *brownstones* in New York City are found in the boroughs of Manhattan and Brooklyn.

6. **AERIE**: an elevated dwelling that's often secluded. The term is frequently used to describe penthouses atop skyscrapers in New York and other cities, as well as homes perched on hills and mountains, like those overlooking Los Angeles. *Aeries* generally have amazing views.

7. **PIED-À-TERRE**: literally a 'foot to the ground' in French, a temporary or secondary house, apartment, or other lodging.

A *pied-à-terre* is usually small, and usually in a city. The term is often applied to apartments in multistory buildings in large cities like New York, London, and Paris.

PLURAL: *pieds-à-terre,* pronounced the same as the singular.

8. **LOFT**: an apartment that consists of one large open space with high ceilings and exposed construction elements, such as pipes, brick, and support beams. Floors are wood or concrete.

BONUS WORDS: True *lofts,* known as **hard lofts**, are located in buildings that originally had commercial or industrial purposes, e.g., the former warehouses of Manhattan's SoHo and NoHo districts, where the concept of loft-living began.

A **soft loft** is an apartment in a new building designed to resemble a *hard loft.*

Our final two words (and two bonus words) describe places you may want to rent (or buy) for vacation use. Two of these describe types of dwellings in Italy, while the others describe typical houses in the South of France.

9. **TUSCAN VILLA**: the region of Tuscany, birthplace of the Italian Renaissance and home to some of the most attractive rural landscapes in Italy, has attracted foreigners for millennia. But the 1996 bestseller ***Under the Tuscan Sun: At Home in Italy,*** by **Frances Mayes**, made the region even more desirable.

A *Tuscan villa* is a formal country house with large rooms and high ceilings that was designed by an architect to shelter between a dozen and three dozen aristocrats.

These *villas,* built of native stone, are generally symmetrical, and usually include a formal garden and a pleasing view.

Tuscan villas may be centuries old, although modern renovations have often added such conveniences as indoor plumbing and swimming pools to the structures.

BONUS WORD: don't confuse a *Tuscan villa* with a Tuscan farmhouse, or **casa colonica** (KAH´-zah koh-LOH´-nee-kah), an Italian residence that began life as a dwelling for peasants, no matter how gentrified it may have become.

Casas colonicas usually started out as small square structures, but over the centuries, farmers added rooms and stories to make space for extended family members.

Because of their haphazard nature, *casas colonicas* may be more picturesque than *villas,* but their rooms are smaller and ceilings lower. They don't necessarily have gardens or views.

10. BASTIDE: the name for a manor house in Provence, the historic region of southeast France known for lavender, sunflowers, and a unique light prized by the Impressionists (we stayed in my *bastide* on Day 11, if you'll remember).

A prime tourist destination since Roman times, Provence got a late-twentieth-century boost from *A Year in Provence* (1989) by **Peter Mayle**. The book increased demand for the purchase and rent of historic houses in the area, most of which are built of native stone and local ceramic tiles.

A *bastide* is similar to a *Tuscan villa* in that both structures are usually architect-designed with large rooms, high ceilings, and lovely views. *Bastides* are generally large, but size varies.

BONUS WORD: a **mas** (mah), in contrast to a *bastide*, is the Provençal version of a Tuscan *casa colonica*. Built by farmers, often in piecemeal fashion, *mas* (the plural is written and pronounced the same as the singular) can be charming, but often lack the spacious rooms and grand views of the more formal *bastides*.

II. NAME THAT LUXURY PROPERTY

As you'll remember, my apartment is on **Fifth Avenue**, facing Central Park, in the section of the Upper East Side known as the **Gold Coast**. This privileged rectangle runs three blocks deep along the bottom third of the park.

Let's take a stroll through the neighborhood, where you'll see that the *avenues* (which run north and south) are lined with luxury high-rise apartment buildings, while the narrower *streets* (which run east and west) are home to townhouses built of brick and brownstone.

As we ogle, match our snob words with their definitions.

duplex   hôtel particulier
prewar apartment   co-op

brownstone	**loft**
bastide	**Tuscan villa**
aerie	**pied-à-terre**

_____ 1. apartment with exposed brick, cement floors, and no interior walls

_____ 2. small temporary or second home

_____ 3. stone townhouse of at least three stories, often in Manhattan or Brooklyn

_____ 4. home in high place with great views

_____ 5. elegant French townhouse set between an entrance court and a garden

_____ 6. aristocratic country house in Tuscany

_____ 7. apartment consisting of two stories

_____ 8. elegant manor house in Provence

_____ 9. spacious, elegant dwelling in a pre-1940s Manhattan building

_____ 10. ownership system in which tenants are investors in a building

ANSWERS: (1) loft; (2) pied-à-terre; (3) brownstone; (4) aerie; (5) hôtel particulier; (6) Tuscan villa; (7) duplex; (8) bastide; (9) prewar apartment; (10) co-op

III. MULTIPLE CHOICE

We've already mentioned that the Upper West Side, another tony Manhattan neighborhood worth a visit, is home to a high concentration of _prewar_ apartment buildings, although the predominantly residential area also has a large number of _brownstones_.

The Upper West Side is also home to the **Lincoln Center for the Performing Arts,** which houses the **Metropolitan Opera** and the **Juilliard School**, one of the premier music and performing arts schools in the U.S.

Let's play the following multiple-choice game as we look around.

1. An asymmetrical home in rural Tuscany with small rooms and low ceilings is a:
    a. *casa colonica*
    b. *Tuscan villa*
    c. *mas*
2. A Provençal house originally built for farmers, rather than aristocrats, is a:
    a. *mas*
    b. *bastide*
    c. *Provençal farmhouse*
3. An apartment with three stories is a:
    a. *tripartment*
    b. *triple-decker*
    c. *triplex*
4. A loft-style apartment in a new building is called a:
    a. *hard loft*
    b. *soft loft*
    c. *loft for softies*
5. A *prewar apartment* has:
    a. generous rooms
    b. high ceilings
    c. both of the above
6. The most sought-after *brownstones* have:
    a. ornate 19th-century details
    b. gourmet kitchens
    c. garden ornaments

7. The literal meaning of *pied-à-terre* is:
   a. 'foot in the air'
   b. 'foot to the ground'
   c. 'house on potato farm'
8. *Co-ops* are known to:
   a. have egalitarian policies
   b. be picky in admitting new members
   c. shun non-Bohemian types
9. You would **not** find an *hôtel particulier* in:
   a. Paris
   b. Madrid
   c. Bordeaux
10. Which is **not** an example of an *aerie?*
    a. a garden apartment in New Jersey
    b. a mansion in the hills overlooking L.A.
    c. a Manhattan penthouse

ANSWERS: (1) a; (2) a; (3) c; (4) b; (5) c; (6) a; (7) b; (8) b; (9) b; (10) a

IV. COMPLETE THE STORY

Greenwich (GREN´-utch) **Village**, or simply "the Village," is another highly coveted section of Manhattan.

Washington Square Park is the centerpiece of the neighborhood, surrounded by **New York University** and a host of narrow, leafy streets (some cobbled) lined with *brownstones.*

As we wander, let's check in with our favorite couple—Marco and Giselle.

Fill the blanks below with snob words and bonus words from this lesson. Each word is used once. Make words plural where necessary.

duplex	**triplex**
prewar apartment	**co-op**
brownstone	**hard loft**

soft loft	mas
bastide	Tuscan villa
aerie	pied-à-terre
casa colonica	hôtel particulier

The Expensive Escapades of
MARCO & GISELLE
Professional Beautiful People

Episode Seven: Musing in Manhattan

After Giselle bravely rescues Marco from the grotto (in the last episode), Marco begins to fall in love with her.

He isn't so sure about her feelings for him, however, so he decides to follow her to New York in hopes of arranging another encounter.

On Thanksgiving afternoon, Marco plants himself in the lobby of the Van de Kamp family's apartment building, a luxurious (1)_____ on Fifth Avenue. When Giselle passes through on her way to Central Park (to walk off those candied yams), she spies Marco, who is partially concealed behind a copy of the *Wall Street Journal.*

GISELLE: Marco! What brings you to New York?

MARCO: Oh, you know—business—business as usual.

GISELLE: What a coincidence to find you here! I was about to take a stroll in the park if you'd care to join me.

MARCO: Well, I am supposed to meet my grandmother in an hour at her (2)_____ in the Village. She wants my advice on moving her kitchen from the ground floor to the parlor floor, but I suppose I could spare a few minutes.

GISELLE: I adore the Village! Maybe I could go with you.

MARCO: Certainly! But you must remember that my grandmother's primary residence is in Buenos Aires. Her house here in New York is not much—really just a (3)_____.

It is nothing compared to your (4)_____. I can only imagine your spacious rooms and high ceilings.

GISELLE: Our apartment isn't as big as you seem to think. It's just a (5)_____—not one of the larger (6)_____ in the building—but it's home.

MARCO: You are being modest. It must be wonderful to live in a(n) (7)_____ with magnificent views of the park.

GISELLE: Park views are overrated. Once you get used to a giant expanse of urban greenery out your windows, you don't see it any more—in fact, we usually keep the drapes closed. I'd rather live in a (8)_____ in SoHo or maybe even one of the new (9)_____ they're building now.

MARCO: I have no experience whatsoever with high-rise living. Our house in Buenos Aires has two stories, our formal (10)_____ in the hills outside Florence has three, and our (11)_____ in Paris has four, but that is as high as it gets for us. I have stayed in high-rise hotels, of course, but I would like to actually *live* in a tall building.

GISELLE: Again, you're not missing anything. I'd much prefer having a place in the Italian countryside, like you have. While I do adore formal villas, I especially like the more rural (12)_____. So homey, so charming!

MARCO: If you like those, I will have to show you the rustic (13)_____ that my uncle owns in Provence. It was originally built by farmers, who added to it over the centuries, but he has installed two new wings, a swimming pool, and tennis courts.

Now it is more like a (14)_____—or aristocratic manor—except for the low ceilings and rather cramped rooms of the original section.

ANSWERS: (1) co-op; (2) brownstone; (3) pied-à-terre; (4) prewar apartment; (5) duplex; (6) triplexes; (7) aerie; (8) hard loft; (9) soft lofts; (10) Tuscan villa; (11) hôtel particulier; (12) casas colonicas; (13) mas; (14) bastide

V. TRUE OR FALSE

We've referred to the Manhattan neighborhood of **SoHo** (or **Soho**, short for **S**outh of **Ho**uston Street), as it relates to *lofts*, but now let's pay it a visit. Once an industrial area, this landmarked district's 19th-century commercial structures, many with elaborate cast-iron facades, have been turned into residential buildings of the most sought-after *hard lofts* in the city.

Originally inhabited by starving artists, these *lofts* are now occupied by well known actors, CEOs, and other multi-millionaires.

As we tour the sector, let's play this true-or-false game:

(T/F)   1. A *prewar apartment* can be located in a new building.
(T/F)   2. *Hard lofts* are set in former industrial buildings.
(T/F)   3. A *duplex* in Manhattan is an apartment created by adjoining two apartments on the same floor.
(T/F)   4. *Bastides* were originally built for the aristocracy.
(T/F)   5. It's easy to become a member of a *co-op*.
(T/F)   6. *Aeries* almost always have good views.
(T/F)   7. Most *brownstones* were built after World War II.
(T/F)   8. A *pied-à-terre* is usually a large country manor.
(T/F)   9. A *Tuscan villa* began life as a simple farmhouse.
(T/F)   10. A Provençal farmhouse is an *hôtel particulier.*

ANSWERS: numbers (2), (4) and (6) are true; the rest are false.

Ready to invest in high-end real estate? Ready to *sell* high-end real estate?

Congratulations! You're one day closer to word snobdom, and ten words closer to getting your broker's license.

Tomorrow you can relax a bit, since we'll be heading to the West Coast to look into ritzy recreation.

Day 14

Got Game?
SNOBBY SPORTS & LEISURE ACTIVITIES

LOCATION: **SANTA BARBARA, CALIFORNIA**

Some sports are meant for the masses: football, baseball, soccer, basketball. But other sports—due to the high expense involved in playing them, their aristocratic origins, or both—remain firmly in the hands of the privileged few.

The ten terms we'll learn today, which relate to snobby athletic and leisure activities, will do more than raise your heart rate: they'll raise your snob quotient.

And where better to study these sporty snob terms than in snooty Santa Barbara, California, the jewel of the posh section of Pacific Coast known as the **American Riviera**.

This privileged locale, with azure water and Mediterranean architecture set against the **Santa Ynez Mountains**, *does* remind one of the persnickety Côte d'Azur.

Today we'll begin our lesson at the lovely **Santa Barbara Polo & Racquet Club,** one of the world's most exclusive private athletic facilities. You'll be welcome as my guest. We'll start our lesson on this dining terrace, with its view of the polo fields and the bright blue Pacific.

Breakfast? Spa-style, of course: wilted dandelion greens and egg whites on manna toast, served with ginger and chia-seed smoothies. Yum! (Not really. Just smile and go with it for now. We'll get some real food later.)

Aside from the interesting food, the club's eighty manicured acres, covered in stables, swimming pools, clubhouses, and tennis courts, should keep us busy...and comfortable.

Since you already know how to pronounce most of today's terms, we'll forego our usual list of phonetic spellings and simply provide pronunciation guides where necessary.

I. DEFINE

Sports

1. **BADMINTON**: you've heard of this sport, but did you know it's one of the most popular pastimes in the United Kingdom? Not so in the United States, of course, where it's still an elitist activity.

Think of *badminton* as a cross between tennis and volleyball.

The game is played by two or four players on what looks like a volleyball court. Instead of using their hands to hit a ball, however, players use rackets to hit a rubber and plastic shuttlecock (or 'birdie') back and forth across the net.

The goal is to avoid letting the birdie touch the ground on one's own side of the court.

Despite the fact *badminton* is known for being played outdoors at garden parties, it likely has indoor origins. The game is thought to have been invented in the early 1870s at Badminton House, the Duke of Beaufort's Gloucestershire, England, estate.

Legend has it that the duke's children devised the game inside the great hall on a rainy day.

Badminton quickly became popular among the British elite, who played it at seaside resorts and as a holiday activity at country estates. Today the game is also played professionally.

2. POLO: you've also heard of this sport, but did you know it was first played in Persia in the 6th century B.C.? The game eventually spread across Asia, where the British discovered it—in India—in the mid-19th century.

British cavalry officers were the first European *polo* enthusiasts, and they introduced the game to the English universities, nobility, and royalty. The sport reached the United States in the 1870s.

Polo has always been a sport of the rich because of the large expense of maintaining a stable of *polo* ponies. But don't let the term "pony" deceive you. These are full-size horses, originally Thoroughbreds, although mixed breeds are now common.

To play a *polo* match, two teams, consisting of four mounted players each, line up at the center of a nine-hundred-foot-long *polo* field. (That's a long field—the length of three American football fields.)

Once the umpire rolls the small plastic ball into play, the players, using mallets, try to hit it toward their respective goalposts at opposite ends of the field.

While England and the United States once dominated *polo,* it's now Argentina that reigns supreme in the sport.

3. CROQUET: no one knows exactly how this game began. There's evidence it was played in London as early as the 16th century, but the game's French name and use of French terminology suggest it was developed earlier in France.

Be that as it may, the rules of *croquet* were standardized in England in 1870, the same year the **All England Croquet Club** at Wimbledon began to host the *croquet* championship.

While *croquet* can be played on any grassy surface, it's properly played on perfectly flat and immaculately groomed courts.

The object of the game, which can be played as singles or doubles, is to hit a solid plastic ball (they were originally wooden) through a series of six or nine metal hoops (called *wickets*) using a wooden mallet.

While the Victorians played *croquet* at private clubs and upper-class garden parties, the game survives today on the lawns of Oxford and Cambridge universities, private clubs, certain stately homes, and a few luxury hotels.

4. **CRICKET**: a game thought to have originated in the British Isles as early as the 13th century, and now second only to soccer as the most popular sport in the world. We consider *cricket* a snob sport, however, because it's so rare in the U.S.

Cricket is played on a large oval field with a rectangular area called the *pitch* at its center. The pitch, twenty-two yards long, has what's known as a *wicket* at each end.

A wicket consists of two wooden *bails,* each shaped something like a miniature rolling pin, that rest horizontally atop three vertical wooden poles called *stumps.* (Stay with me.)

To play the game, the *bowler* of one team pitches the ball to a *striker* from the opposite team, who is standing in front of a wicket. The bowler's goal is to hit the wicket and knock the bails off the stumps, causing the striker to be 'out.'

The striker's goal, on the other hand, is to defend the wicket by hitting the ball with a flat bat. If successful, he or she runs to the other wicket to score a point. (The game is actually a little more complicated than this, but you get the general idea.)

Cricket teams have eleven members. The length of a match can vary from a few hours to a maximum of five days. (Yikes!)

Ski Terms

5. **PISTE** (peest): the French term for a downhill ski trail, run, or slope that is marked, maintained, and supervised by resort staff.

The term is used in English to refer to ski trails at uppity resorts, not only in France, but around the world.

The related phrase **en piste** (ahng PEEST′) refers to being on an established ski trail or ski run, and roughly corresponds to the English phrase 'on the slopes.'

- I was *en piste* when I spotted former President Obama and his daughters.

6. OFF-PISTE (off-peest): refers to being *off* an established ski run and skiing, instead, on a slope that's unmarked, unsupervised, and unmaintained.

In regular English, this is called skiing the 'backcountry.'

7. APRÈS-SKI (ap′-ray-SKEE′): French for 'after-ski,' the activities in which skiers participate after a day (or morning, or afternoon) on the slopes, or *pistes*.

More broadly, *après-ski* refers to any activity at a winter resort other than skiing.

These activities may include dining, shopping, dancing, snowmobiling, sleighing, driving ice go-carts—even sunbathing (they do it in St. Moritz) and playing snow polo (yes, it does exist).

Après-ski functions as both a noun and an adjective:

- Aspen has fabulous *après-ski*.

- The pizza place on Park City's Main Street is a popular *après-ski* hangout.

8. SKI-IN, SKI-OUT: this term is tricky, with multiple meanings, so use caution when booking a property that claims to be *ski-in, ski-out*.

In a best-case scenario, or the arrangement most beneficial to you, the skier, the term means that a property (house, condo, hotel) is situated directly on a ski slope, somewhere between the base and summit of a chair lift or gondola.

This allows you to simply ski out your door (or the door of a "ski room," in the case of some hotels), down the slope to the lift. At the end of the day, you simply ski from the top of the lift directly back to your lodging (or ski room).

The beauty of this type of *ski-in, ski-out* situation is that you don't have to walk across a ski village in ski boots or take a private vehicle, bus, tram, or any other kind of transportation to get to the slopes.

However, *ski-in, ski-out* can also have less favorable meanings. One of these is that a lodging provides transportation to the ski lifts so that you don't need to walk or use a private vehicle. Better than nothing, but not as convenient as skiing out your door.

A final meaning of the term is that a hotel or other lodging provides a "valet" service that takes your ski gear (but not you) to the lift or gondola (so you don't have to carry it), and then takes it away and stows it when you're through with it.

Of course, if you're a true ski snob, you won't consider staying anywhere that's not *ski-in, ski-out* in one form or another.

Equestrian Events

9. **DRESSAGE** (druh-SAHZH′): French for 'training,' a classical form of horse training, as well as a sport designed to gauge how well a horse has responded to this training.

In a *dressage* competition, a horse must execute a variety of movements, called *airs,* in response to barely perceptible signals from its rider.

Judges take into account a horse's pace and bearing as it executes walks, trots, pirouettes, canters, and other maneuvers.

Dressage is divided into two levels: the elementary **campagne** and the advanced **haute école.**

10. **STEEPLECHASE**: a distance horse race in which competitors jump obstacles in the form of ditches and fences.

The name of the competition comes from early races in Ireland, where the sport originated. Horses and riders were required to race across the countryside, from one church steeple to another, jumping fences, ditches, and other obstacles in their way.

Steeplechases are now held on special courses with artificial obstacles. The sport is still practiced in Ireland, but it also has a significant following in the United Kingdom, the United States, Canada, and France.

II. PLAY BALL!

Let's take a tour of the stables while we review the words we've just learned. (The stables, of course, are where the polo ponies are kept.)

As we admire these magnificent animals, fill each of the following blanks with one of the snob sports listed below, each of which requires a ball.

In contrast to our usual instructions, each term may be used **more than once.**

polo	**croquet**
badminton	**cricket**

_____ 1. employs a 'bowler' who sends a ball across a 'pitch' to a 'striker'

_____ 2. requires players to hit a 'birdie' across a net

_____ 3. likely has French origins

_____ 4. requires mounted players to hit a ball with mallets

_____ 5. makes use of 'wickets' comprised of 'stumps' and 'bails'

_____ 6. has four mounted players on each team

_____ 7. uses 'wickets' made of metal hoops

_____ 8. has indoor, aristocratic origins

_____ 9. makes use of a flat bat; has British origins

_____ 10. is currently dominated by Argentina

ANSWERS: (1) cricket; (2) badminton; (3) croquet; (4) polo; (5) cricket; (6) polo; (7) croquet; (8) badminton; (9) cricket; (10) polo

III. MULTIPLE CHOICE

Now let's pull ourselves away from this exclusive compound long enough to visit Santa Barbara's **State Street**, the city's lushly landscaped principal thoroughfare. Here we'll find restaurants, boutiques, and day spas in picturesque Spanish-style buildings.

As we traverse this palm-lined snobevard, let's play the following multiple-choice game:

1. Skiing *off-piste* means skiing:
    a. the backcountry
    b. off-kilter
    c. off a runway
2. In *dressage,* a horse and rider must show off:
    a. fancy wardrobes
    b. elaborate and difficult movements
    c. quick costume-change skills
3. The term *ski-in, ski-out:*
    a. always means you can ski directly to your door
    b. has several meanings
    c. always means a valet service will drop off your ski equipment at the lift

4. *Piste* is a fancy French word for:
    a. a post-skiing party
    b. high-quality snow
    c. a ski slope, run, or trail

5. *Badminton* was originally:
    a. played in bad parts of London
    b. played on a tennis court
    c. an indoor game

6. *Après-ski* does **not** usually include:
    a. dining
    b. scrapbooking
    c. shopping

7. *Polo* ponies are:
    a. full-sized horses
    b. always Thoroughbreds
    c. Shetland ponies

8. The metal hoops in *croquet* are called:
    a. crickets
    b. briquettes
    c. wickets

9. A *cricket* team has how many players?
    a. seven
    b. eleven
    c. fifteen

10. A *steeplechase:*
    a. is held in a churchyard
    b. requires horse and rider to jump obstacles
    c. is so named because horses and riders were
       originally required to jump over steeples

ANSWERS: (1) a; (2) b; (3) b; (4) c; (5) c; (6) b; (7) a; (8) c; (9) b; (10) b

IV. CLEAN THAT CLOSET

It's time for a tour of **Mission Santa Barbara**, one of the largest (and most beautiful) of the historic California missions. The complex, which dates to 1786, has lovely courtyards and priceless religious art hidden behind its distinctive pink and white façade.

As we gawk at the gardens and peruse the paintings, let's play the following game.

Your mother (or significant other) gives you an ultimatum: organize all that sports equipment that's falling out of your closet...or it's all going to the dump!

Fill each blank below with the snob sport from this lesson that coincides with the equipment indicated. (We realize that some of the items mentioned won't actually fit in a closet.)

Each snob sport may be used **more than once**.

cricket	croquet
badminton	polo
steeplechase	

_____	1. flat bats
_____	2. wickets made of metal hoops
_____	3. rackets
_____	4. stumps
_____	5. birdies
_____	6. bails
_____	7. fences and ditches
_____	8. shuttlecocks
_____	9. ponies
_____	10. wickets made of stumps and bails

ANSWERS: (1) cricket; (2) croquet; (3) badminton; (4) cricket; (5) badminton; (6) cricket; (7) steeplechase; (8) badminton; (9) polo; (10) cricket

V. SKI TRIP

To finish our lesson, let's return to the Santa Barbara Polo & Racquet Club, where we'll lounge by the pool awhile.

As you've noticed, Santa Barbara has a Mediterranean climate, which means mild weather year round. There's no skiing here, of course, but at some point you'll want to leave this paradise for the slopes.

The following is a snippet of a conversation you have with a snobby travel agent as you book your next European ski trip.

Fill each blank with the appropriate ski term from this lesson. Make words plural where appropriate.

ski-in, ski-out   **après-ski**
piste   **off-piste**

AGENT: Do you plan to spend the majority of your time on the (1)_____? Or are you more interested in (2)_____ activites, such as dining, shopping, and dancing?

YOU: Well, both. I'm also pretty adventurous, so I'd like to try some (3)_____ skiing in the backcountry.

AGENT: And what about your hotel? Are you interested in (4)_____ so you won't have to lug around your ski equipment?

ANSWERS: (1) pistes; (2) après-ski; (3) off-piste; (4) ski-in, ski-out

Are your muscles sore from just thinking about all these athletic activities?

Shall we hit the spa? Or are you up for a game of badminton?

Maybe some other time, you say?

That's fine. Let's get some rest, because tomorrow we head back to England to study performing arts terms.

Day 15

Encore!
PERFORMING ARTS TERMS

LOCATION: **LONDON, ENGLAND**

Do you find cultural performances painful? Do you suffer through ballets and operas wishing the whole time you were at a monster-truck show instead?

The problem could be that you've never been taught the language of culture, which we hope to remedy during this lesson. The performing arts aren't really that mysterious—you just need to learn some basics.

For example, you already know that **Broadway** is home to New York City's theater district. But you may not know that the hub of London theater is the **West End**, the most uppity part of the city.

We'll head to the *West End* now, where we'll stay at my red-brick Georgian townhouse that overlooks the lovely and peaceful **Grosvenor Square**. As we take a brief stroll through this leafy oasis, let's go over the following terms, which will help you enjoy (or at least survive) any performance.

I. PRONOUNCE & DEFINE

1. **intermezzo** (in-ter-METS′-oh)
2. **libretto** (luh-BRET′-oh)
3. **bel canto** (bell′-KAHN′-toh)
4. **opera seria** (OH′-pehr-uh SEHR′-ee-uh)/
   opera buffa (OH′-pehr-uh BOOF′-uh)
5. **virtuoso** (ver-chew-OH′-soh)
6. **en pointe** (ahn POINT′)
7. **pas de deux** (paw′ duh DU′, with final *U*
   pronounced as *u* in *put*)
8. **bravo** (BRAH′-voh)
9. **West End** (London)
10. **Stanislavsky method** (stan-uh-SLAHV′-skee)

1. **INTERMEZZO**: ('interlude' in Italian) historically, any short entertainment, dance, or musical piece performed between the acts of a play or an opera.

Today the term is generally reserved for opera, meaning an instrumental interlude performed halfway through the work.

- The opera featured a delightful orchestral *intermezzo,* but Harry, of course, snored all the way through it.

The use of *intermezzi* (the proper plural) began in 15th-century Italy, where they consisted of short segments of song, dance, or spoken dialogue—or any combination of the three elements—used to break up a longer performance.

During the 17th and 18th centuries, however, *intermezzi* became comic spectacles performed between the acts of serious opera, or **opera seria** (see below). These *intermezzi* often attracted more attention than the operas themselves, which led to the development of the more comic **opera buffa** (also defined below).

By the 19th century, the definition of *intermezzo* had come to mean a short instrumental piece filling the gap between two sections of any relatively long theatrical presentation.

One well known orchestral *intermezzo* is that belonging to ***Cavalleria rusticana*** (1889), an opera by Italian composer **Pietro Mascagni** (1863-1945).

NOTE: *intermezzo* is also used currently to refer to a small serving of sorbet or other palate-cleanser offered midway through a multicourse meal.

2. **LIBRETTO**: (Italian, 'little book') the words that are sung or spoken in musical works for the theater, including operas, operettas, and *oratorios* (defined below). The author is called the **librettist**.

- I love the music to *The Marriage of Figaro,* but since the *libretto* is in Italian, I can't understand the words.

The term *libretto* dates to the late 16th century, when the text of musical works began to be printed in small books, or *libretti* (the proper plural). Audiences used these *libretti* to follow the performances.

While the term *libretto* is occasionally applied to the script (and in some cases, the script and lyrics) of contemporary musical theater productions, the terms **book** (for the spoken words) and **lyrics** (sung words) are more common, as in, "Book by Jane Doe, lyrics by John Doe."

3. **BEL CANTO**: (Italian, 'beautiful singing') a lyrical, melodic style of singing that contrasts with a more dramatic, speech-like style.

The *bel canto* technique began in the mid-17th century and dominated opera for nearly two hundred years.

By the mid-19th century, however, trends encouraged heavier and more dramatic singing, and by 1900, *bel canto* was almost dead.

But the late 20th century brought a resurgence of the technique, and many opera singers returned to the more expressive, smooth, and melodic style, placing renewed emphasis on vocal agility, tonal quality, and phrasing.

- If you take away *bel canto,* opera is nothing more than actors yelling at the audience.

4. OPERA SERIA/OPERA BUFFA: unless you're already an opera buff, you probably think all opera is quite somber. But in reality, there are two types of opera: *seria,* which is serious, and *buffa,* which is comic.

Knowing this distinction, as well as some basics about opera in general, will not only save you from embarrassment, but will greatly increase your cultural snob cred if you flaunt your knowledge appropriately.

Opera seria developed first, emerging in late 17th-century Naples. The new genre featured tragic and heroic themes taken from history and mythology, and the focus was on elegant verse and expert vocal display.

You won't recognize them, but Handel's **Rinaldo** (1711) and Mozart's **Idomeneo** (1781) are two examples of *opera seria.*

Now let's turn to the more entertaining *opera buffa,* which, as we mentioned in the definition of *intermezzo,* got its start in the form of short *intermezzi* performed between the acts of serious operas. As noted, these comic pieces, which focused on characters of low social station drawn from real life, were often more popular than the operas into which they were inserted.

With time, these *intermezzi* came to include characters of higher social status (especially heroines with high morals), which paved the way for the short spectacles to eventually become full, stand-alone, comic operas.

Well known examples of *opera buffa* include Mozart's **The Marriage of Figaro** (1786) and Rossini's **The Barber of Seville** (1813). Chances are, you *have* heard of these, since they've been widely parodied and otherwise incorporated into popular culture. (You know, "Figaro, Figaro, FI....GA....RO!")

- I simply cannot stomach *opera seria*. If I'm going to spend several hours watching something in a foreign language, it must at least be funny...in other words, *opera buffa*.

5. VIRTUOSO: as a noun, usually an instrumental performer with exceptional technical skill, although the term may also be applied to highly talented vocal and other types of performers.

- Craig is certainly a *virtuoso* on the piano. He plays Mozart's sonatinas at lightning speed with perfect accuracy.

A female with *virtuoso* qualities may be called a **virtuosa**; however, the masculine form is often used for both sexes.
PLURAL: **virtuosi** (ver-chew-OH´-see)

- There are several *virtuosi* flautists in the orchestra.

As an adjective, *virtuoso* means 'excellent' or 'highly skilled,' as in "a *virtuoso* performance."

6. EN POINTE: refers to the ballet technique of **pointe work**, usually reserved for females, in which a dancer supports all of her body weight on the tips of fully extended toes.
It takes years of training and conditioning for a dancer to perfom *en pointe*. Special shoes distribute the dancer's weight throughout her feet, lessening the possibility of injury.

- After ten years of ballet classes, Justine is finally dancing *en pointe*.

The anglicized pronunciation (ahn POINT´) is used by most ballet dancers and aficionados in the U.S., but for greater snob appeal, use the French pronunciation: ahng PWAHNT´.

7. PAS DE DEUX: (literal French, 'step for two') a dance for two performers.

Most ballets feature at least one *pas de deux,* usually performed by a male and a female.

- My favorite part of *The Nutcracker* is when the Sugar Plum Fairy and Prince Coqueluche dance the *pas de deux.*

While *pas de deux* is most often used in relation to ballet, it can be applied to any style of dance.

The term can also refer to any intricate activity or relationship involving two parties or things.

- Congress and the President are in a *pas de deux* over tariffs.

PLURAL: written and pronounced the same as the singular: one *pas de deux,* two *pas de deux,* etc.

8. BRAVO: as you already know, it's appropriate to shout *"Bravo!"* when you've enjoyed a live dramatic, musical, or dance performance.

But you may not realize that true Italians shout *"Bravo!"* only when they're expressing praise for a single male performer. If it's a single *female* perfomer they wish to honor, they shout *"Brava!"* (BRAH´-vuh).

If Italians are applauding a group effort by more than one male, or by a mixed group of males and females, they shout *"Bravi!"* (BRAH´-vee).

And to praise the efforts of more than one female, the correct term is *"Brave!"* (BRAH´-vay).

- The all-female ensemble in Claire's school musical was so good that I couldn't stop shouting *"brave!"*

9. **WEST END**: short for *the West End of London,* or *London's West End,* one of the most vibrant and expensive areas of the British capital, known for historic sites, shopping, and most notably, theater.

- We saw *Dreamgirls* in the *West End* last night.

The *West End's* boundaries are vague, but roughly include the districts of Mayfair, Bloomsbury, Covent Garden, and Soho, along with parts of St. James's, King's Cross, and Marylebone.

While the entire *West End* is fashionable, the most uppity area is **Mayfair**, home to the exclusive shopping mecca of **Bond Street**, with its old and new sections.

When seen on a map of today's Greater London, the *West End* does not seem to be "west" at all, but rather quite central. When the term came into being, however, in the early 19th century, it referred to all the fashionable areas of London that then existed west of Charing Cross.

London's *West End* theater district, known as **Theatreland**, forms a rough rectangle east of Mayfair. This area is home to more than forty theaters, with **Shaftesbury Avenue** having the greatest concentration of venues.

London also has more than a hundred "fringe," or **off-West End,** theaters (equivalent to off-Broadway theaters) located in various parts of the city.

The British capital is widely considered the greatest theater city in the world for its variety and quality of productions.

10. **STANISLAVSKY METHOD:** an acting technique developed by Russian theater director and actor **Konstantin Stanislavsky** (1863-1938) and refined by Russian-American acting teacher **Lee Strasberg** (1901-82).

Stanislavsky encouraged his actors to develop a realistic, believable style of acting that contrasted with the artificial and stylized performances common in the late 19th century.

In order to achieve this, he advised actors to take a psychological approach to the development of a character by putting themselves in the character's place. To aid in this process, he encouraged actors to recall their own past experiences and emotions, and to carefully observe the emotions of others.

- Marie became severely depressed after using the *Stanislavsky method* to prepare for the role of Juliet.

Strasberg implemented Stanislavsky's system (which came to be known as **the Method,** or **Method acting**) at the Actors Studio in New York City, where he was artistic director from 1948 to 1982.

Actors who use *the Method* are know as **method actors**.

- I think this roll calls for a *method actor*.

II. POP QUIZ

Isn't London lovely? So civilized. And frankly, a little boring compared to many of the other places we've visited.

But that's part of London's charm—the unexpected rarely happens.

And what could be more *expected* in London than afternoon tea? (Yes, believe it or not, it's 3 p.m.! Those definitions took longer than usual.)

Let's take a short walk to **Claridge's**, a quintessential London hotel with a quintessential afternoon tea service.

Don't drink tea? Neither do I, but since "tea" is actually a meal here, we'll gorge ourselves (in a polite way) on dainty cucumber sandwiches, freshly baked scones, clotted cream, lemon curd, cookies, cakes, muffins, éclairs, tarts....

Meanwhile, I'll test you on our new snob words.

1. A dance by two performers is a(n):
    a. *en pointe*
    b. *pas de deux*
    c. *intermezzo*
2. The *West End* is home to:
    a. London's theater district
    b. the *Stanislavsky method*
    c. *opera buffa*

3. *Bel canto* is:

    a. an acting method

    b. a ballet technique

    c. a sweet style of singing

4. The technique ballet dancers use to perform on the tips of their toes is called:

    a. dancing *bel canto*

    b. dancing *en pointe*

    c. dancing *pas de deux*

5. The correct form of *bravo* to use to show appreciation for the efforts of a group of female performers is:

    a. *bravi*

    b. *brava*

    c. *brave*

6. The *Stanislavsky method* encourages actors to:

    a. use past emotions to make their acting more believable

    b. forget the past and focus on the present

    c. focus on historic figures

7. An instrumental or vocal performer with extreme technical skill is a:

    a. *bravo*

    b. *bel canto*

    c. *virtuoso*

8. *Opera buffa* is:

    a. boring

    b. light and humorous

    c. serious and tragic

9. The term *libretto* refers to:

    a. comic opera

    b. a short entertainment between the acts of a play or an opera

    c. the text of an opera or other musical production

10. The correct plural of *intermezzo* is:

    a. *intermezzos*

    b. *intermezzi*

    c. *intermezzoes*

ANSWERS: (1) b; (2) a; (3) c; (4) b; (5) c; (6) a; (7) c; (8) b; (9) c; (10) b

III. FILL IN THE BLANKS

Isn't this the life? There's nothing more reassuring than afternoon tea in London, even sans the tea. Especially on a cold, gray, rainy day like today.

Now that we can't eat enother bite, let's burn some calories by taking a little longer walk to Shaftesbury Avenue, which, as we've mentioned, is home to more theaters than any other street in the *West End*. It's a rather narrow street, which makes it easy to marvel at the venues' ornate façades on either side.

As we huddle under our umbrellas and try to keep our feet dry, let's review one of the more complicated words from this lesson: *bravo*. First, go back and review its definition on page 178. Then fill each blank below with the correct form of the word to express appreciation for each group of performers.

_____ 1. three female ballet dancers

_____ 2. one male opera singer

_____ 3. two male rappers

_____ 4. one actress

_____ 5. two female dancers, one male dancer

_____ 6. a choir of thirty-six women

_____ 7. one male actor

_____ 8. two female opera singers

_____ 9. three female, two male opera singers

_____ 10. one comedienne

ANSWERS: (1) brave; (2) bravo; (3) bravi; (4) brava; (5) bravi; (6) brave; (7) bravo; (8) brave; (9) bravi; (10) brava

If you got nine or more questions correct, congratulations. If you didn't, go back and do the exercise again (and again, if necessary) until you do.

IV. SENTENCE PAIRS

Meanwhile, let's continue walking to the **Strand,** one of the *West End's* major boulevards. Here we'll actually attend a musical at the **Savoy Theater,** often cited as the most beautiful theater in London.

Originally built in 1887, and rebuilt and restored several times since, the Art Deco venue now features a ceiling meant to mimic the color of the April sky, as well as multicolored seats that suggest flowers.

During intermission, fill the blanks in the following sentence pairs with snob words from this lesson. Alter words for number and gender where appropriate.

intermezzo	**en pointe**
libretto	**pas de deux**
opera seria	**bravo**
opera buffa	**West End**
virtuoso	**Stanislavsky method**

1. As part of a ballet, a male and a female dancer perform a duet. This is called a _____.
2. You're watching a live theatrical production in the British capital. You're likely in the _____ of the city.
3. A female dancer has just finished performing an amazing solo. You clap and shout, "_____!"
4. Between the two acts of a very long and serious play, some jugglers come on stage and entertain the audience for a few minutes. This is called a(n) _____.

5. You know an actor who uses his past emotional experience to infuse his performances with realism. He's using some form of the _____.

6. You're watching an opera that's light and full of humor. The work is an example of _____.

7. For whatever reason, you really identify with the text of the opera *Nixon in China*. This text is known as the opera's

    _____.

8. Ballet dancers often dance on the tips of their toes. This technique is called dancing _____.

9. An opera with a tragic theme taken from Greek mythology would be an example of _____.

10. You've just watched a world-famous concert pianist perform Rachmaninoff's *Piano Concerto No. 2* with absolute perfection. The pianist is truly a _____.

ANSWERS: (1) pas de deux; (2) West End; (3) brava; (4) intermezzo; (5) Stanislavsky method; (6) opera buffa; (7) libretto; (8) en pointe; (9) opera seria; (10) virtuoso

V. COMPLETE THE STORY

Before we call it a night, let's check in with Marco and Giselle. Use this lesson's snob words to fill the blanks in the following selection. Alter words to fit context where necessary.

The Expensive Escapades of
MARCO & GISELLE
Professional Beautiful People

Episode Eight: Lucky in London

virtuoso	Stanislavsky method
intermezzo	en pointe
libretto	pas de deux
bel canto	bravo
opera seria/opera buffa	West End

As luck would have it, the next meeting of our hero and heroine takes place in London, where each—unbeknownst to the other—buys a ticket to a live theatrical performance of Disney's *Beauty and the Beast*.

As luck would also have it, their seats turn out to be right next to each other. (It could happen.)

MARCO: Can it be that this beast—meaning myself—has the pleasure of sitting next to the greatest beauty on earth?

GISELLE: Marco! What brings you to the (1)_____?

MARCO: Business—and my love of (2)_____. I have not yet seen this particular show, but the actress who plays Belle has a lovely voice with sweet, melodic qualities.

GISELLE: Indeed. Last night she gave a (3)_____ performance, but I'm here again for the (4)_____. When she and the beast danced, I melted!

I must say, though, that I'm surprised to see *you* at a Disney musical.

(The lights dim and the music begins.)

MARCO: Oh, I adore Disney musicals. Some of the books, or (5)_____, leave something to be desired, and the acting—well, sometimes it seems as if no one is familiar with the (6)_____—but the music is always delightful. In fact, I find it so enchanting that I wish every Disney musical included an instrumental (7)_____ for the orchestra to play between acts.

GISELLE: One can only wish. But do you like any of the other performing arts?

MARCO: I enjoy opera, especially the lighter and more humorous (8)_____. It is much more entertaining than the stale and serious (9)_____.

GISELLE: And ballet?

(Belle comes onstage and begins to sing her opening number.)

MARCO: I must confess to being very unfamiliar with any type of dance. And you?

GISELLE: I absolutely adore it, of course! When I was younger,

I wanted to be a professional ballerina, but I could never dance (10)_____. I have a problem with my Achilles tendon.

MARCO: So your Achilles tendon was literally your Achilles heel?

GISELLE: I don't get it.

(Belle finishes her number and the audience applauds.)

MARCO: *(shouts politely)* (11)_____!

ANSWERS: (1) West End; (2) bel canto; (3) virtuoso; (4) pas de deux; (5) libretti; (6) Stanislavsky method; (7) intermezzo; (8) opera buffa; (9) opera seria; (10) en pointe; (11) brava

Now it's my turn to shout *"brava!"* or *"bravo!"* to you (choose the term that applies).

You're now prepared for a cultural night out.

It's getting late, however, so let's get back to the townhouse and get some shut-eye. Tomorrow we'll travel to Rome for our second Latin lesson.

Day 16

Et tu, Brute?
LATIN WORDS & PHRASES

LOCATION: **ROME, ITALY**

Etymologists say English is fifty-percent Latin. So why aren't we Anglophones fifty-percent fluent in the language of the Romans?

Why don't we understand half of a Latin mass? Or half the medical and legal terms that doctors and lawyers throw at us?

Probably because we speakers of English have always preferred to use short Anglo-Saxon words in our daily conversation and writing, leaving Latin-based words, for the most part, to specialized fields.

Nevertheless, there are certain Latin words and phrases that every word snob must know. Remember, while French is the snob language of style and etiquette, Latin is the equivalent when it comes to law, medicine, and academia in general.

We'll present today's lesson here in Rome. Where better to learn Latin than in the City of the Seven Hills itself? We'll be based in this opulent apartment I own in a *palazzo* near the famous **Spanish Steps**. Help yourself to *prosciutto* (Italian ham, see Day 17) with figs and deep-fried zucchini flowers (they're actually quite tasty) as we begin our lesson.

I. PRONOUNCE & DEFINE

Say each of the following words aloud until they roll off your tongue like rain off the dome of the **Pantheon** (c. 126 A.D.), the only ancient Roman monument to have survived completely intact.

1. **quid pro quo** (kwid′ proh KWOH′)
2. **ad infinitum** (ad′ in-fun-EYE′-dum)
3. **pro bono** (proh BOH′-noh)
4. **de facto** (duh FACK′-tow)
5. **gravitas** (GRAV′-uh-toss)
6. **persona non grata** (per-SOHN′-uh nawn GRAW′-duh)
7. **rara avis** (raw′-ruh AH′-wuhs)
8. **in situ** (in SIT′-yooh)
9. **ad nauseam** (ad NAW′-zee-um)
10. **ad hoc** (ad hawk′)

Now look at the words in sentences.

1. The mayor suggested a *quid pro quo.* The city will allow Roger to build a gas station on Main Street if he'll give the city two acres on Oak Avenue to use as a park.
2. Tom and I will never reach agreement on this point—we'll be arguing *ad infinitum.*
3. This custody battle is killing me! My ex-wife has no legal fees, since her attorney is working *pro bono,* but I'm paying my lawyer four hundred dollars an hour.
4. Mr. Palmer is the CEO, but the *de facto* head of the company is his assistant, Mrs. Jones.

5. I like Mayor Smith's ideas, but with his grunge attire, blue hair, and multiple piercings, he lacks the *gravitas* to be governor.

6. Jessica burned down our garden shed and put bubble bath in our pool, so she's now *persona non grata* at our house.

7. Now that everyone has a cell phone, a public pay phone is a *rara avis*.

8. Carl loves Roquefort cheese, so for his birthday, his wife planned a trip to France to allow him to sample it *in situ*.

9. Marge talks about her grandchildren *ad nauseam*. I know the names, ages, and accomplishments of all twenty-six.

10. Because the school's cooling system was not working, we made an *ad hoc* decision to allow students to wear shorts until it could be fixed.

II. QUICK DEFINITIONS

First off, let's explore the **Piazza di Spagna**, one of Rome's most impressive public spaces. The centerpiece of the plaza is the **Fontana della Barcaccia** (c. 1628), a boat-shaped fountain designed by sculptor **Pietro Bernini** (1562-1629).

Directly east of the fountain is Europe's largest staircase, the monumental Spanish Steps. We'll climb these later in the course, but just so you know, they're named for the Spanish Embassy to the Vatican, which was once located nearby.

As we enjoy the area, which is always full of interesting tourists and locals, look at some brief definitions of our new words, along with some additional sentences.

1. QUID PRO QUO: ('something for something') an agreement in which one thing is exchanged for another. In other words, I'll give you what *you* want, if you give me what *I* want.
PLURAL: *quid pro quos* (kwid′ proh KWOZE′)

• Janice and I reached a *quid pro quo:* I would pretend to be her boyfriend if she would clean my apartment twice a week.

2. **AD INFINITUM**: ('to infinity') forever, or what seems like forever.

- The thirty-day course seemed to go on *ad infinitum*.

3. **PRO BONO**: ('for the good') donated for the public good. In the legal world, work done without charge for those who can't afford attorneys' fees.
Also applies to other free services.

- It was clear that the woman couldn't afford to pay for the surgery, so the hospital and doctor provided it *pro bono*.

4. **DE FACTO**: ('by way of fact') actual; existing in fact, but not necessarily legal, approved, or accepted.

- Clyde's home is his *de facto* office, since that's where he meets with patients and performs psychotherapy.

5. **GRAVITAS**: an air of seriousness and decorum. Judges usually possess it; comedians do not.

- To me, Jimmy Smith, who played a clown for years on a kids' television show, lacks the *gravitas* to serve on the city council.

6. **PERSONA NON GRATA**: ('unwelcome person') the diplomatic term for a person rejected as an emissary to a foreign government. Also, an unwelcome person in any situation.
PLURAL: *personae non gratae* (per-SOHN´-ay nawn GRAW´-tay)

- After I spilled borscht on the white carpet, my wife and I were *personae non gratae* at the dinner party.

7. **RARA AVIS**: ('rare bird') something, or someone, rare or unusual.
Remember, the *v* in *avis* is pronunced like a *w*.
PLURAL: *rarae aves* (rah´-rye AH´-ways)

- Rose and Harry are *rarae aves*. They have millions of dollars in stocks, but they live in a camper parked at Walmart.

8. **IN SITU**: ('in place') in place or on site; in the natural or original position.

- Sure, we could save money by using a prefabricated vinyl shell, but I'd rather build the pool *in situ*.

9. **AD NAUSEAM**: ('to the point of nausea') excessive to the point of making one want to throw up.

- Over the past two years, the phrase "Russian collusion" has been repeated *ad nauseam*.

10. **AD HOC**: temporary or one-time-only; to fulfill a particular purpose.

- We made some *ad hoc* changes to the menu last night when two dozen vegans showed up at our barbecue restaurant.

Ad hoc is often used to describe committees designed to be temporary.

- After the tornado hit, the mayor convened an *ad hoc* committee to oversee repairs.

III. MATCHING

Let's take a ten-minute walk to the **Trevi Fountain,** another important Roman landmark. This assemblage of statues, rocks, and innumerable water jets is Baroque theater at its finest.

According to legend, if you throw a coin over your back and into the fountain, you'll return to the Eternal City. Let's try it!

Now match our snob words with their definitions:

____ 1. *ad nauseam*   a. in place
____ 2. *gravitas*   b. excessive; to the point of nausea
____ 3. *pro bono*   c. something for something
____ 4. *in situ*   d. in reality; actually
____ 5. *quid pro quo*   e. without limit or end
____ 6. *ad infinitum*   f. a rarity
____ 7. *ad hoc*   g. an unwelcome person
____ 8. *de facto*   h. for a particular purpose
____ 9. *rara avis*   i. for the public good; without charge
____ 10. *persona non grata*   j. seriousness in bearing and manner

ANSWERS: (1) b; (2) j; (3) i; (4) a; (5) c; (6) e; (7) h; (8) d; (9) f; (10) g

IV. SENSE...OR NONSENSE?

Time for a gelato break? I thought you'd agree. There's a great little place around the corner.

Be sure to try the coconut *(noce di cocco),* which is divine combined with raspberry *(lampone).*

Now let's head to the **Roman Forum**, where, with a little imagination (more honestly, a lot of imagination), we can catch a glimpse of the grandeur of ancient Rome.

Now in ruins, the Forum was the heart of the Roman Republic, the seat of the Senate, and the principal gathering spot for citizens.

As we explore, check each sentence that makes sense:

____ 1. How about a *quid pro quo?* You can use the car if you promise to wash it, wax it, and change the oil.
____ 2. Since the facility will house an orphanage, the Governor asked if we could build it *pro bono*.
____ 3. If Lola keeps making changes to the house plans, the cost overruns will continue *ad infinitum.*

____ 4. Roger needs to loosen up a bit. His personality could use a little more fun, a little more *gravitas*.

____ 5. When Lily's tourist visa expired, she suddenly became *persona non grata*.

____ 6. The U.S. president is the *de facto* leader of the free world.

____ 7. Like a *rara avis*. Kim Kardashian is everywhere.

____ 8. Mia's bedroom contains figurines *ad nauseam*.

____ 9. We thought of having our company Christmas party at a restaurant, but in the end, we held it *in situ*.

____ 10. I declined the invitation to sit on the *ad hoc* committee because I didn't want a lifetime commitment.

ANSWERS: all but (4), (7), and (10) should be checked.

V. MULTIPLE CHOICE

How are you feeling about these words by now?

As we continue to work with them, our next stop will be ancient Rome's most impressive monument—the **Colosseum**.

This grand venue could seat fifty thousand bloodthirsty spectators in its heyday, and thanks to a system of tunnels and elevators below the arena floor, it provided them with a constant flow of gladiators and exotic animals to be sacrificed.

As we inspect this ancient Astrodome, answer the following questions:

1. The term *rara avis* refers to:
   a. a division of a rental car company
   b. undercooked poultry
   c. a rare or unusual thing
2. *Ad hoc* means:
   a. temporary
   b. permanent
   c. in place

3. *Ad nauseam* means:
    a. excessive
    b. ulcer-inducing
    c. nausea-reducing

4. *De facto* means:
    a. the legal state of things
    b. the actual state of things
    c. just the facts, ma'am

5. A *persona non grata* is someone who is:
    a. pleasant; not grating
    b. greeted with open arms
    c. unwelcome

6. A man with *gravitas* is likely to:
    a. wear a bathrobe in public
    b. wear a business suit
    c. wear a Hawaiian shirt

7. If something is *pro bono,* it is:
    a. free
    b. for the public good
    c. both of the above

8. The term *in situ* is pronounced:
    a. IN´ suh-too
    b. in´ SIT´-yoo
    c. een´ CITE´-yoo

9. A *quid pro quo* is:
    a. an exchange of one thing for another
    b. a Roman seafood preparation
    c. an agreement with its terms written in Latin

10. If something goes on *ad infinitum,* it continues:
    a. forever (or seemingly forever)
    b. until it's finished
    c. for a finite period

ANSWERS: (1) c; (2) a; (3) a; (4) b; (5) c; (6) b; (7) c; (8) b; (9) a; (10) a

VI. SNOB STATEMENTS

As we wrap up this lesson, let's travel to the working-class neighborhood of **Ostiense** to sample authentic Roman pizza (we'll look into the actual origins of pizza when we visit Naples on Day 25).

The term Roman pizza (*pizza romana*) is often used outside Rome, but not by Romans, who know their city offers *two* distinct varieties of the product: **pizza al taglio**, a thick-crust pizza sold by the slice for snacking, and **pizza tonda**, a cracker-thin version sold as complete pies in sit-down restaurants.

Let's squeeze into this packed pizzeria and sample the *pizza tonda* topped with zucchini flowers, anchovies, and mozzarella.

As we mingle with hungry locals, fill the blanks below with snob words from this lesson.

Each word is used only once. Alter words to fit context.

quid pro quo	**persona non grata**
ad infinitum	**rara avis**
pro bono	**in situ**
de facto	**ad nauseam**
gravitas	**ad hoc**

1. I dread Professor Smith's class because he talks about his experiences in Antartica _____.
2. It seems as if each class will go on _____.
3. The class is supposed to be a beginning zoology course, but it's a _____ penguin-appreciation fest.
4. It might be bearable if Professor Smith had a comedic personality, but he offers nothing but _____.
5. The professor is also something of a _____. Some days he actually wears a penguin suit to class.
6. The course would also be better if we left the classroom once in awhile and observed some real animals _____.

7. One day, when I went to the professor's office, he gave me a look that made me feel like _____.

8. In fact, he was so condescending that he acted as if he were meeting with me _____, when it's well known that he receives a large salary.

9. I asked the professor to make some _____ changes to the syllabus, but he refused.

10. In the end, we reached a _____: I would leave his office and he would destroy the penguin suit.

ANSWERS: (1) ad nauseam; (2) ad infinitum; (3) de facto; (4) gravitas; (5) rara avis; (6) in situ; (7) persona non grata; (8) pro bono; (9) ad hoc; (10) quid pro quo

VII. FINAL CAVEAT

Lamentably, we must now bid *arrivederci* to the ancient *Caput Mundi,* or capital of the world. Regrettably, we didn't make it to all of Rome's famous landmarks.

But we'll be back. We threw coins into the Trevi Fountain, remember?

As we leave, we take with us ten important Latin terms as souvenirs.

Now get some sleep and attempt to cleanse your snobcabulary palate, because tomorrow we head back to France for a look at fancy food.

Day 17

Foodie University, Part Deux
ESTEEMED EDIBLES

LOCATION: **LOIRE VALLEY, FRANCE**

You already know that caviar is expensive. But what about *truffles?* Would you pay ten thousand dollars a pound for balls of fungus dug out from under oak trees by pigs?

Maybe not, but plenty of people would, and *do,* making *truffles*—which grow wild in the forests of France and Italy—the world's most expensive food.

Other coveted foodstuffs, including certain fruits and vegetables, are much less costly, but just as highly prized by connoisseurs.

In this lesson, we introduce you to ten sought-after victuals.

To do that, we'll return to France, to the lovely **Loire Valley**, where I own a small château with a large kitchen garden, or *potager,* as the French call them.

I also have a wonderful private chef, Jean-Luc, who cooks the bounty.

Come inside the garden gate, and we'll begin our lesson right here by the peas and beans.

I. PRONOUNCE & DEFINE

1. **petits pois** (puh-TEE′ PWAH′)
2. **haricots verts** (AHR′-ee-coh VEHR′)
3. **crème fraîche** (krem′ FRESH′)
4. **fraises des bois** (frez′ day BWAH′)
5. **prosciutto** (pro-SHOO′-toh)
6. **mozzarella di bufala** (moats′-a-RAY′-lah dee BOO′-fah-lah)
7. **jamón ibérico** (hah-MOHN′ ee-BEHR′-ee-coh)
8. **Wagyu** (WAG′-you)
9. **truffles** (TRUH′-fuls)
10. **foie gras** (fwah GRAH′)

1. PETITS POIS: literally, 'small peas;' to the French, however, the phrase simply means 'peas,' because citizens of France refuse to eat the marble-sized peas consumed in other countries.

Why? Because little peas are sweeter and more tender than super-sized peas. *Petits pois* are best from your own *potager,* raw or lightly steamed, with a little salt and butter. Mmmmm.

2. HARICOTS VERTS: French for 'green beans' in general, although the term is usually only applied to green beans that conform to French tastes: young, narrow, and with tiny seeds.

As with their *petits pois,* the French refuse to eat the old, fat, tough green beans (with seeds the size of golf balls) that we often put up with in America.

3. CRÈME FRAÎCHE: (French, 'fresh cream') the default cream of France. Not fresh cream at all, but rather cream that has been allowed to ferment until it takes on a rich, nutty flavor and thick texture.

4. FRAISES DES BOIS: (literal French, 'strawberries of the woods') wild strawberries *(Fragaria vesca)* native to much of the northern hemisphere, but especially prized in France.

Fraises des bois, also known as woodland or wild strawberries, are tiny, deep red, and covered in prominent seeds. Berries gathered from the woods can be found in French street markets and in some French restaurants from June through September. The berries are also grown commercially in France on a limited scale.

The French eat *fraises des bois* plain, with a little sugar, or with *crème fraîche.*

5. PROSCIUTTO: Italian dry-cured ham, usually sliced thin and served raw. The variety produced in Parma (**prosciutto di Parma**), salted and air-dried for at least eight months (and up to twenty-four months) is considered the best.

Prosciutto has a sweet, delicate taste. It's often served with cantaloupe, or added to pastas and risottos.

Don't confuse *prosciutto,* which comes from the pig's hind legs, with **pancetta** (basically unsmoked bacon), which is taken from the pig's belly.

6. MOZZARELLA DI BUFALA: the name for authentic mozzarella cheese, produced in the **Campania** region of Italy (around Naples) from the milk of domestic water buffalo. The cheese is worked into balls or braids and then packed in cream, brine, or myrtle leaves to preserve its flavor.

Mozzarella di bufala, a vital ingredient of authentic Italian pizza, is whiter, creamier, and more moist than mozzarella-type cheeses made of cow's milk.

7. JAMÓN IBÉRICO: (literally, 'Iberian ham') a deep red Spanish ham with a buttery texture, often considered the best ham in the world. Made from a special breed of black-hooved pigs, *jamón ibérico* sells for up to $100 per pound in the U.S.

All *jamón ibérico* meets strict quality standards, but **jamón ibérico de bellota**, made from free-range, acorn-fed pigs, and cured for more than two years, is considered the best.

8. **Wagyu**: in Japanese, *wa* means 'Japanese' and *gyu* means 'beef,' so the term *Wagyu* refers to all beef produced in Japan. Therefore, it's redundant to say *Wagyu beef.*

That said, all breeds of Japanese cattle have a tendency for fat to marble evenly throughout their muscle, resulting in the world's most tender and buttery beef. But these qualities come at a price: small steaks can cost upwards of $200 each.

Good as all *Wagyu* is, however, the type called **Kobe**, named for the region where it's produced, is considered the very best. The *Kobe* designation is highly protected in Japan, and standards are so rigorous that fewer than 4,000 head of cattle receive the distinction each year.

That makes *Kobe beef* a rarity in Japan, and almost impossible to obtain in the rest of the world, since only ten percent of *Kobe beef* is exported.

Only a small fraction of that ten percent reaches the U.S., a situation that has led to fraud in the meat-packing and restaurant industries. *Caveat emptor!*

Some beef with Japanese bloodlines is now being produced in the U.S. and in Australia, but most of this is not pure: it's *Wagyu* stock crossbred with other types of cattle. Nevertheless, this beef is often labeled "Wagyu." It's also sold as "Japanese beef," "Japanese Wagyu," and "Domestic Wagyu."

9. **truffles**: round masses of fungus, about the size of golf balls, that grow in certain oak forests of France and Italy. *Truffles* are highly prized for their pungent aroma and flavor.

Specially trained pigs are used to locate *truffles*, the price of which can reach up to ten thousand dollars per pound depending on quality. White *truffles* are considered more desirable than black *truffles*.

Because of their high cost, *truffles* are used sparingly. They are often shaved onto egg, seafood, and pasta dishes, or worked into soups and risottos.

10. **FOIE GRAS:** (literal French, 'fat liver') the livers of force-fed ducks and geese, especially prized by the French.
Foie gras is generally prepared using low heat (in order to preserve its velvety texture), and served cold in the form of terrines, mousses, and pâtés.
Producers and devotees of *foie gras* claim the force-feeding process—the only way to produce the fat livers—does not harm the ducks or geese, but the practice generates some controversy. Most *foie gras* is produced in France.

II. ON THE MENU

Is your mouth watering yet? Try some of these fresh-picked peas, straight out of the shell.
According to historians, that's the way Louis XIV liked them. Who can argue with the Sun King?
Now match each snob food below with its description.

___	1. *haricots verts*	a. strawberries from the woods
___	2. *Wagyu*	b. top-quality Spanish ham
___	3. *petits pois*	c. world's most expensive food
___	4. *truffles*	d. cheese made of buffalo milk
___	5. *fraises des bois*	e. tiny and tender green beans
___	6. *prosciutto*	f. livers of force-fed ducks and geese
___	7. *jamón ibérico*	g. meat from Japanese cows
___	8. *crème fraîche*	h. fermented French cream
___	9. *mozzarella di bufala*	i. small peas
___	10. *foie gras*	j. Italian dry-cured ham

ANSWERS: (1) e; (2) g; (3) i; (4) c; (5) a; (6) j; (7) b; (8) h; (9) d; (10) f

III. TRUE OR FALSE

Let's move over to the fruit section of my *potager*, where I have a strawberry patch.

My berries aren't quite as good as the wild *fraises des bois*, but they're a hundred times better than what you find in the supermarket.

Why don't we pick a few to have for lunch?

Yes, go ahead and sample them now, no need to wash them. We don't use pesticides.

Divine, aren't they?

As we pick, let's play the following true-or-false game:

(T/F) 1. Every piece of meat labeled *Wagyu* has the quality of *Kobe beef*.

(T/F) 2. *Foie gras* exists naturally.

(T/F) 3. *Petits pois* are large peas bursting out of their pods.

(T/F) 4. *Fraises des bois* are smaller, but more flavorful, than supermarket strawberries.

(T/F) 5. To be considered *haricots verts*, green beans must be thin and tender.

(T/F) 6. *Truffles* are commonly eaten by French peasants.

(T/F) 7. The best *jamón ibérico* is cured for more than two years.

(T/F) 8. *Crème fraîche* is cream straight out of the cow.

(T/F) 9. True *mozzarella di bufala* is made from the milk of domestic water buffalo.

(T/F) 10. *Prosciutto* is made from black-hooved Spanish pigs.

ANSWERS: all false except (4), (5), (7), and (9).

IV. MULTIPLE CHOICE

For our dinner tonight, I asked Jean-Luc to prepare a glorious meal using every ingredient from this lesson.

For the *entrée* (a first course in France), we'll have *haricots verts au gratin,* a dish consisting of tender green beans baked with seasoned breadcrumbs and bubbly *mozzarella di bufala.*

The smell alone is nasal nirvana.

Don't you agree?

As we begin our fantastic meal in my equally fantastic garden, with its wonderful view of the river, let's play a multiple-choice game.

1. Wild strawberries gathered in the woods are called:
    a. *fraise de bois*
    b. *fraises des bois*
    c. *bois des fraises*

2. *Prosciutto* is:
    a. made from a pig's hind leg
    b. made from a pig's belly
    c. often served with watermelon

3. The finest type of *Wagyu* is:
    a. Kobe
    b. Coby
    c. Kobi

4. True *mozzarella di bufala* is:
    a. made in Italy's Campania region
    b. whiter, creamier, and more moist than similar cheeses made of cow's milk
    c. both of the above

5. *Foie gras* is usually cooked:
    a. at high temperatures to enhance flavor
    b. at low temperatures to preserve texture
    c. in microwave ovens

6. *Petits pois* are:
    a. large and green
    b. small and black
    c. small and green

7. *Jamón ibérico* is often considered:
    a. suitable only for informal meals
    b. the world's best ham
    c. dangerous because it's served raw
8. Which *truffles* are considered most desirable?
    a. black
    b. white
    c. gray
9. The French cream for everyday use is called:
    a. *fraîche crème*
    b. *crème du jour*
    c. *crème fraîche*
10. Tender green beans with small seeds are called:
    a. *haricot vert*
    b. *haricots verts*
    c. *verts haricots*

ANSWERS: (1) b; (2) a; (3) a; (4) c; (5) b; (6) c; (7) b; (8) b; (9) c; (10) b

V. SHOPPING

Enjoying the meal? Time to cleanse our palates, which we'll do with a small cup of sorbet made from *petits pois*.

Never tried sorbet made from *peas,* you say? It's much better than it sounds, and actually quite delicious.

As you give your tongue this much-deserved rest, match the food items below with their countries of origin.

    a. France   **c. Japan**
    b. Italy   **d. Spain**

____ 1. jamón ibérico   ____ 4. crème fraiche
____ 2. mozzarella di   ____ 5. Wagyu
       bufala   ____ 6. truffles
____ 3. foie gras   ____ 7. prosciutto

ANSWERS: (1) d; (2) b; (3) a; (4) a; (5) c; (6) a, b; (7) b

VI. NAME THAT SNOB FOOD!

Now it's time for the main course: grilled *Wagyu* fillets (wrapped in strips of *prosciutto* and *jamón ibérico*) topped with *foie gras* and shavings of white *truffles*.

Talk about an embarrassment of culinary riches!

As we indulge, pretend you're a contestant on a game show. Match the correct snob food from this lesson with each of the following clues.

Set a timer for 60 seconds. Go!

mozzarella di bufala	**Wagyu**
truffles	**prosciutto**
fraises des bois	**foie gras**
crème fraîche	**petits pois**
jamón ibérico	**haricots verts**

_____ 1. This snob food is sliced thin and often paired with cantaloupe.

_____ 2. Pigs are used to locate these, the world's most expensive food.

_____ 3. This snob meat is in such short supply that you should beware of counterfeits.

_____ 4. These round snob vegetables are picked when young and tender.

_____ 5. These snob fruits are tinier and tastier than their supermarket counterparts.

_____ 6. The French prefer these legumes thinner than those usually consumed in the U.S.

_____ 7. The authentic version of this cheese is not made from the milk of cows, sheep, or goats.

_____ 8. This snob food is controversial because of feeding practices used to produce it.

_____ 9. This snob food is fermented, though its name implies freshness.

_____10. The animals that produce the highest grade of this snob meat are fed on acorns.

Time's up!

Now tally your score.

A perfect '10' won't get you a new car, but it *will* give you ten new snob terms to add to your snob arsenal.

ANSWERS: (1) prosciutto; (2) truffles; (3) Wagyu; (4) petits pois; (5) fraises des bois; (6) haricots verts; (7) mozzarella di bufala; (8) foie gras; (9) crème fraîche; (10) jamón ibérico

VII. COMPLETE THE STORY

Ready for dessert?

Jean-Luc has prepared *fraises des bois* (which he picked himself less than an hour ago in the woods behind the château) with sweetened *crème fraîche* and candied violets. So simple, yet so elegant.

As we partake of this after-meal ambrosia, we'll be entertained by—you guessed it!—our friends Marco and Giselle.

Fill the blanks below with snob words from this lesson.

mozzarella di bufala	**Wagyu**
truffles	**prosciutto**
fraises des bois	**foie gras**
crème fraîche	**petits pois**
jamón ibérico	**haricots verts**

The Expensive Escapades of
MARCO & GISELLE
Professional Beautiful People

Episode Nine: Picky in Paris

Marco is now madly in love with Giselle, and the next time they meet—in Paris—he invites her to lunch at a certain Michelin three-star restaurant located inside an exclusive hotel.

Marco decides on lunch, rather than dinner, to save money. As of late, he's been strapped for cash because his parents have cut his monthly allowance in half. (By so doing, they hope to convince him to stop playing polo and return to Argentina to help run the family *estancia*.)

GISELLE: This is one of my favorite places! *(Marco helps her sit down in a Louis XVI* fauteuil *in the elegant gray and gold dining room.)* I think I'll order one of everything.

MARCO: *(looking shocked)* Uhhh....

GISELLE: I'm just kidding!

MARCO: *(Laughs, then breathes a sigh of relief as he scans the menu for the least expensive main course.)* Do you know what you'd like, my dear?

GISELLE: Well, the (1)_____ sounds good, but Japan doesn't export beef to Europe. So the restaurant is lying about that.

MARCO: Really? I can't imagine establishments of this caliber being dishonest about the sources of their food.

GISELLE: Don't be naïve! They do it all the time. I've had what was billed as (2)_____ in three-star restaurants in Italy that I'm certain was made with cow's milk. I've ordered *pâté de* (3)_____ right here in Paris that was obviously made of chicken livers. And I've read about a case in which a top restaurant in Spain was serving what it billed as (4)_____, but which turned out to be from the U.S.

MARCO: What insolence!

GISELLE: Yes, restaurants skimp on all kinds of things. They often substitute flavored oil for actual (5)_____, which saves them a lot of money. Oh, and get this: I once ordered (6)_____ *di Parma* that turned out to be from Cleveland.

MARCO: How did you know?

GISELLE: I demanded to see the package! That's why I like to stick with vegetables when I eat at restaurants. It's difficult to counterfeit (7)_____. They're either small or they're not. The same with (8)_____. It's impossible to disguise tough old green beans!

MARCO: All this discussion of faux food has caused me to completely lose my appetite. I think I'll just order dessert. Some (9)_____ with a little (10)_____ should do nicely.

"And you?"

ANSWERS: (1) Wagyu; (2) mozzarella di bufala; (3) foie gras; (4) jamón ibérico; (5) truffles; (6) prosciutto; (7) petits pois; (8) haricots verts; (9) fraises des bois; (10) crème fraîche

Aren't Giselle and Marco two of the most delightful people you've ever met?

And wasn't the feast that Jean-Luc prepared one of the best meals—if not *the* best meal—you've ever had?

Unfortunately, you won't have much time to sleep it off.

We'll be up at the crack of dawn to head to Venice, Italy, where we'll learn some exciting new design terms.

Day 18

You Got Shagreen in My Venetian Plaster!
MORE INTERIOR DESIGN

LOCATION: **VENICE, ITALY**

If we can trust the pages of *Architectural Digest* (and why shouldn't we?), every movie star in the world has his or her walls covered in something called *Venetian plaster*.

What is this mystery material? Does it really come from Venice? And why does it appeal to movie stars?

Stay tuned for breaking news on this, as well as for nine additional snob terms that describe hoity-toity techniques and imperious materials from the world of interior design.

To get to the bottom of the *Venetian plaster* issue, let's go straight to Venice, where I own a 15th-century *palazzo* on the **Grand Canal**. Like Venice itself, the palazzo is faded, decadent, and long past its prime...yet irresistible.

Come right in—yes, the *chintz* is disintegrating in places, and the *papier peint* is flaking off the walls, but I can't bear to replace anything. New materials would ruin the ambience.

Go ahead, put your feet up on that ottoman. Yes, it's covered in *shagreen,* but you won't hurt it.

I. PRONOUNCE

1. **verre églomisé** (VEHR´ ay´-gloh-mee-ZAY´)
2. **papier peint** (pop´-ee-yay PAN´)
3. **ormolu** (OR´-muh-loo)
4. **shagreen** (shuh-GREEN´)
5. **Venetian plaster**
6. **marquetry** (MAR´-kuh-tree)
7. **boulle** (bool)
8. **chintz** (chints)
9. **parquet de Versailles** (par-KAY´ duh vehr-SIGH´)
10. **faux marbre** (foh MAHR´-bruh)

II. DEFINE

1. **VERRE ÉGLOMISÉ**: glass that's been decorated on the reverse side with paint and gold (or silver) leaf. The *verre églomisé* process results in a gleaming, luxurious finish that's often used on screens, dividers, or entire walls.

To create *verre églomisé,* an artisan first paints a design on the back of a glass panel. He or she then applies gold or silver leaf on top of the design to cover the panel's entire reverse side, creating a mirror-type finish when seen from the front.

Finally, the artisan seals the panel with varnish or another piece of glass.

Verre églomisé gives wow factor to private homes as well as public places, such as restaurants and hotel lobbies.

2. **PAPIER PEINT**: simply 'wallpaper' in French, but when used in English, the term usually refers to wallpaper that's hand painted, block printed, antique, or otherwise rare and expensive.

Papier peint was used extensively in 18th-century dining rooms on both sides of the Atlantic. Much of this wallpaper was made to form panoramas—often tropical and exotic in nature—that covered entire walls. This antique *papier peint* is in high demand today.

3. ORMOLU: gilt bronze, meant to resemble gold, applied as decoration to furniture in the form of mounts, moldings, and medallions. The use of *ormolu* was especially popular during the reign of **Louis XIV** (1643-1715) of France.

True *ormolu* (from *or moulu*, French for 'gold paste') is made through a process in which powdered gold is mixed with mercury and brushed onto a bronze form. The form is then fired, which causes the mercury to evaporate, leaving the surface covered in gold.

Bronze can also be gilt through a process of electrolysis, but the resulting finish is not considered true *ormolu.*

4. SHAGREEN: a pricey material made from the untanned skins of horses, mules, sharks, and rays. The skins are finished with a granular surface and dyed green.

Shagreen was widely used in the 18th century to cover small pieces of furniture and *objets d'art*. It was also used extensively in the 1920s and 1930s to cover **Art Deco** items such as jewelry boxes. The material is still used today as a luxury finish.

5. **VENETIAN PLASTER**: a wall treatment that results in a highly polished, rock-hard finish similar to marble. To achieve this effect, plaster is mixed with marble dust and pigment. It's then applied to walls in thin multiple layers with a trowel.

Once dry, the plaster is polished. This allows patterns from the various layers to show through, giving the final result depth and texture similar to real marble.

Venetian plaster is thought to have been invented in Venice, where many 16th-century examples of the technique survive.

But now for the $64,000 question: why do movie stars seem to love this stuff? It's exclusive, expensive, and it helps get their faces in *Architectural Digest*. What's not to love?

6. MARQUETRY: a technique used to decorate furniture in which thin, shaped pieces of wood or other materials are glued onto a surface to form a shallow mosaic veneer.

Marquetry is used on all types of furniture, including tables, bureaus, consoles, and desks. Patterns are non-geometric, and include floral, arabesque, and landscape designs.

Don't confuse *marquetry* with **inlay**, a technique in which pieces are cut out of solid wood furniture and filled with different woods or other materials for decorative effect. *Marquetry* always involves placing a patterned veneer on top of an inferior surface material.

Feeling especially snobby? Spell *marquetry* the French way: *marqueterie*.

7. BOULLE: a type of *marquetry* developed by **André-Charles Boulle** (1642-1732), the furniture maker to Louis XIV responsible for many of the original furnishings at the French Palace of Versailles.

Boulle is often referred to as **boulle marquetry** or **boulle work**.

The *boulle* technique is accomplished by fusing a thin sheet of tortoiseshell to a thin sheet of brass and cutting complex designs from the composite sheet. The cut-outs are then separated into their respective layers to form two types of veneer.

The tortoiseshell veneer is glued to the surface of a piece of wooden furniture, such as a bureau, table, or clock. The holes, or negative spaces in the tortoiseshell design, are then filled in with the brass cut-outs, creating an intricate brown and gold design known as **premiere partie**.

The reverse, known as **contre partie**, uses brass to form the positive design and tortoiseshell to fill the negative spaces.

The process can be executed using ivory, ebony, and other materials in lieu of tortoiseshell, and by using silver-colored pewter rather than brass.

8. **CHINTZ**: a thin cotton fabric, of Chinese and Indian origin, introduced to Europe in the early 17th century by the British East India Company.

The original *chintzes*—bright floral patterns on light backgrounds, finished with a shiny glaze—were used for draperies and upholstery. They were so popular that both France and England eventually banned their import in order to save their own textile industries.

The bans did not completely stop the flow of *chintz* into Europe, however, and it continued to be used in aristocratic houses.

In the mid-18th century, Europe began to produce its own *chintz*, and the fabric became so widely used that the term *chintzy* came to mean 'cheap' or 'common.'

Chintz is still popular today as a drapery and upholstery material, especially in the **English country house** style.

9. **PARQUET DE VERSAILLES**: a style of *parquet* famous for its use at the Palace of Versailles. (*Parquet* is flooring made of small wooden pieces fit together to form a geometric pattern.)

The *Versailles* pattern consists of large squares filled in with smaller wooden rectangles set on the diagonal (google it). While found throughout the palace, the best-known example of the pattern is in the **Hall of Mirrors**.

The term *parquet de Versailles* may refer to any parquet in the basic *Versailles* pattern, but parquet of this type that dates to the 17th and 18th centuries is known as **antique parquet de Versailles.**

This antique flooring—salvaged from demolished townhomes and other structures, and in demand for use in newer buildings—is known for its beauty and durability.

10. **FAUX MARBRE**: (French for 'fake marble') a decorative painting technique used to make wood, plaster, and other materials appear to be marble.

The technique is often used on mantels, columns, walls, floors, and furniture as a less expensive alternative to real marble. The *faux marbre* technique is also used when real marble would be too heavy for a particular application.

III. POP QUIZ!

Feeling overwhelmed? Relax. Go to the balcony and take in the parade of gondolas making its way down the canal.

Now take a deep breath and match each snob term below with its definition:

____ 1. *parquet de Versailles*   a. process in which glass is painted on its reverse side

____ 2. *marquetry*   b. wall treatment made of multiple coats of plaster

____ 3. *verre églomisé*   c. printed cotton fabric used for upholstery and draperies

____ 4. *chintz*   d. wooden flooring with distinct diagonal pattern

____ 5. *shagreen*   e. non-geometric mosaic veneer of different woods or other materials

____ 6. *boulle*   f. green material made of horse, mule, shark, or ray skin

____ 7. *faux marbre*   g. gilt bronze

____ 8. *Venetian plaster*   h. marquetry executed in brass and tortoiseshell

____ 9. *ormolu*   i. rare and expensive wallpaper

____ 10. *papier peint*   j. painted to resemble marble

ANSWERS: (1) d; (2) e; (3) a; (4) c; (5) f; (6) h; (7) j; (8) b; (9) g; (10) i

IV. DECORATE YOUR DREAM ROOM

How was the quiz? Don't fret, it's still early in the lesson.

Let's take a break and walk over to **Piazza San Marco**, the largest and most important square in Venice, and home to the city's cathedral, the **Basilica di San Marco** (c. 1092).

The piazza is also home to **Caffè Florian**, established in 1720, which bills itself as the most beautiful café in the world. What do you think?

Since it's sunny (although a bit chilly), let's have a seat outside on the square and order *cioccolata con panna* (hot chocolate with whipped cream) and a *crostata di frutta fresca* (fresh fruit tart).

As we eat, let's plan your dream living room (or great room, sitting room, salon—whatever you want to call it) with the help of a top interior designer. Fill the blanks below with snob words from this chapter. Each word is used once.

verre églomisé	**marquetry**
papier peint	**parquet de Versailles**
ormolu	**chintz**
shagreen	**boulle**
Venetian plaster	**faux marbre**

DESIGNER: First of all, what level of formality are you looking for? Are we talking about Louis Quinze pieces with glittering (1)_____ mounts and walls covered in (2)_____?

YOU: Oh, no, nothing as showy as all that. I *do* appreciate (3)_____ work, for example, with its intricate veneers of tortoiseshell and brass, but I don't want my house to look like a museum.

The same with (4)_____—I find its gleaming glass surfaces impressive, but I don't need that much wow factor in my daily life.

DESIGNER: So, according to what you've just said, I assume (5)_____ is out for the walls.

YOU: Yes, that polished, marble-like finish is too rich and formal for my taste. But I *would* like a little luxury on the floors—perhaps highly waxed (6)_____.

DESIGNER: Keep it coming! I'm seeing your vision! Do you own any special pieces of furniture or *objets d'art* that we'll need to work in?

YOU: Yes, I have a Charles II cabinet decorated with floral (7)_____. Its designs, executed in wooden veneer, of course, are intricate and beautiful, but not as flashy as *boulle* work. I also have an Art Deco box covered in (8)_____ that I'd like to display on the coffee table.

DESIGNER: We like to call them *cocktail* tables.

YOU: Have it your way—I don't drink coffee *or* cocktails.

DESIGNER: Give me a second...it's all coming together. The English country look! A mixture of luxe and practicality, where your dogs can climb up onto the (9)_____ upholstery—

YOU: I don't have dogs.

DESIGNER: You will once you're living in this room! It will be *fantastic!* And what about some classical elements? I picture several (10)_____ columns (real marble would be too heavy, as well as unnecessarily costly) to give the room *gravitas* and proportion.

ANSWERS: (1) ormolu; (2) papier peint; (3) boulle; (4) verre églomisé; (5) Venetian plaster; (6) parquet de Versailles; (7) marquetry; (8) shagreen; (9) chintz; (10) faux marbre

V. TRUE OR FALSE

Did you get your living room design worked out?

Before we leave Piazza San Marco, let's take a quick elevator ride to the top of the **Campanile**, or bell tower, the highest structure in the city. From the observation area, three hundred feet up, we can look out over the Byzantine cupolas of the Basilica to the red-tile roofs of the city and the distant lagoon.

As we gaze, let's play a true-or-false game:

(T/F)   1. *Marquetry* involves placing very thin pieces of desirable material over inferior types of wood.

(T/F)   2. Only flooring that was originally installed in the Palace of Versailles may be considered true *parquet de Versailles.*

(T/F)   3. Objects made of *shagreen* are generally expensive.

(T/F)   4. *Chintz* is a cotton fabric with origins in China and India.

(T/F)   5. *Venetian plaster* was born in Venice, California.

(T/F)   6. *Papier peint* is used for draperies and upholstery.

(T/F)   7. True *ormolu* is made through a process that fuses gold to bronze using mercury.

(T/F)   8. A *faux marbre* floor is painted to resemble a marble floor.

(T/F)   9. *Boulle* refers to any item made of tortoiseshell.

(T/F) 10. *Verre eglomisé* produces an elegant, shiny finish.

ANSWERS: all true except (2), (5), (6), and (9).

VI. MULTIPLE CHOICE

Now it's time for a ride in my private gondola with my personal gondolier. You ask if he sings? Of course he does, but I've banned the tired *'O Sole Mio.* Any other requests?

As we admire the faded façades of this floating city, I have a multiple-choice game for you:

1. *Parquet de Versailles* is:
     a. a small park at the Palace of Versailles
     b. wooden flooring in a certain diagonal pattern
     c. a butter substitute served at Versailles

2. Gilt bronze used as decoration on furniture is:
    a. *boulle*
    b. *shagreen*
    c. *ormolu*
3. *Venetian plaster* is a wall treatment that resembles:
    a. marble
    b. *boulle*
    c. *chintz*
4. The French term for 'fake marble' is:
    a. *faux marble*
    b. *fake marbre*
    c. *faux marbre*
5. Rare and expensive wallpaper is known as:
    a. *paper peint*
    b. *papier peint*
    c. *papier paint*
6. A material made from untanned skins dyed green is:
    a. *shagreen*
    b. *papier peint*
    c. *boulle*
7. Glass that is painted and gilt on its reverse side is:
    a. *boulle*
    b. *ormolu*
    c. *verre églomisé*
8. *Boulle* work generally consists of:
    a. tortoiseshell
    b. brass
    c. both of the above
9. A thin cotton fabric composed of bright colors on a light background is:
    a. *shagreen*
    b. *chintz*
    c. *ormolu*

10. *Marquetry* is:
    a. a type of wood flooring
    b. decoration formed by applying veneers in geometric patterns
    c. decoration formed by applying veneers in non-geometric patterns

ANSWERS: (1) b; (2) c; (3) a; (4) c; (5) b; (6) a; (7) c; (8) c; (9) b; (10) c

VII. SENSE...OR NONSENSE?

Put a check beside each sentence that makes sense.

____ 1. The expensive curtains were made of *faux marbre*.

____ 2. The desk was decorated with *boulle* executed in ivory and pewter.

____ 3. We decided to cover the kitchen floor in *ormolu*.

____ 4. The exterior of my husband's new car is decorated with *marquetry*.

____ 5. *Parquet de Versailles* seemed like the best flooring to go with the foyer's antique *papier peint*.

____ 6. Stella's country house features *verre églomisé* on the kitchen floor.

____ 7. The dining room is quite elegant, with *shagreen* on the banquette and *Venetian plaster* on the walls.

____ 8. The thing I love most about Julia's bedroom is the *parquet de Versailles* on the ceiling.

____ 9. It's just the garage, so we decided to go cheap and do the walls in *Venetian plaster*.

____ 10. I love the *chintz* countertops in Emma's kitchen.

ANSWERS: numbers (2), (5), and (7) should be checked.

VIII. COMPLETE THE STORY

For our entertainment this evening, we'll attend a performance at **La Fenice**, the 18th-century Venetian opera house that's played an important role in operatic history.

This neo-Baroque theater has hosted dozens of important opera premieres, including that of Verdi's *La Traviata* in 1853.

As we marvel at the acoustics, and rub shoulders with duchesses and bricklayers (everyone in Venice loves opera), let's check in with Marco and Giselle.

Use this lesson's snob words to fill the blanks in the following passage. Each word is used once.

verre églomisé	marquetry
papier peint	parquet de Versailles
ormolu	chintz
shagreen	boulle
Venetian plaster	faux marbre

The Expensive Escapades of
MARCO & GISELLE
Professional Beautiful People

Episode Ten: Emoting through Email

Because of Marco's reduced financial situation, he has sold his seven-bedroom chalet in **St. Moritz**, Switzerland, and purchased a one-bedroom apartment in the less pricey winter resort area of **Baqueira-Beret**, Spain.

What follows is an email he writes to Giselle asking for interior design suggestions, along with her reply.

My Dearest Giselle,

I write to ask your advice on decorating my new *pied-à-terre* in Baqueira-Beret. I want it to be classic and elegant, yet not so museum-like that I cannot put my feet up and relax after a day on the slopes.

The place has a small elevator vestibule, a medium-sized living/dining area, a small kitchen, a small bedroom with bath, and a powder room for guests.

Your ideas?

Yours Forever,
Marco

And now for Giselle's response:

Dearest Marco,

I'm flattered that you would ask for my advice. I'm certainly no professional designer, but I have learned a thing or two from my mother and the dozens of decorators she has hired over the years.

Let's start with something jawdropping in the vestibule. Cover the walls with custom (1)_____ panels painted with a mountain and pine tree motif. This will be expensive, but the shiny, golden surfaces will knock your socks off the moment you get out of the elevator.

I'd also flank the entrance door with two columns painted in (2)_____, which will be cheaper than the real thing, yet just as effective.

The only piece of furniture I suggest you put in the vestibule is a console covered in (3)_____ work—in brass and tortoiseshell—and equipped with shiny (4)_____ mounts.

I'd choose a honey-colored (5)_____ for the bedroom walls because it will take on a warm, marble-like look at night. Spectacular!

Yes, this technique is also expensive, since it requires multiple applications, but it will give the apartment the elegance you're looking for.

As for the living/dining area, I'd cover the floors in antique (6)_____ and the walls in antique (7)_____, preferably an exotic panorama.

I would upholster the couches and the chairs in the same (8)_____—you know, a cotton fabric with a light background and colorful print—that you use for curtains.

For the dining table, I'd choose something show stopping. Let me see...how about a Louis Quatorze piece covered in floral (9)_____? I'd also suggest a credenza covered in (10)_____ (that nubby, green material) to serve as an elegant buffet for the dining area.

All my best,
Giselle

ANSWERS: (1) verre églomisé; (2) faux marbre; (3) boulle; (4) ormolu; (5) Venetian plaster; (6) parquet de Versailles; (7) papier peint; (8) chintz; (9) marquetry; (10) shagreen

Congratulations! You can now pick up a design magazine without a French dictionary (or French dictionary app) in your other hand.

Now head to your suite, take one last look at the twinkling lights along the Grand Canal, and get some sleep.

Tomorrow we head to the **Italian Riviera**, where we'll focus on snob words and snob phrases with Italian origins.

Day 19

La Dolce Vita
ITALIAN WORDS & PHRASES

LOCATION: **PORTOFINO, ITALY**

So far in this course, we've focused heavily on French, but the Italians have also made extensive contributions to our repertoire of snob words.

During the Renaissance, Italy was the cultural leader of Europe, and during that period, the Italians exported many of their culinary and artistic innovations to France. For example, the Italian wife of Henry II, **Catherine de' Medici** (1519-89), is credited with introducing the fork, olive oil, and ice cream to the French court. And **Leonardo da Vinci** (1452-1519), an Italian who spent the last three years of his life in France, is responsible for the most famous work in the **Louvre**—the *Mona Lisa.*

The Italians, therefore, are no slouches in the snobbery department: we must learn Italian-based snob words.

However, a word of warning is in order. While the words and phrases in this chapter *do* have Italian origins, some of them are *not* used in modern Italian.

For example, English adopted the term *cognoscente* from Italian in the 18th century, but now it's obsolete in its mother tongue. *Litterati*, which gave birth to the English *literati*, is also now extinct in Italian.

Likewise, the term *alfresco,* an Italian borrowing that signifies 'outdoors,' or 'in the open air' in English, has morphed to mean 'in jail' in modern Italian, as we mentioned on Day 1. (When today's Italian's eat outdoors, they dine *all'aperto*.)

So, to repeat our earlier warning: use these terms as snob words in *English*, but not with native speakers of Italian.

For today's lesson, we return to the Mediterranean, where we'll meet on the Italian Riviera, or **Riviera Ligure**. This croissant-shaped piece of snob coast is divided into two parts: the **Riviera di Ponente** (Western Riviera), which runs northeast from the French border to the Italian city of Genoa, and the **Riviera di Levante** (Eastern Riviera), which continues southeast to the border of the Tuscany region.

We'll be based here at my villa in the hills above **Portofino**, an exclusive enclave on the Riviera di Levante. This one-time fishing village is a storybook town—that is, if the stories you read are full of mega-yachts, designer boutiques, and panoramic views of the sapphire **Ligurian Sea**.

I. PRONOUNCE & DEFINE

As you settle into your room, with its bougainvillea-covered terrace overlooking the harbor, say our new words aloud.

1. **bravado** (bruh-VAH´-doh)
2. **imbroglio** (im-BROLL´-yo)
3. **sprezzatura** (spraits´-uh-TOO´-ruh)
4. **sotto voce** (soh´-toh VOH´-cheh)
5. **il dolce far niente** (ill DOHL´-chay far NYEN´-tay)

Now consider these words in the following sentences:

1. After an hour of watching Jake and his brothers attempt to outdo each other by diving off increasingly higher cliffs, Amy tired of their *bravado* and went inside the houseboat.

2. Eliza was engaged to Tom when Tom decided he was in love with Alice, who was engaged to Brian. Then Brian proposed to Eliza. What an *imbroglio!*

3. Kyle missed swim practice half the time, but still won every event. He also maintained a 3.9 grade point average without ever seeming to study. His *sprezzatura*—or apparent lack of effort—was the envy of everyone.

4. During the board meeting, Danielle told me, *sotto voce* (so no one else would hear), that Clarice had a curler sticking out the back of her coiffure.

5. We had no reason to go to the Italian Riviera except to partake of *il dolce far niente*, the sweetness of doing nothing.

II. FILL IN THE BLANKS

Let's walk down to the harbor, where we'll have breakfast at what you and I would call a *café*, but which Italians call a *bar* (roll the *r* when you say it).

The locals usually have strong coffee with their breakfast pastries, but I order the wonderfully frothy hot chocolate. As we bite into our *cornettos* and *crostatas,* match each definition below with one of the five snob terms we've just introduced.

1. _____ 'the sweetness of doing nothing'
2. _____ spoken softly; under one's breath
3. _____ the ability to do something well
without seeming to work at it
4. _____ talk or behavior designed to impress
5. _____ a complicated misunderstanding or
altercation

ANSWERS: (1) il dolce far niente; (2) sotto voce; (3) sprezzatura; (4) bravado; (5) imbroglio

III. PRONOUNCE & DEFINE

Now let's board my yacht for a quick trip to **Cinque Terre** (Five Lands), a supremely picturesque area protected as a national park.

The five fishing and wine-making villages within the park, which form an eleven-mile coastal chain, are perched on the sides of dramatic cliffs at the southeastern tip of the Riviera di Levante.

My favorite of the five villages is **Corniglia**, where we'll stop to hike through the terraced vineyards and olive groves that hover above the pastel houses.

As we enjoy amazing views, let's pronounce five additional snob words with Italian origins.

> 6. **literati** (li´-der-AH´-dee)
> 7. **alfresco** or **al fresco** (all-FRES´-coh)
> 8. **gusto** (GUS´-toh)
> 9. **la dolce vita** (lah DOL´-chay VEE´-tah)
> 10. **cognoscente** (con-yuh-SHEN´-tee)

NOTE: the plural of *cognoscente* is *cognoscenti*, pronounced the same as the singular.

Now let's try to guess at the definitions of these words from their use in the following sentences:

1. The *literati* may look down their noses at the *Harry Potter* series, but whether or not the books have artistic merit, I happen to like them.
2. Due to the rain, we began the meal in the formal dining room. But once the sun came out, we moved to the terrace in order to dine *alfresco*.
3. After returning from two years in the Ecuadorian jungle, Jim devoured the burger with *gusto*.

4. What Carol wanted was *la dolce vita:* an easy, carefree, and luxurious life.

5. Armed with a doctorate in art history, Arthur often gives advice, as a *cognoscente*, on high-profile art sales.

IV. FILL IN THE BLANKS

There's nothing like a good hike to whet your appetite, so let's finish our visit to Cinque Terre with lunch in a *ristorante* in **Monterosso al Mare**, another quaint town with gelato-colored buildings overlooking a rocky beach.

Here we'll dine on **minestrone, focaccia** (similar to pizza), and pasta with **pesto**, all of which are Ligurian specialties.

As we eat, match the words from the previous section with their definitions below.

1. _____ Italian for 'the sweet life'
2. _____ an expert or connoisseur
3. _____ in the open air; outdoors
4. _____ relish; enjoyment; enthusiasm
5. _____ intellectuals; the educated class

ANSWERS: (1) la dolce vita; (2) cognoscente; (3) alfresco; (4) gusto; (5) literati

V. TRUE OR FALSE

As we continue our long and drawn-out meal (a three-hour lunch is not uncommon here), let's play the following game to reinforce what you've learned.

(T/F)   1. A person who seems to put a great deal of effort into his or her dress, and succeeds in always looking elegant, exhibits *sprezzatura*.

(T/F) 2. A man may use *bravado* to attempt to impress women.

(T/F) 3. An *imbroglio* is a minor problem.

(T/F) 4. Jessica is living *la dolce vita:* her husband left her with three kids, she can't find a job, and she has a serious heart problem.

(T/F) 5. If you're eating *alfresco,* you're eating outside.

(T/F) 6. *Cognoscenti* are experts in a particular field.

(T/F) 7. If one speaks at all during an opera, one should do so *sotto voce*.

(T/F) 8. People show *gusto* toward things they don't like.

(T/F) 9. Professional athletes are generally **not** members of the *literati*.

(T/F) 10. Manhattan's Wall Street is a good place to practice *il dolce far niente*.

ANSWERS: numbers (1), (3), (4), (8), and (10) are false.

VI. OPPOSITES

So far we've spent our time here on the Italian Riviera on the eastern half of the famed coastline, or the Riviera di Levante. Now let's pay a visit to **San Remo**, the most elegant and cosmopolitan resort town on the western half, or Riviera di Ponente.

In the late nineteenth and early twentieth centuries, San Remo, like many towns on the nearby Côte D'Azur, was an aristocratic winter destination favored by English and Russian nobles.

These foreigners have now been replaced by Italian families, but San Remo retains remnants of its patrician past: the **Russian Orthodox Church**, the grand **Casino**, and the **Corso Imperatrice**, a promenade named after Russian Empress Maria Alexandrovna, who visited in the 1870s.

As we wander this city's palm-lined avenues, built to give the nobles a place to promenade, match each word below with the definition most **opposite** its true meaning.

____	1. *literati*	a. to seemingly put great effort into everything
____	2. *alfresco*	b. spoken loudly
____	3. *gusto*	c. a sad life full of difficulties
____	4. *il dolce far niente*	d. a tiny misunderstanding
____	5. *bravado*	e. the illiterate masses
____	6. *sotto voce*	f. taking place indoors
____	7. *la dolce vita*	g. a novice or amateur
____	8. *sprezzatura*	h. a lack of interest
____	9. *imbroglio*	i. a strong work ethic
____	10. *cognoscente*	j. timid and modest behavior

ANSWERS: (1) e; (2) f; (3) h; (4) i; (5) j; (6) b; (7) c; (8) a; (9) d; (10) g

VII. MULTIPLE CHOICE

Let's climb up to the **Giardini Regina Elena**, a beautiful park that cascades down a steep slope, where we'll have amazing sunset views of San Remo.

While we hike, let's play a multiple-choice game.

1. If something is said *sotto voce,* it is uttered:
   a. sweetly
   b. softly, or under one's breath
   c. as loudly as possible

2. An *imbroglio* is:
   a. an Italian stew
   b. an expert or connoisseur
   c. a complicated or embarrassing situation

3. Members of the *literati* must be:
   a. well educated
   b. literary geniuses
   c. literature majors

229

4. A person who displays *sprezzatura:*
   - a. likes to express himself
   - b. makes success look effortless
   - c. likes to do nothing

5. The plural of *cognoscente* is:
   - a. *cognoscenti*
   - b. *cognoscentum*
   - c. *cognoscentes*

6. Which would **not** constitute a display of *bravado?*
   - a. bragging, loudly, about one's business acumen
   - b. jumping into the ocean from a tall cliff
   - c. sitting in a corner reading Shakespeare

7. If you're a proponent of *il dolce far niente,* you enjoy:
   - a. speaking softly
   - b. doing nothing
   - c. uncomfortable situations

8. If you have plenty of money, love, and leisure time, you may be living:
   - a. *c'est la vie*
   - b. *la vida loca*
   - c. *la dolce vita*

9. When you eat outdoors, you're dining:
   - a. *alfresco*
   - b. *al fresco*
   - c. the term can be spelled either way

10. If you do something with *gusto,* you do it with:
    - a. enthusiasm
    - b. disdain
    - c. both of the above

ANSWERS: (1) b; (2) c; (3) a; (4) b; (5) a; (6) c; (7) b; (8) c; (9) c; (10) a

VIII. SNOB APPEAL

I realize it's only been a few hours since we finished a big, long lunch, but at this point, a little pre-bedtime snack might be in order.

Piazza Bresca, next to the **Porto Vecchio** (Old Port), is home to restaurants that serve local specialties like freshly caught prawns, **ravioli** filled with ricotta and chard, and **sardenaria**, a type of focaccia topped with tomato sauce, onions, olives, capers, and anchovies. *Delizioso!*

While we wait for our food to arrive, fill the blanks in the following statements with the most appropriate snob words from this lesson.

Each word is used once.

bravado	imbroglio
sprezzatura	sotto voce
il dolce far niente	literati
alfresco	gusto
la dolce vita	cognoscente

1. The _____ began when Henrietta told Lynette that her house was a dump, and Lynette responded by posting on Facebook that Henrietta's physician husband was not actually licensed.
2. We were in a restaurant in St. Moritz when Donna leaned over to me and revealed, _____, that there was a fly in her soup.
3. Who has time for _____ when work takes up fifteen hours of every day?
4. Yes, I do enjoy expensive French cheeses, but I wouldn't consider myself a _____.
5. Oh, how I wish I had Bob's _____. He wins at everything, but never seems to expend any effort.

6. Don't believe Jacob's _____. He claims to be the best salesman in the company, but the figures show otherwise.

7. Pauline didn't seem at all happy about buying the penthouse. She sat there, bored, as we signed the papers, without displaying the slightest bit of _____.

8. _____ is the only way to eat at The Four Unicorns. The indoor dining room is crowded, loud, and decorated with black-velvet paintings.

9. Yes, the restaurant is popular with blue-collar workers. It's not usually frequented by the _____.

10. Running a place like The Four Unicorns isn't exactly conducive to _____. According to the owner, hours are long, customers are abusive, and profits aren't great. Does that sound like a sweet life?

ANSWERS: (1) imbroglio; (2) sotto voce; (3) il dolce far niente; (4) cognoscente; (5) sprezzatura; (6) bravado; (7) gusto; (8) alfresco; (9) literati; (10) la dolce vita

Congratulazioni! I'm proud of you! You're one day closer to word snobdom and to livin' *la dolce vita.*

Get to bed early, though, because tomorrow you'll take your second mid-term exam, which will cover all the snob words we've learned up to this point.

Day 20

Second Midterm Exam
LET'S TEST YOUR SNOB CRED

LOCATION: **COTOPAXI PROVINCE, ECUADOR**

The second day of reckoning has arrived! Time to see if you're worthy to receive your master of snobcabulary degree. But where should we go to administer this important ex— I mean, *learning game?*

I have the perfect spot.

You may not be especially familiar with Ecuador, the tiny South American country that straddles the equator, and even if you are, you may not associate it with snobbery. But I happen to own a 17th-century *hacienda* an hour south of Quito, the country's capital, where you can play this game in Latin American splendor.

The hacienda, with its forty-room mansion, is truly in the middle of nowhere, so you won't be distracted. The surrounding pastures were once home to an enormous llama empire—ten thousand head at its peak—but we now have about one third that number.

I have wonderful staff members here who'll treat you to Ecuadorian specialities like **patacones** (crispy fried plantains) and **llapingachos** (potato pancakes filled with cheese, served with peanut sauce). Then they'll leave you to luxuriate in the master suite, which has astounding views of the estate's gardens and of snow-capped **Cotopaxi**, one of the world's most symmetrical and beautiful volcanoes.

Welcome to paradise!

But back to the midterm, which contains 180 questions in a variety of formats. It's difficult, so please review the words from the first two parts of this course before you begin.

Once you're ready to take the test—I mean, play the game— set a timer for thirty minutes...and go!

¡Buena suerte!

I. MULTIPLE CHOICE

1. A *faux pas* is:
   a. a fake fur
   b. a social mistake
   c. an insincere handshake
2. A business that targets wealthy clients caters to the:
   a. *hoi polloi*
   b. *carriage trade*
   c. *glitterati*
3. If you're having breakfast in an outdoor covered area attached to a house, you could be eating on a:
   a. *baranda*
   b. *porte-cochère*
   c. *veranda*
4. A symmetrical garden feature composed of elements such as flower beds, paths, and fountains is a:
   a. *parterre*
   b. *parquet de Versailles*
   c. *pergola*

5. *Chamber music* is:
>   a. music composed for a small group of musicians and meant to be performed in a small venue
>   b. music composed for large chambers
>   c. music that originated in bedchambers

6. A *duplex* in Manhattan is a:
>   a. house built for two families
>   b. pricey two-story apartment in a high-rise building
>   c. movie complex with two theaters

7. A man who just wants to fill his stomach is a:
>   a. *gourmet*
>   b. *gourmand*
>   c. *gastronome*

8. The sport of *badminton*:
>   a. is one of the most popular sports in the U.K.
>   b. was originally played indoors
>   c. both of the above

9. The "bible" of the women's fashion industry is:
>   a. *Women's Wear Daily*
>   b. *Vogue*
>   c. *Harper's Bazaar*

10. *Bel canto* is:
>   a. a lyrical, melodic style of singing
>   b. a heavy, dramatic style of singing
>   c. a form of Gregorian chant

11. *Ancien régime* furniture comes from:
>   a. ancient cultures
>   b. pre-revolutionary France
>   c. ancient Greece and Rome

12. An agreement in which one thing is exchanged for another is a(n):
>   a. *pro bono*
>   b. *quid pro quo*
>   c. *ad hoc*

13. To be *au courant* is to:
    a. be up to date on current trends and events
    b. be current on utility bills
    c. have plenty of currency

14. The practice of force-feeding geese or ducks results in:
    a. *foie gras*
    b. *truffles*
    c. *prosciutto*

15. An artwork consisting of three panels is a:
    a. *diptych*
    b. *triptych*
    c. *dipstick*

16. The term *chichi*:
    a. is usually used in a negative sense
    b. means 'showy' in a way meant to impress
    c. both of the above

17. The technique in which glass is painted and gilt on its reverse side is called:
    a. *boulle*
    b. *verre églomisé*
    c. *shagreen*

18. Forcing paint through a screen onto paper results in an artwork called a:
    a. *silkscreen*
    b. *screen print*
    c. *silkscreen print*

19. Good-natured teasing or banter is:
    a. *bonhomie*
    b. *bastide*
    c. *badinage*

20. A *belvedere* is:
    a. a garden structure that provides a view
    b. a manservant
    c. an Italian belfry

ANSWERS: (1) b; (2) b; (3) c; (4) a; (5) a; (6) b; (7) b; (8) c; (9) a; (10) a; (11) b; (12) b; (13) a; (14) a; (15) b; (16) c; (17) b; (18) b; (19) c; (20) a

II. TRUE OR FALSE

(T/F)   1. The proper way to pronounce *chaise longue* is 'chase lounge.'

(T/F)   2. *Repartee* is angry conversation.

(T/F)   3. *Haute couture* is custom women's clothing by top designers.

(T/F)   4. *Pergolas* are a common feature inside houses.

(T/F)   5. A *locavore* is a person who eats crazy things.

(T/F)   6. All *prewar apartments* were built before World War I.

(T/F)   7. *Polo* players must hit a plastic ball through the opposing team's goalpost while on horseback.

(T/F)   8. It's possible for birds and insects to join you as you dine on a *loggia*.

(T/F)   9. In *pizzicato*, strings are plucked rather than played with a bow.

(T/F) 10. To be *en pointe* means to stay on task.

(T/F) 11. The term *Old Master* refers to artists who worked (roughly) between the years 1350 and 1800, as well as to their works.

(T/F) 12. *Ad infinitum* means 'forever,' or 'to infinity.'

(T/F) 13. *Par excellence* means 'less than excellent.'

(T/F) 14. *Truffles* (not the chocolate kind) are the world's most expensive food.

(T/F) 15. The term *étagère* is French for 'stranger.'

(T/F) 16. *Jamón ibérico* is top-quality Spanish ham, often considered the best in the world.

(T/F) 17. A *dernier cri* is a cry for help.

(T/F) 18. *Nouvelle cuisine* is lighter and healthier than *cuisine classique*.

(T/F) 19. *Bon chic, bon genre* refers to a certain lower-class French lifestyle.

(T/F) 20. *Trompe l'oeil* is used to trick the eye.

ANSWERS: all true but (1), (2), (4), (5), (6), (10), (13), (15), (17), (19)

III. MATCHING

Match the snob words below with their definitions.

____ 1. *scion*	a.	Paris, New York, Milan, London
____ 2. *ad nauseam*	b.	elegantly dressed and groomed
____ 3. *gastronome*	c.	to a sickening degree
____ 4. *fashion's Big Four*	d.	string of aligned doorways providing a long interior view
____ 5. *chiaroscuro*	e.	furniture and decoration that feature Chinese motifs
____ 6. *enfilade*	f.	descendant of a notable family
____ 7. *sonata*	g.	musical composition for a soloist and full orchestra
____ 8. *concerto*	h.	one with knowledge of food and who enjoys good food
____ 9. *soigné*	i.	instrumental composition with several contrasting movements
____ 10. *chinoiserie*	j.	extreme contrast between light and dark areas in a painting

ANSWERS: (1) f; (2) c; (3) h; (4) a; (5) j; (6) d; (7) i; (8) g; (9) b; (10) e

IV. SNOB STATEMENTS

Let's take a break and gaze out at the llamas grazing on the verdant pastures of the estate.

Feeling the need for an emotional support animal? Have at it! You've got three thousand of them.

Now use this chapter's snob words to fill the blanks in the statements below. Each word is used only once.

bonhomie	**la dolce vita**
casa colonica	**orangerie**
cricket	**shagreen**
de facto	**imbroglio**
fraises des bois	**Stanislavsky method**

1. "Mary's family was polite, but during the weekend I spent with them, I felt they lacked genuine _____."
2. "I know the house is valued at four million dollars, but it's a _____ dump."
3. "The wedding turned into a(n)_____, with the bride's mother slapping the groom, and the groom's mother dumping a pitcher of ice water on the bride."
4. "Tell her to cover the coffee table in a material that screams rare and expensive— _____, perhaps."
5. "I get bored at baseball games. I don't know how you Brits can handle hour after hour of _____."
6. "The acting was so unnatural! It was as if no one in the entire cast had ever heard of the _____."
7. "No, we're not looking for a Tuscan villa. We want a more rustic and charming _____."
8. "Jane just graduated from Juilliard, her acting career is taking off, and she's engaged to the heir of a Greek shipping fortune. She's living _____."
9. "If we're going to add lemon trees to the Southampton garden, we'll have to have a(n) _____ in which to house them during the winter."
10. "No, I *can't* duplicate the strawberry tart we had in Paris because I don't have _____."

ANSWERS: (1) bonhomie; (2) de facto; (3) imbroglio; (4) shagreen; (5) cricket; (6) Stanislavsky method; (7) casa colonica; (8) la dolce vita; (9) orangerie; (10) fraises des bois

V. SENSE...OR NONSENSE?

Check each of the following sentences that makes sense.

____ 1. The Impressionists often painted *en plein air.*

____ 2. When dining out, the Napa Valley *cognoscenti* favor La Toque over The French Laundry.

____ 3. There's only one *fashion week* in the world, and it takes place in Los Angeles.

____ 4. Once you turn off the main road, you'll take a right onto an *allée* that leads to the manor.

____ 5. A *chic* woman has confidence in her own style.

____ 6. Juanita likes to buy *objets d'art* at French bakeries.

____ 7. Imelda pretends to be a *gourmet,* but her elaborate meals are actually warmed-up take-out.

____ 8. After years of looking at properties, we finally purchased an *hôtel particulier* in Paris.

____ 9. Juan must not feel well today because he's acting *off-piste.*

____ 10. The *beautiful people* have fame and money, but not necessarily looks.

____ 11. I will never be friends with that *arriviste* Hélène.

____ 12. Ellen's performance of *Für Elise* was a little too *staccato* for my taste.

____ 13. I'm not a *fashionista*—I spend most of my time at fashion shows and in expensive boutiques.

____ 14. I'm afraid her vocal range wasn't equal to the *tessitura* of the piece.

____ 15. The façade featured a *colonnade* in the style of a southern plantation house.

____ 16. I liked the music from the new opera, but I didn't care for its *libretto.*

____ 17. Anne played several wrong notes and actually dropped her violin at one point, which made for a *virtuoso* performance.

___ 18. After being convicted of removing ancient pottery from the country, Blair was *persona non grata* in Peru.

___ 19. At the zoo, we saw elephants, giraffes, and *mozzarella di bufala.*

___ 20. Alex has the *joie de vivre* of a five-year-old at a waterpark.

ANSWERS: all should be checked except (3), (6), (9), (13), (17), and (19).

VI. MORE MATCHING

___	1. *co-op*	a. gilt bronze used to adorn furniture
___	2. *ormolu*	b. reckless or daring acts performed with the intent to show off
___	3. *pro bono*	c. painted to look like marble
___	4. *intermezzo*	d. knowing what to do in any social situation
___	5. *savoir faire*	e. for the public good
___	6. *bravado*	f. building owned by shareholders who have use of its apartments
___	7. *crème fraîche*	g. short entertainment between acts of a play or an opera
___	8. *faux marbre*	h. game properly played on a perfectly flat grass court
___	9. *folly*	i. thick, cultured French cream
___	10. *croquet*	j. an architectural ornament in a garden, often rather costly

ANSWERS: (1) f; (2) a; (3) e; (4) g; (5) d; (6) b; (7) i; (8) c; (9) j; (10) h

VII. MORE SNOB STATEMENTS

Fill the blanks below with snob words from this lesson. Each word is used once. Alter words as needed to fit context.

241

bastide	en piste
entre nous	espalier
gravitas	gusto
opera buffa	prosciutto
Venetian plaster	sotto voce

1. "I actually prefer course stucco for the walls, but if we're ever going to make the pages of *Architectural Digest*, we'd better go with _____."

2. "He *does* possess a certain level of _____, but I'm not sure that qualifies him to be CEO."

3. "To be perfectly honest, I don't like opera in general, but I much prefer _____ to the serious, dramatic works."

4. "Claire tried to corner me in the skiwear boutique about that endorsement she wants, but I told her I had to meet someone _____."

5. "Margaret leaned over and said, _____, 'I think Brigitte had a facelift.'"

6. "_____, I think Brigitte's facelift was a mistake."

7. "Of course I requested a _____! We rented a *mas* the last time we were here, and we got low ceilings, cramped rooms, and no view."

8. "Felipe must not have eaten for a week. He attacked that pizza with _____!"

9. "The charming garden, which has a fountain at its center, has orange and lemon _____ covering its stone walls."

10. "Unless it's served with real Italian _____, I refuse to eat cantaloupe."

ANSWERS: (1) Venetian plaster; (2) gravitas; (3) opera buffa; (4) en piste; (5) sotto voce; (6) entre nous; (7) bastide; (8) gusto; (9) espaliers; (10) prosciutto

VIII. FILL IN THE BLANKS

ad hoc   dressage
flâneur   flâneuse
loft   marquetry
West End   steeplechase
papier peint   pied-à-terre

1. _____ French for 'wallpaper'
2. _____ man who wanders a city observing society and seeking adventure
3. _____ decoration that uses veneers to make non-geometric designs
4. _____ small second home or apartment
5. _____ for the case at hand only
6. _____ one-room apartment in a former industrial building
7. _____ equestrian event designed to showcase a horse's training
8. _____ hub of London theater
9. _____ horse race over fences and ditches
10. _____ a female *flâneur*

ANSWERS: (1) papier peint; (2) flâneur; (3) marquetry; (4) pied-à-terre; (5) ad hoc; (6) loft; (7) dressage; (8) West End; (9) steeplechase; (10) flâneuse

IX. SNOB SEARCH

What would you be most likely to find (or hear) in each of the following places? Circle the best answer.

1. art supply store: *sfumato   gouache   trompe l'oeil*
2. Italian countryside: *de rigueur   Tuscan villa   glitterati*
3. art gallery: *lithograph   bel canto   prosciutto*
4. formal garden: *de rigueur   treillage   foie gras*

5. *Old Master* painting: *pro bono   sfumato   glitterati*
6. brunch at the Paris Ritz: *beau monde   de trop   portico*
7. concert hall: *opera seria   rara avis   veranda*
8. department store: *trompe l'oeil   prêt-à-porter   treillage*
9. entrance of a grand house: *portico   virtuoso   forage*
10. film premiere: *petits pois   glitterati   lanai*
11. working-class *bistro: bon appétit   dressage   ad hoc*
12. ground floor of a residence: *aerie   veranda   oratorio*
13. French refrigerator: *crème fraîche   Wagyu   ormolu*
14. new building: *hard loft   soft loft   prewar apartment*
15. Provençal countryside: *mas   casa colonica   Tuscan villa*

ANSWERS: (1) gouache; (2) Tuscan villa; (3) lithograph; (4) treillage; (5) sfumato; (6) beau monde; (7) opera seria; (8) prêt-à-porter; (9) portico; (10) glitterati; (11) bon appétit (12) veranda; (13) crème fraîche; (14) soft loft; (15) mas

X. EVEN MORE MATCHING

____ 1. *haricots verts*   a. originated in Japan; very pricey

____ 2. *rara avis*   b. one who likes good food, parties

____ 3. *Wagyu*   c. dining, shopping, and ice skating, among other activities

____ 4. *brownstone*   d. French for 'green beans'

____ 5. *bon vivant*   e. dance for two performers

____ 6. *il dolce far niente* f. Latin for 'rare bird'

____ 7. *après-ski*   g. dwelling common in Manhattan

____ 8. *pas de deux*   h. cave in a garden, usually man-made

____ 9. *grotto*   i. type of furniture decoration made of brass and tortoiseshell

____ 10. *boulle*   j. 'the sweetness of doing nothing'

ANSWERS: (1) d; (2) f; (3) a; (4) g; (5) b; (6) j; (7) c; (8) e; (9) h; (10) i

XI. MORE TRUE OR FALSE

(T/F)   1. A *fauteuil* is heavy and difficult to move.

(T/F)   2. *Chintz* is often used as a floor covering.

(T/F)   3. *Cuisine classique* is classic French *haute cuisine*.

(T/F)   4. *Parquet de Versailles* is a popular wallcovering.

(T/F)   5. An *aria* is a lyrical song often used to reflect on the action in an opera.

(T/F)   6. Members of the *literati* are likely to be college educated.

(T/F)   7. A *pilaster* is a round column made of plaster.

(T/F)   8. A *mauvais quart d'heure* is a pleasant experience.

(T/F)   9. *Noblesse oblige* means 'if you're noble, do whatever you want.'

(T/F) 10. *Sprezzatura* is the act of spraying oneself with fragrance.

(T/F) 11. A *tapis vert* could be a good place for a game of croquet.

(T/F) 12. Handel's *Messiah* is an *oratorio*.

(T/F) 13. *Aeries* are generally located in gorges, hollows, and other low-lying areas.

(T/F) 14. *Haute cuisine* applies to French food only.

(T/F) 15. At a *ski-in, ski-out* hotel, you can get to and from the slopes without using a private car.

(T/F) 16. To dine *alfresco* is to dine outside.

(T/F) 17. If several females have just completed an excellent performance, the appropriate term to shout is *"Brava!"*

(T/F) 18. *In situ* means 'on site.'

(T/F) 19. *Petits pois* is the French term for 'green beans.'

(T/F) 20. The technique of painting an object to resemble marble is called *faux marbre*.

ANSWERS: all false except (3), (5), (6), (11), (12), (15), (16), (18), and (20).

XII. COMPLETE THE STORY

Time to check in with Giselle and Marco.

Use the following words to fill blanks in the passage below. Each word is used once. Alter words to fit context as necessary.

atelier

bergère

boiserie

cantata

Coco Chanel

comme il faut

couturier

couturière

de rigueur

de trop

diptych

entablature

epicure

etching

forage

gauche

haute bourgeoisie

jet set

lanai

magnum opus

nouveau riche

outré

Palladian window

passementerie

triplex

The Expensive Escapades of
MARCO & GISELLE
Professional Beautiful People

Episode Eleven: Angst-Ridden in Argentina

As we've mentioned, Marco's parents have drastically reduced his monthly allowance. This is a problem because now that he's madly in love with Giselle, he has to constantly search for cheap date ideas, which are hard to come by.

Fortunately, after paying four hundred dollars for lunch with his beloved in *Episode Nine*, in Paris (the last time they met), Marco has a *Eureka!* moment—he'll invite Giselle and her mother to his family's *estancia* in Argentina, where entertaining the two will not cost him a dime.

Giselle and her mother accept his offer. They are now in Argentina, and we join the two women as they converse alone for a moment in the *sala grande* of the Grimaldi home.

MRS. VAN DE KAMP: Look at this divine, eclectic room! The classical (1)_____ that forms the fireplace mantel, this wonderful, wide (2)_____ made of a cattle-horn frame and leather upholstery, the walls covered in (3)_____ of tropical woods, and the fabulous light streaming in through this massive (4) _____!

GISELLE: Mother, *au contraire* in the most *au contrairian* way! This room is *not* (5)_____. In fact, that chair, with its cattle references, is (6)_____, and quite frankly, I find this whole *estancia* rather over the top— (7)_____, even. To add insult to injury, you know how I detest (8)_____ on curtains!

(Marco enters the room with his parents.)

MARCO: Mrs. Van de Kamp and Giselle, may I present my parents, Alessandra and Ignacio Grimaldi.

(Everyone hugs and kisses.)

MRS. VAN DE KAMP: How wonderful to meet you! We were just admiring your lovely living room!

MRS. GRIMALDI: Thank you, but I wish we were hosting you in our Buenos Aires home. Out here on the *estancia*, things are a little cattle-centric, as you can see. For example, my husband insists I hang these (9)_____ he makes of his favorite cows. He has hundreds more of them (artworks, not cows) in his (10)_____, where he produces them.

MRS. VAN DE KAMP: No need to apologize! Cattle art would seem to be (11)_____ on an *estancia*.

MR. GRIMALDI: *Muchas gracias* for understanding, *señora*. My (12)_____ is hanging in the dining room. It is a (13)_____, with two separate panels hanging side by side. You will see it shortly. And then we will tour my garage of antique cars and my stable of prize-winning bulls.

MRS. GRIMALDI: Please, *mi cielo*, they've only just arrived. It would be (14)_____ to show them the *estancia* before they've had a chance to rest.

MR. GRIMALDI: Right you are, *mi amor*. Marco, show the ladies to their rooms for now. We can continue our conversation at dinner, after which I plan to present the (15)_____ I just finished composing, which I have titled "Ode to Cows."

MARCO: *(grimacing)* Thank you, father, we look forward to hearing that.

MRS. VAN DE KAMP: *(turning to Mrs. Grimaldi)* May I just say that you look even more lovely in person than in the pictures I've seen of you in *Women's Wear Daily*.

MRS. GRIMALDI: *Ay, gracias*, and *merci beaucoup*, but *you* are the one looking lovely. I adore your ensemble! Who is your favorite (16)_____?

MRS. VAN DE KAMP: Well, of all time, (17)_____, of course. But the truth is, I don't think I've never met a designer I didn't like. Lately I've been buying the work of a new (18)_____ in Paris. She's not well known, yet— but she will be.

(As the mothers continue to chat, Marco shows Giselle to her room on the second floor.)

GISELLE: How lovely! It has a door leading outside to a private (19)_____!

MARCO: Here in Argentina it is known as a *terraza*, but call it what you like.

GISELLE: Whatever it's called, it's lovely, and it reminds me of a (20)_____ we own in Dubai—each of its three floors has a *terraza* (I'll use *your* word) just like this.

MARCO: So happy you like it. By the way, after you rest awhile, would you like to (21)_____ for some berries with me? My mother is something of a(n) (22)_____, and only *fraises des bois* will do for tonight's dessert.

GISELLE: Certainly. What girl wouldn't love to gather berries?

MARCO: *(Nervously)* One other thing. I hope you will excuse my father. He has lived on this *estancia* for so long that he no longer knows how to relate to members of the (23)_____, well-traveled people like you and your mother.

I know he seems (24)_____, always bragging about his cars and bulls, but he should know better—he was born into the (25)_____ of Buenos Aires.

ANSWERS: (1) entablature; (2) bergère; (3) boiserie; (4) Palladian window; (5) comme il faut; (6) de trop; (7) outré; (8) passementerie; (9) etchings; (10) atelier; (11) de rigueur; (12) magnum opus; (13) diptych; (14) gauche; (15) cantata; (16) couturier; (17) Coco Chanel; (18) couturière; (19) lanai; (20) triplex; (21) forage; (22) epicure; (23) jet set; (24) nouveau riche; (25) haute bourgeoisie

XIII. HOW DID YOU DO?

I'll assume you passed the exam with flying colors. Who could fail a test in this wholesome, uncontaminated Ecuadorian air? With so many adorable llamas at the ready?

Tally your score and consult the following table to see which degree you've earned.

175-180 **Master of Arts in Snobcabulary,** *magna cum laude*
165-175 **Master of Arts in Snobcabulary,** *summa cum laude*
150-165 **Master of Arts in Snobcabulary,** *cum laude*
130-150 **Master of Arts in Snobcabulary**
100-130 **40 credits** toward your Master's in Snobcabulary
  0-100 **Sorry, you failed.** Go back and try again!

It's now time to say *adiós* to Ecuador and get set for PART THREE of this course, in which we cover more French and more Latin, as well as film, high-end travel, snobby dining, and ritzy retail, among other topics.

We'll begin by traveling to the Spanish capital of Madrid for another fascinating lesson on Latin phrases.

PART THREE

Day 21

Et Cetera
MORE LATIN SNOB TERMS

LOCATION: **MADRID, SPAIN**

Latin—the language that brought us Italian, French, Spanish, Portuguese, Catalan, and Romanian—is also the root of many other languages you've probably never heard of.

One of the most fruitful places for the evolution of these obscure Romance tongues was the **Iberian Peninsula**, once an important part of the Roman Empire, and home today to Spain and Portugal. More than half a dozen distinct languages developed here from Latin, including Galician, Asturian, Leonese, Aragonese, and Castilian.

The latter, which evolved in the area around Madrid, eventually became modern Spanish, Latin's greatest legacy, which now has more than 500 million native speakers worldwide.

But as we've pointed out in previous lessons, the mother tongue of the Romance languages also lives on in English (a prolific poacher of Latin terms), which is why we must study Latin snob words.

Since we've already been to Rome, and haven't yet explored Spain, we'll have today's Latin lesson here in the Spanish capital, a sophisticated and elegant city of grand imperial boulevards, royal palaces, manicured parks, and world-class museums.

We'll stay at my *pied-à-terre,* a *duplex* in a 19th-century building on the leafy **Paseo de la Castellana**. This avenue, which runs through the posh **Salamanca** district, is Madrid's answer to the French capital's Champs-Élysées.

But first, since I imagine you're hungry, let's walk a few blocks to **Gran Café Gijón**, a historic eatery that's been serving this neighborhood—and Madrid's *literati*—since 1888.

Here, at a marble-topped table surrounded by mirrors and red-velvet banquettes, we'll snack on *jamón ibérico,* or premium Spanish ham (Day 17), and **queso manchego**, a sheep's milk cheese made in the nearby region of **La Mancha**.

Our little repast should hold us over until dinner, which no self-respecting *Madrileño* will eat before 10 p.m.

As the ham and cheese melts on our tongues, let's go over our new words, which don't fit any particular category except that they're Latin terms that every word snob should know.

Pay close attention!

I. PRONOUNCE & DEFINE

1. **terra firma** (tehr´-uh FUR´-muh)
2. **carpe diem** (car´-pay DEE´-uhm)
3. **i.e.** *(id est)* (id-EST´)
4. **e.g.** *(exempli gratia)* (ig-zem´-plee GRAW´-tee-ah)
5. **modus operandi** (moh´-duhs ah-per-AN´-dee)
6. **ne plus ultra** (nay plus OL´-truh)
7. **mea culpa** (may´-uh COOL´-puh)
8. **deus ex machina** (day´-uhs ex MAH´-kuhn-uh)
9. **ex post facto** (ex´ post FAK´-toh)
10. **ipso facto** (IP´-soh FAK´-toh)

1. **TERRA FIRMA**: ('firm land') dry and solid ground as compared to air or water.

- After our three-week cruise, we were happy to be back on *terra firma*.

2. **CARPE DIEM**: ('pluck the day') usually translated 'seize the day,' the philosophy that one should enjoy life's pleasures while they last without much concern for the future.

- Bryce took a *carpe diem* attitude toward junk food without worrying about its effect on his waistline.

The phrase is also used as a command (*Carpe diem!*) to urge taking advantage of the present situation.

3. **I.E.**: (abbreviation of *id est*, 'that is') a concise replacement for 'in other words' or 'that is to say' when introducing a clarification or restatement.

- The bathroom was covered in faux marbre, *i.e.,* imitation marble.

Always use a comma before and after *i.e.*

4. **E.G.**: (abbreviation of *exempli gratia*, 'for example') a concise way to introduce one or more examples.

- We own homes in some of the world's most important cities, *e.g.,* Paris, London, and Tokyo.

As with *i.e.,* always use a comma before and after *e.g.*

5. **MODUS OPERANDI**: ('method of operating') often abbreviated **m.o.**, a usual and distinct way of doing something.

PLURAL: *modi operandi* (moh´-dee ah-per-AN´-dee)

- Lies, passive aggression, and micromanagement were all part of Sadie's *modus operandi.*

6. **NE PLUS ULTRA:** ('not further beyond') the ultimate; the perfect or most extreme example of its type; the zenith, summit, or peak.

- Adidas athletic shoes are the current *ne plus ultra* of fashion footwear among U.S. high school students.

7. **MEA CULPA:** ('my fault') a formal acknowledgment of personal fault or error.

- After issuing a public *mea culpa,* the Governor tweeted that he wasn't actually sorry at all.

8. **DEUS EX MACHINA:** ('god from a machine') an unexpected power or event that appears suddenly and solves a seemingly hopeless situation, especially as a contrived plot device in a play or novel.

The term comes from ancient Greek and Roman drama, in which a god often appears above the stage (with the help of a crane, the *machine*) and saves the day.

- The film had a few good moments, but the chance arrival of the Queen—a *deus ex machina* if there ever was one—was hard to swallow.

9. **EX POST FACTO:** ('from a thing done afterward') with retrospective action or force; after the fact.

- After Carl renounced his American citizenship to avoid paying U.S. taxes, Congress, passed an *ex post facto* law banning him and other tax emigrés from ever re-entering the country.

10. **IPSO FACTO**: ('by the fact itself') as an inevitable result; by the very fact or act.

- Claire believed that *Old Master* paintings were *ipso facto* better than anything produced today.

II. MATCHING

How about those definitions?

Not so clear, you say?

Relax, give them time to percolate through your brain as we explore the Salamanca neighborhood.

This area is equivalent to the Triangle D'or in Paris, with **Calle de José Ortega y Gasset** playing the role of *l'avenue Montaigne,* or snootiest shopping street.

Here, and on adjoining side streets, we'll find upscale retailers like Cartier, Jimmy Choo, Chanel, Escada, Valentino, Louis Vuitton, Lladró, Omega, Dior, Hermès, Saint Laurent, Tiffany, Gucci, Bulgari, Balenciaga, and Dolce & Gabbana.

As we walk and gawk down this attractive avenue, match our new snob words with their definitions.

____ 1. *ipso facto*   a. land; dry ground

____ 2. *carpe diem*   b. an admission of guilt

____ 3. *terra firma*   c. 'seize the day'

____ 4. *ex post facto*   d. 'by the very fact'

____ 5. *deus ex machina*   e. usual way of operating

____ 6. *i.e.*   f. 'that is;' 'in other words'

____ 7. *ne plus ultra*   g. 'god of the machine'

____ 8. *mea culpa*   h. 'for example'

____ 9. *e.g.*   i. 'after the fact'

____ 10. *modus operandi*   j. the highest level possible

ANSWERS: (1) d; (2) c; (3) a; (4) i; (5) g; (6) f; (7) j; (8) b; (9) h; (10) e

III. FILL IN THE BLANKS

My chauffeur, Jorge Luis, will now drive us (in my black Maserati Gran Turismo, but who's dropping luxury brand names?) to the **Plaza Mayor**, the center of Madrid's historic district.

Please sit in front—I'll take the back seat, which is a bit cramped.

As we drive, fill each blank below with a snob word from this lesson. Each word is used only once.

terra firma	ipso facto
carpe diem	ex post facto
i.e.	deus ex machina
e.g.	mea culpa
modus operandi	ne plus ultra

1. After the ten-hour flight, it was a huge relief to set foot on _____.

2. Switzerland's swank St. Moritz is the _____ of fashionable winter resorts.

3. Europe is also home to several other *chic* winter resorts, _____, Courchevel, Megève, and Cortina.

4. Since the 1960s, Gstaad, in the Swiss Alps, has been popular with the *jet set*, _____, people with time and money to travel the world in search of pleasure.

5. After falling and breaking her leg, Brigitte confessed to us, _____, that she'd never learned to ski.

6. She then performed a tearful _____, begging everyone's forgiveness for ruining the trip.

7. The poor girl assumed—quite wrongly—that her broken leg would _____ end the ski trip for all of us.

8. "_____!" I said to the group. "We're wasting precious slope time by worrying about Brigitte's leg."

9. Then came the _____: a renowned orthopedic surgeon, who happened to be staying at our hotel,
   performed a revolutionary surgical technique, and Brigitte
   returned to the slopes immediately.
10. This time she had a ski instructor, with whom she flirted
    unceasingly. That's her _____, of course.

ANSWERS: (1) terra firma; (2) ne plus ultra; (3) e.g.; (4) i.e.; (5) ex post facto;
(6) mea culpa; (7) ipso facto; (8) carpe diem; (9) deus ex machina; (10) modus
operandi

IV. SENSE...OR NONSENSE?

Aren't these terms delightful? They have the advantage of
making you sound snobby *and* erudite—a double threat.

We're almost to the Plaza Mayor, but since it's off-limits
to motor vehicles, we'll have to get out here and walk to the
actual square.

First, let's pass through this arch, the **Arco de Cuchilleros**
(Arch of the Knifemakers), named for the tradesmen who once
had their workshops here. Then we'll climb this narrow stairway, and *voilà!* The plaza suddenly opens before us. Does it
remind you of anything? How about the Place des Vosges in
Paris (though smaller, and without the greenery)?

As we admire this architectural *tour de force* (see Day 22)—
which was originally completed in the 17th century, but took
its current form in the 19th—and as we peruse the shops and
cafés in its ground-level arcades, read the following statements
and place a check next to those that make sense.

____ 1. The thief's *modus operandi*—leaving a banana peel
        at every crime scene—led to his capture.
____ 2. Her *mea culpa* didn't convince me to put her back
        on the finance committee.
____ 3. Al ordered *coq au vin;* his date ordered *carpe diem.*

___ 4. I know you like cruises, but I prefer *terra firma*.

___ 5. Dan likes most individual sports, *i.e.,* tennis, swimming, croquet, and ping pong.

___ 6. The fact that Juan is from Spain does not mean, *ex post facto,* that he likes flamenco music.

___ 7. The plot was weak: Santa, an unlikely *deus ex machina*, rescues the tsunami survivors on Christmas Eve.

___ 8. Brock plays the sousaphone, *e.g.*, one of those huge brass horns you see in marching bands.

___ 9. Jim was fired after the general manager made an *ipso facto* rule against eating in cubicles.

___ 10. Jill says the Range Rover is the *ne plus ultra* of SUVs.

ANSWERS: numbers (1), (2), (4), (7), and (10) should be checked.

V. TRUE OR FALSE

Our next stop is the **Museo del Prado**, the Spanish art museum that rivals the Louvre in Paris. Here we'll see one of the museum's most famous works: ***Las Meninas*** (1656), by **Diego Velázquez** (1599-1660), who is often considered the greatest painter of the **Spanish Golden Age** (1492-1681).

As we gaze at this lovely, enigmatic masterpiece, in which Velázquez painted himself painting the Spanish princess, let's play a true-or-false game.

(T/F)   1. If something is the *ne plus ultra*, there are better things in its class.

(T/F)   2. A politician might perform a *mea culpa* in order to appease his or her constituents.

(T/F)   3. The term *i.e.* stands for *id est*, or 'that is.'

(T/F)   4. If a fictional character escapes the Nazis by swimming the English Channel, the author has made use of a *deus ex machina*.

(T/F)   5. A person with a *carpe diem* philosophy hoards money and rarely leaves home.

(T/F)   6. A person who asks permission *ex post facto* has already done whatever he or she wanted to do.

(T/F)   7. To introduce a clarification, use *e.g.*

(T/F)   8. *Ipso facto* describes something that happened 'after the fact.'

(T/F)   9. A person who swims the English Channel will be glad to eventually reach *terra firma*.

(T/F) 10. *Modus operandi* is often abbreviated *m.o.*

ANSWERS: (2), (3), (6), (9), and (10) are true; the rest are false.

VI. COMPLETE THE STORY

Before we leave Madrid, we must visit **El Retiro,** a huge expanse of urban greenery similar to Manhattan's Central Park. Originally built as a royal retreat, the park became public in the 19th century.

El Retiro is lovely, with formal gardens, fountains, a lake, cafés, and an enormous and fanciful greenhouse, the **Palacio de Cristal**. Inaugurated in 1887, the glass palace was built to house tropical plants from the Philippines, a Spanish possession at the time.

As we continue to wander the park, let's check in with Marco and Giselle.

Use snob words from this lesson to fill the blanks in the following passage. Each word is used once.

terra firma	ipso facto
carpe diem	ex post facto
i.e.	deus ex machina
e.g.	mea culpa
modus operandi	ne plus ultra

The Expensive Escapades of
MARCO & GISELLE
Professional Beautiful People

Episode Twelve: Latin Dancing

In our last episode, Giselle and her mother traveled to Argentina to visit Marco and his parents at their *estancia,* or cattle ranch.

As our current episode opens, all of our characters are still in Argentina, and Marco has taken Giselle to Buenos Aires (in his private jet) for a night on the town.

Our couple visits a night club in posh **Palermo**, where Marco plans to show off his dancing skills. The evening, however, does not go as smoothly as he hopes.

MARCO: Allow me to offer a sincere (1)_____ for our disastrous flight. I imagine you are glad to be back on (2)_____.

GISELLE: Yes, running out of fuel in mid-air—with nowhere to land—is (3)_____ stressful.

MARCO: Yes, but we could not have asked for a better (4)_____ than the military tanker that appeared out of nowhere and refueled us.

GISELLE: Yes, thank heavens for the Argentine Air Force! I honestly thought we were going to die. I guess it's time to adopt a (5)_____ philosophy: one never knows when the Grim Reaper may arrive.

MARCO: Yes, it certainly is time to "seize the day"—or *night*, as it were. Would you care to dance, my dear?

GISELLE: Dance?

MARCO: Yes, dance, (6)_____, move around on the dance floor?

GISELLE: Oh, that. Um, no, I don't dance.

MARCO: How can you say you don't dance? Everyone dances!

Dancing is the (7)_____ of all polite social interactions.

GISELLE: Oh, I see your (8)_____—I wasn't born *mañana*.

MARCO: I think you mean you weren't born *ayer*, or 'yesterday.' *Mañana* means 'tomorrow.'

GISELLE: Don't try to capture my heart with your smooth Spanish phrases! You're just like all the other Latin men I've met! You bring me to this impossibly romantic place, convince me to dance, and I'll end up falling in love with you, right on the dance floor.

Then tomorrow we'll have a(n) (9)_____ "talk" about our "relationship," and you'll tell me you just want to be friends.

You know, I can think of several appropriate ways to describe you, (10)_____, heartbreaker, flirt, tease, Casanova, Lothario, and Don Juan!

ANSWERS: (1) mea culpa; (2) terra firma; (3) ipso facto; (4) deus ex machina; (5) carpe diem; (6) i.e.; (7) ne plus ultra; (8) modus operandi; (9) ex post facto; (10) e.g.

How's that for a plot twist? And you thought a lesson on Latin words would be *ipso facto* boring.

As we say *hasta luego* to Giselle and Marco, as well as to the Spanish capital, let's ease back into French mode. Tomorrow we travel to the coast of Normandy to learn more Gallic snob phrases.

Day 22

Au Contraire, Mon Frère
USEFUL FRENCH PHRASES

LOCATION: **DEAUVILLE, FRANCE**

Many of France's *chic* seaside resorts, especially those of the Côte d'Azur, began life as fishing villages and eventually became gentrified. Not so **Deauville** (DOE′-veal), known as the queen of Norman beach towns, which was designed from the ground up to be the northern playground of rich Parisians.

The **Duc de Morny** (1811-65), businessman and half-brother of **Emperor Napoleon III** (1808-73), established Deauville in 1859, and he immediately equipped the town with racetracks, a yacht harbor, beachside villas, a casino, and luxury hotels. More than a century and a half later, the town is still the most *bon chic, bon genre* beach resort in France.

Set on the **English Channel**, Deauville is a mere two hours from Paris by car. Consequently, well-heeled Parisians spend so much time here that they often refer to the town as the twenty-first *arrondissement* (in case you're not aware, Paris is divided into twenty districts, or *arrondissements*).

At any rate, Deauville is the perfect place to learn today's useful and very snooty French phrases.

Sometimes a sentence, written or spoken, needs a little *je ne sais quoi* (definition below) to spice it up. An uppity French phrase can usually do the trick.

Elegant, arrogant, and absolutely snobbish, these terms pack a punch when spelled and pronounced correctly.

I. PRONOUNCE & DEFINE

Let's start our lesson with a stroll along the **Promenade des Planches**, the elegant boardwalk that runs along Deauville's wide, sandy beach. In fact, this beach is so wide, and contains so much sand, that one wonders why the French government doesn't take half of it and dump it onto the uncomfortably pebbly beaches of the Cote d'Azur.

Be that as it may, the low buildings you see lining the promenade are changing cabins, each marked with the name of a movie star who once attended the annual **Deauville American Film Festival**. Many of the names belong to Hollywood royalty from decades past: Kim Novak, Robert Duvall, and Lauren Bacall, to name just a few.

As we continue our walk, let's take our first look at today's words:

1. **au contraire** (oh´ cohn-TRAIR´)
2. **je ne sais quoi** (zhuh´ nuh say KWAH´)
3. **c'est la vie** (say lah VEE´)
4. **cause célèbre** (kawz´ suh-LEB´)
5. **carte blanche** (cart´ BLAWNSH´)
6. **fait accompli** (FAY´ tah-cohm-PLEE´)
7. **comme ci, comme ça** (kum SEE´ kum SAW´)
8. **en famille** (ahn fah-MEE´)
9. **tour de force** (tor duh FORCE´)
10. **tête-à-tête** (tet´-ah-TET´)

1. **AU CONTRAIRE**: ('on the contrary') used in English to disagree in a snobby way.

- Nadine said Carol was a slob. *Au contraire!* Yesterday she came to work in a perfectly-tailored Chanel suit and an impeccable coiffure.

2. **JE NE SAIS QUOI**: (archaic French, 'I don't know what') an intangible, elusive quality, especially a pleasing one, that is difficult to put into words.

- Paul is not conventionally attractive, but he has a certain *je ne sais quoi* that makes him quite popular with the ladies.

3. **C'EST LA VIE**: ('that's life') used in English to express resignation in a snooty manner.

- Today I wrecked my Bentley, broke my back in the process, and found out I'm being audited. *C'est la vie!*

4. **CAUSE CÉLÈBRE**: ('celebrated case') a notorious legal case, incident, person, or thing that excites widespread interest.

- President Trump's criticism of NFL players who kneel during the national anthem turned the issue into a *cause célèbre.*

5. **CARTE BLANCHE**: ('blank document') complete freedom to act; permission to do something in any way one chooses.

- Midge gave me *carte blanche* to overhaul the employee lounge, so I spent ten thousand dollars on massage chairs.

6. **FAIT ACCOMPLI**: an accomplished fact; a reality.

- Despite the fact the city ordered construction to cease three months ago, the Smiths' new tennis court is a *fait accompli.*

7. **COMME CI, COMME ÇA:** so-so; not great, but not terrible.

- It hadn't been a good day or a bad day, so when Janice asked me how I was, I replied, *"comme ci, comme ça."*

8. **EN FAMILLE:** ('in family') as a family.

- On weekdays, we grab meals whenever we can, but on weekends, we all sit down together and dine *en famille.*

9. **TOUR DE FORCE:** a thing done exceptionally well; a display of skill, strength, or ingenuity.

- The mayor's supporters called his speech a *tour de force*—the best he'd ever given—but his opponents disagreed.

10. **TÊTE-À-TÊTE:** ('head to head') a face-to-face conversation between two people.

- John and I were alone, ready for a romantic *tête-à-tête*, when my little brother barged in and ruined the moment.

II. TRUE OR FALSE

As we explore Deauville, you may feel as if you've wandered into **Fantasyland** at one of the Disney parks.

That's because the **Norman Revival** architecture—consisting of half-timbered buildings embellished with fanciful turrets, gables, chimneys, and balconies—looks like it's straight out of a fairy tale. (Deauville's housing prices, however, which are similar to those of Paris, are straight out of a nightmare.)

Let's stop by my villa to relax a moment before we continue our explorations. Luckily for us, my housekeeper, Estelle, has just pulled a **tarte normande** from the oven.

This Norman treat is made of local apples and local *crème fraîche*, a rich and delightful cream made from the milk of

Norman cows. (These cows, by the way, have distinctive black circles around their eyes that look like sunglasses. *Très chic.*)

As we sample this edible miracle (the tart, not the cows), let's play the following true-or-false game:

(T/F) 1. If something is a *fait accompli*, there's a slight possibility it will happen.

(T/F) 2. When you travel *en famille*, you travel as a family.

(T/F) 3. The best time to shout *"c'est la vie!"* is when life is good.

(T/F) 4. Something done very well is a *tour de force*.

(T/F) 5. A *tête-à-tête* takes place between no more than two people.

(T/F) 6. A *cause célèbre* is something few people know about.

(T/F) 7. To have *carte blanche* is to have a blank check to do whatever you think needs to be done.

(T/F) 8. If something is *comme ci comme ça,* it's not great, but not bad, either.

(T/F) 9. It's appropriate to say *"au contraire"* when you disagree with something.

(T/F) 10. *Je ne sais quoi* is an appropriate expression to use when you're faced with two good choices.

ANSWERS: (1), (3), (6), and (10) are false; the rest are true.

III. SENSE...OR NONSENSE?

We learned about the late fashion designer **Coco Chanel** on Day 5, but we didn't mention that Deauville was the site she chose for her first boutique, which opened in 1913.

Here Chanel revolutionized women's fashion by ditching the corseted silhouette of the **Belle Epoque** (1871-1914, the period between the Franco-Prussian War and World War I) and replacing it with a male-inspired look consisting of separates like striped shirts and yachting pants.

Alas, there's no longer a Chanel outlet in Deauville, but as we explore the luxury retail district around **Place du Casino**, home to Hermès, Ralph Lauren, and Louis Vuitton, read the following sentences and check those that make sense.

____ 1. I really like Claire's wedding dress—it has a certain *au contraire.*

____ 2. The desk was decorated with *carte blanche* executed in ivory and pewter.

____ 3. Jan's kitchen has a certain *je ne sais quoi.* It really speaks to me.

____ 4. The living room couches are upholstered in *fait accompli.*

____ 5. We thought we'd be invited to Joe's bar mitzvah, but in the end, the event was celebrated *en famille.*

____ 6. Aunt Mabel took Jeremy on a *tour de force:* she made him see Germany, Switzerland, and Luxembourg in just three days.

____ 7. When bad things happen, it's appropriate to sigh and murmur, *"C'est la vie."*

____ 8. The restaurant was highly recommended; unfortunately, its food was *comme ci, comme ça.*

____ 9. Francine suggested a neighborhood *tête-à-tête* to discuss the matter.

____10. The search for the mayor's daughter, who was kidnapped by her nanny, became a *cause célèbre.*

ANSWERS: numbers (3), (5), (7), (8), and (10) should be checked.

IV. SNOB SITUATION

Are you a golfer? I'm more of a croquet person myself, as you know, but Deauville does have some lovely links.

Let's play a few holes at **Hôtel Barrière L'Hôtel du Golf**, which has three of the most beautiful golf courses in France.

As we are thus engaged, fill the blanks in the following snob situation with snob words from this lesson.

tête-à-tête	fait accompli
tour de force	comme ci, comme ça
en famille	c'est la vie
au contraire	carte blanche
je ne sais quoi	cause célèbre

1. Three teachers at Strathmore Preparatory Academy—the drama master, the vocal master, and the orchestra master, were charged with selecting a musical for the students to perform the following year. Since the drama master had already purchased the rights to *Beauty and the Beast,* however, the other two teachers were presented with what amounted to a _____.

2. "_____," said the vocal master, who had wanted to do *Cinderella.* "I can't always get my way."

3. The orchestra master, however, who had also had his heart set on *Cinderella,* was not about to give up. "If we perform *Cinderella,* it will be a _____," he said. "If we attempt *Beauty and the Beast,* it will be a flop."

4. The headmaster suggested a _____ between the drama master and the orchestra master to discuss the problem, but the drama master refused.

5. Most theater students were unenthusiastic about the issue. They thought both options were _____.

6. Parents tried to discuss the conflict at home, but students didn't seem to wish to discuss it _____.

7. Then the orchestra master appealed to the school board, claiming that the drama master should not have been given _____ in choosing the musical.

8. "_____," replied the drama master when the board confronted him. "I am the theater expert."

9. "*Cinderella* is okay," he said, but *Beauty and the Beast* has a certain _____."

10. The issue, which became a local _____, was covered by area newspapers and television stations.

ANSWERS: (1) fait accompli; (2) c'est la vie; (3) tour de force; (4) tête-à-tête; (5) comme ci, comme ça; (6) en famille; (7) carte blanche; (8) au contraire; (9) je ne sais quoi; (10) cause célèbre

V. SHORT DEFINITIONS

Before we leave Deauville, we must visit the outdoor market in the **Place du Marché**. This charming square, surrounded by storybook houses dripping geraniums from window boxes, is where Snow White and Cinderella would come if they were to need groceries.

And they'd be impressed, because this is where Normandy's finest produce, poultry, meat, seafood, and dairy products all come together—the picky Parisian customers insist on the *crème de la crème*.

As we salivate over perfectly ripe Camembert cheeses, crisp apples and pears from nearby orchards, freshly caught scallops, and butter from nearby **Isigny-sur-Mer** (the best butter in the world, according to the French), let's do a final review of our snob phrases by matching them with their definitions.

tête-à-tête	**fait accompli**
tour de force	**comme ci, comme ça**
en famille	**c'est la vie**
au contraire	**carte blanche**
je ne sais quoi	**cause célèbre**

1. _____ a notorious incident, person, or thing that excites broad interest

2. _____ permission to do something in any way one chooses

3. _____ 'that's life'
4. _____ refers to a quality or attribute that's difficult to describe or express
5. _____ 'on the contrary'
6. _____ a face-to-face conversation between two people
7. _____ a thing done exceptionally well
8. _____ 'as a family'
9. _____ an accomplished fact; a reality
10. _____ not great, but not terrible; okay

ANSWERS: (1) cause célèbre; (2) carte blanche; (3) c'est la vie; (4) je ne sais quoi; (5) au contraire; (6) tête-à-tête; (7) tour de force; (8) en famille; (9) fait accompli; (10) comme ci, comme ça

You're making excellent progress! You've now mastered 190 of the 250 snob words in this course.

You may want to turn in early tonight. You'll need plenty of energy tomorrow because we'll be traveling to luxury retail locations all around the world.

Day 23

Platinum Cards at the Ready
EXCLUSIVE SHOPPING DISTRICTS

LOCATION: **WORLD'S PRICIEST RETAIL PROPERTIES**

We've been working hard at improving your snobcabulary now for twenty-two days. Why not take a break and engage in some retail therapy?

Today, rather than basing our lesson in one particular place, we'll travel to ten of the world's most exclusive shopping streets, as well as one exclusive shopping square. (It'll be tough, but with the Learjet, I'm confident we can do it.)

Why learn the names of exclusive shopping streets? Isn't it obvious? So we can visit them, buy snobby things, and brag about them...especially about *where* we bought them!

As we shop today, we'll learn how to drop the names of these thoroughfares—full-fledged snob terms if there ever were any—into conversation and social media posts. (High-end products from high-rent areas really get the envy flowing.)

The exclusive shopping districts that we've selected, half in Europe, half in the United States, will give you plenty to gloat about. We've already become familiar with some of their home cities during this course (New York, Paris, London, Milan, and Rome), but today's visits will focus exclusively on luxury retail.

After we've strolled each snob street, and taken a good look at the bounty, we'll check out the most exclusive hotels and restaurants in the vicinity so you can also drop *their* names—like little snob bombs—into your chosen means of communication. ("We stayed at the *Mandarin Oriental* and dined at *Seta* during our shopping spree on *Via Monte Napoleone*.")

For our U.S. hotel options, we've selected properties that currently have five diamonds (the highest rating) from the **AAA Diamond** ratings system (aaa.com). For cities outside the U.S., we've listed hotels with five stars (also the highest rating) from the **Forbes Travel Guide** (forbestravelguide.com).

For restaurants, wherever possible, we've chosen starred establishments from the **Michelin Guide** (guide.michelin.com), often considered the gold standard for restaurant reviews. Michelin's top rating is three stars, but we've also included restaurants with one and two stars. For cities not covered by Michelin, we've used other criteria noted in the text.

Hang on to your credit cards, because here we go!

I. SHOPPING DESTINATIONS

1. **Fifth Avenue/Madison Avenue**, New York City
2. **Avenue Montaigne** (moan-TAN´-yuh), Paris
3. **Bond Street**, London
4. **Via Monte Napoleone** (VEE´-uh MOAN´-tay nah-poh-lay-OH´-nay), Milan
5. **Worth Avenue**, Palm Beach, Florida
6. **Via dei Condotti** (VEE´-uh day cohn-DOH´-tee), Rome
7. **North Michigan Avenue** (Magnificent Mile), Chicago
8. **Bahnhofstrasse** (BAHN´-hoaf-stross-uh), Zurich

9. **Union Square**, San Francisco, California
10. **Rodeo Drive** (roh-DAY'-oh), Beverly Hills, California

II. DESCRIPTIONS

1. **FIFTH AVENUE/MADISON AVENUE** (New York City): Upscale retail is found throughout Manhattan, with several new malls and the SoHo district currently *en vogue.* But the most concentrated luxury shopping in the Big Apple is spread over two luxe avenues and one short street that connects them.

• **FIFTH AVENUE:** Manhattan's traditional stretch of luxury retail has been upstaged in recent decades by *Madison Avenue,* but *Fifth* is still home to a relatively short section of high-end shopping, beginning around **Rockefeller Center** (48th Street) in **Midtown,** and running north to the **Plaza Hotel** (58th Street).

As you can see, while there's a plethora of luxe loot to be found here, the street is not especially exclusive: sumptuous department stores and opulent boutiques rub shoulders with banks, souvenir shops, and mass retailers like Forever 21.

Still, *Fifth Avenue* retains some elegance, although heavy traffic, construction, and very tall buildings (which make the avenue feel like a tunnel) detract from the pedestrian experience. We're using my car and driver now, of course, but when you return, make sure you have a limo.

RITZY RETAIL: Bergdorf Goodman, Bottega Veneta, Bulgari, Cartier, Coach, Giorgio Armani, Harry Winston, Henri Bendel, Louis Vuitton, Piaget, Prada, Rolex, Saks Fifth Avenue, Tiffany, Valentino, Van Cleef & Arpels, Zegna.

MICHELIN-STARRED RESTAURANTS: Le Bernardin ★★★; The Modern ★★; Aquavit ★★.

AAA FIVE-DIAMOND HOTELS: the Ritz-Carlton Central Park; the Peninsula; Park Hyatt New York.

277

EXPERIENCES: After exploring Rockefeller Center, we'll gaze up at **Trump Tower** (East 57th Street) before checking out the original **Saks Fifth Avenue** outlet (between East 49th and East 50th streets), an eight-story emporium with a top floor dedicated entirely to women's shoes.

• **MADISON AVENUE:** as we've mentioned, the bulk of Manhattan's snobbiest retail establishments are now found on *Madison*, packed into a twenty-block stretch between East 58th and East 78th streets. Retail rents here are the highest in the Big Apple, and some of the highest in the world.

This posh section of *Madison Avenue* is located on the **Upper East Side**, two blocks east of **Central Park**, and I think you'll agree that the pedestrian experience is better here than on *Fifth*. Buildings are shorter, allowing more light to reach the street, traffic is lighter, and there's somewhat more greenery.

RITZY RETAIL: Alexander McQueen, Baccarat, Balenciaga, BCBG Max Azria, Bottega Veneta, Calvin Klein, Canali, Carolina Herrera, Cartier, Céline, Chanel, Chloé, Chopard, Christian Louboutin, David Yurman, Dior, Dolce & Gabbana, Elie Saab, Fendi, Frette, Giorgio Armani, Gucci, Hermès, Jil Sander, John Varvatos, Ladurée, Lalique, Lanvin, Max Mara, Michael Kors, Montblanc, Oscar de la Renta, Pucci, Ralph Lauren, Sonia Rykiel, Stella McCartney, Tod's, Tory Burch, Vacheron Constantin, Vera Wang.

MICHELIN-STARRED RESTAURANTS: Daniel★★; Caviar Russe★.

AAA FIVE-DIAMOND HOTELS: the Pierre; Four Seasons New York.

EXPERIENCE: We'll pause to examine the elaborate French Renaissance Revival architecture of the **Gertrude Rhinelander Waldo Mansion** (at East 72nd Street), which dates to 1898. It now houses the Ralph Lauren men's flagship store.

• The section of **EAST 57TH STREET** of interest to luxury shoppers like us is only one block long, the piece that runs between *Fifth* and *Madison* avenues. Curiously, this segment of *East 57th* unites the northernmost block of luxury shopping on *Fifth Avenue* with the southernmost block of luxe retail on *Madison* (*Fifth* and *Madison* run parallel).

This allows one to traverse thirty-one continuous blocks of Manhattan luxury shopping without any interruption. And you thought the American Dream was dead!

RITZY RETAIL: In addition to Louis Vuitton and Tiffany, which are at the corners of *East 57th Street* and *Fifth Avenue*, this short stretch is home to Burberry, Chanel, Dior, Fendi, Miu Miu, and Saint Laurent.

NOTE: two of Manhattan's most famous upscale retailers are not on *Fifth* or *Madison*. **Macy's**, which bills itself as the world's largest department store, is at Broadway and Herald Square; the classier **Bloomingdale's** is at 59th Street and Lexington.

2. AVENUE MONTAIGNE (Paris): As you'll remember, we took a brief stroll here on Day 3, but today we'll take an in-depth look at this awesome avenue.

Forming one side of the Parisian luxury district known as the **Golden Triangle** (*Triangle d'Or*), *l'avenue Montaigne* (the way the French write it), is currently the most exclusive shopping street in the City of Light. It's also one of the most, if not *the* most, beautiful and intriguing stretches of luxury retail in the world.

Dating to the mid-19th century, *Avenue Montaigne* was originally residential, but now, as you can see, its stately townhouses and apartment buildings host top fashion labels and other pricey retailers on their ground floors.

Everything about the street is tasteful and understated: signs are so small as to be almost non-existent; clipped box hedges hide behind low, wrought-iron fences; and neat rows of linden trees add greenery and elegance.

Avenue Montaigne isn't short—it's about a kilometer in length. Even so, not every luxury retailer in the world can be accommodated here, so additional stores spill out onto surrounding streets.

RITZY RETAIL:

Avenue Montaigne: Bottega Veneta, Céline, Chanel, Chloé, Diane von Furstenberg, Dior, Dolce & Gabbana, Elie Saab, Emanuel Ungaro, Escada, Fendi, Ferragamo, Giorgio Armani, Giuseppe Zanotti, Givenchy, Gucci, Harry Winston, Jil Sander, Loro Piana, Louis Vuitton, Max Mara, Nina Ricci, Paul & Joe, Prada, Pucci, Ralph Lauren, Saint Laurent, Valentino, Versace, Vionnet.

Nearby: Alaïa, Boss, Brunello Cucinelli, Cartier, Massimo Dutti, Montblanc, Omega, Paco Rabanne, Swarovski, Tiffany, Zadig & Voltaire.

MICHELIN-STARRED RESTAURANTS: Alléno Paris au Pavillon Ledoyen ★★★; Le Cinq ★★★; Alain Ducasse au Plaza Athénée ★★★.

FORBES FIVE-STAR HOTELS: Four Seasons George V Paris; La Réserve Paris; Hotel Plaza Athénée Paris.

EXPERIENCE: Let's take a break for brunch on the terrace of **L'Avenue,** the restaurant at the corner of *Avenue Montaigne* and Rue François 1er.

We'll watch for celebs as we dine on *foie gras, escargots,* and heart of smoked salmon served with **blini** (thin buckwheat pancakes of Russian origin) and *crème fraîche.*

3. **BOND STREET** (London): Consisting of *Old Bond* and *New Bond* streets, this thoroughfare, which runs through the posh **Mayfair** district (which we visited on Day 15), has been known as a luxury shopping destination since it was laid out in the 1720s. *Old Bond Street* begins at **Piccadilly** in the south and runs north to the intersection of **Burlington Gardens.** There it becomes *New Bond Street*, which continues northwest to **Oxford Street.**

Both *Old* and *New Bond* streets are narrow—for the most part, single lanes—and flanked by historic Georgian architecture strictly protected by the city. Understated signage and window displays, along with a few topiaries for good measure, create a luxurious, yet restrained, ambience.

New Bond Street is by far the longest segment of the thoroughfare, and is considered the more prestigious.

RITZY RETAIL:

New Bond: Anne Fontaine, Bally, Boss, Bulgari, Burberry, Canali, Cartier, Chanel, Chloé, Corneliani, Dior, Emporio Armani, Fendi, Harry Winston, Hermès, Jimmy Choo, Longchamp, Loro Piana, Louis Vuitton, Mephisto, Miu Miu, Montblanc, Pal Zileri, Philipp Plein, Piaget, Ralph Lauren, Tory Burch, Van Cleef & Arpels, Victorinox, Zegna.

Old Bond: Alexander McQueen, Bottega Veneta, Cartier, De Beers, DKNY, Dolce & Gabbana, Ferragamo, Gucci, Max Mara, Moncler, Omega, Prada, Rolex, Saint Laurent, Tiffany, Tod's, Valentino.

Nearby: Luxury retailers in the blocks surrounding *Bond Street* include Alexander Wang, Christian Louboutin, Fabergé, Michael Kors, Moschino, Patek Philippe, and Vivienne Westwood.

MICHELIN-STARRED RESTAURANTS: Alain Ducasse at the Dorchester ★★★; Umu ★★.

FORBES FIVE-STAR HOTELS: the Connaught; Claridge's; the Dorchester; the Berkeley.

EXPERIENCES: Tired of window shopping? Let's walk over to **Berkeley Square**, a grassy, tree-filled oval surrounded by fine Georgian houses and pricey auto showrooms (Bentley and Rolls-Royce). Here we'll relax on a bench in the shade and feed the pigeons.

Then we'll resume our retail quest and take a quick walk to the flagship stores of two British luxury chains: **Fortnum & Mason**, founded in 1707, and **Selfridges**, founded in 1909.

4. **VIA MONTE NAPOLEONE** (Milan): This narrow street, which we visited in our fashion chapter, is sometimes referred to as *Via Montenapoleone*, although the street signs spell *Monte Napoleone* as two words.

At any rate, as you'll remember, the *via,* which cuts through the middle of Milan's fashion district, known as the **Quadrilatero della Moda***,* is lined with neoclassical mansions built for early 19th-century aristocrats.

These mansions—constructed of stone, brick, and stucco—are severe, as you can see, with nothing but a bit of greenery hanging from their balconies to soften their predominantly white and gray façades.

RITZY RETAIL: Bally, Boss, Bottega Veneta, Brioni, Bulgari, Cartier, Céline, Dolce & Gabbana, Falconeri, Fendi, Ferragamo, Giorgio Armani, Giuseppe Zanotti, Gucci, Hermès, Loro Piana, Louis Vuitton, Moncler, Montblanc, Omega, Prada, Pucci, Roberto Cavalli, Rolex, Valentino, Van Cleef & Arpels, Versace, Zegna.

NOTE: Neighboring streets, some cobbled and even narrower than *Via Monte Napoleone*, are also home to luxury retailers such as Alexander McQueen, Canali, Chanel, Givenchy, Issy Miyake, Jimmy Choo, Kenzo, Miu Miu, Moschino, Pal Zileri, Tiffany, Tod's, and Tom Ford.

MICHELIN-STARRED RESTAURANT: Seta ★★.

FORBES FIVE-STAR HOTEL: Mandarin Oriental Milan.

EXPERIENCE: Ready for lunch? Let's do it at **Emporio Armani Caffè***.* Think sleek lines, stainless steel, red accents. We'll follow the fashion crowd and share an *insalata di Cesare* made with iceberg lettuce. (It's okay—iceberg's cool here.) Then we'll splurge on the hazelnut-banana-passion fruit ice cream.

5. **WORTH AVENUE** (Palm Beach, Florida): This lovely and tidy stretch of retail nirvana runs the full width, from east to west, of the barrier island that's home to the patrician enclave of Palm Beach.

The two-lane, one-way avenue is open to motor vehicles (mainly Range Rovers, Mercedes, and BMWs), with plenty of parallel parking on each side, but because of its wide sidewalks, palm trees, and lush subtropical landscaping, the street is also a delight for pedestrians. Many of the street's sidewalks run under arcades, so it if rains (and it will), we're literally covered.

You like the architecture? I'd describe it as Mediterranean fusion, a mixture of Spanish and Italian elements featuring red-tile roofs, arches, columns, balconies, and pergolas.

In contrast to some of our other luxury shopping streets, *Worth Avenue* has nearly as many unique and lesser-known boutiques (albeit still very pricey) as it does world-famous luxury outlets. (We've listed only well known retailers below.)

The street gets increasingly snooty the closer it gets to the Atlantic, ending with **Saks Fifth Avenue** and **Neiman Marcus** (facing each other) before terminating in white sand and turquoise water.

RITZY RETAIL: Bottega Veneta, Brioni, Brooks Brothers, Cartier, Chanel, Christofle, Ferragamo, Gucci, Hermès, Hervé Léger, Jimmy Choo, Louis Vuitton, Max Mara, Michael Kors, Omega, Pucci, Ralph Lauren, St. John, Tiffany, Valentino, Van Cleef & Arpels.

RESTAURANTS: Michelin doesn't rate Florida restaurants, but try **Café Boulud**, which has four stars out of five from Forbes Travel Guide, and **Buccan**, which has four and a half stars out of five from OpenTable (opentable.com).

AAA FIVE-DIAMOND HOTELS: Four Seasons Resort Palm Beach; The Breakers.

EXPERIENCE: Let's check out the pedestrian walkways, called *vias,* that lead behind the *Worth Avenue* façades. These take us to additional boutiques and galleries surrounding lush, tropical courtyards. **Via Mario**, between Ralph Lauren and Maus & Hoffman, is especially beautiful.

6. **VIA DEI CONDOTTI** (Rome): I told you we'd come back to Rome. We threw coins in the fountain, remember? This time, however, we're concentrating on a single street, *Via dei Condotti,* by far the most gritty of the world's exclusive shopping strips. The cracked and peeling façades here (in shades of ocher, red,

and orange)—as well as the narrow street itself—look as if they could use a good power wash.

But that's just Rome.

On a positive note, this is a short and compact street, with lots of luxury shopping packed into a brief and vibrant walk.

We'll begin here at **Largo Carlo Gondoni**, the small square that's home to the Fendi outlet. Then we'll take *Via dei Condotti* northeast all the way to **Piazza di Spagna**, home to the **Spanish Steps** (which we first glimpsed during our fashion lesson).

RITZY RETAIL: Alberta Ferreti, Brioni, Bulgari, Burberry, Cartier, Céline, Damiani, Dior, Ferragamo, Giorgio Armani, Harry Winston, Hermès, Louis Vuitton, Max Mara, Michael Kors, Missoni, Montblanc, Omega, Prada, Swarovski, Tiffany, Tod's, Van Cleef & Arpels, Zegna.

MICHELIN-STARRED RESTAURANT: Il Convivio-Troiani★.

FORBES FIVE-STAR HOTELS: Hotel Eden; Hassler Roma; J.K. Place Roma.

EXPERIENCE: I told you back on Day 16 that we'd eventually climb the Spanish Steps. The time is now.

There are exactly 135 of these travertine beauties, which lead to a terrace in front of **Trinità dei Monti** (c. 1585), an impressive late Renaissance church.

A tiring hike, but look at the view!

7. **NORTH MICHIGAN AVENUE** (Chicago): also known as the **Magnificent Mile**, **Mag Mile**, or simply *Michigan Avenue*, the luxe shopping on the Midwest's snobbiest piece of pavement is indeed concentrated on the north end of this long thoroughfare, namely on the thirteen blocks that run between the Chicago River and East Oak Street.

Think of the Windy City's premier shopping street as a wider, sunnier, and cleaner version of New York's *Fifth Avenue*. Three lanes of traffic in each direction, landscaped medians, and very wide sidewalks furnished with trees and flower beds make for an exceptionally pleasant pedestrian experience.

While *North Michigan Avenue* does have some very tall buildings, as you can see, these alternate with shorter buildings, so they don't block light or air circulation.

In addition to the luxury stores located on *North Michigan Avenue* itself, we'll explore three posh indoor malls on the Mag Mile: **The Shops at North Bridge** (anchored by Nordstrom); **900 North Michigan Shops** (Bloomingdale's); and **Water Tower Place** (Macy's).

Some of the retail outlets we list below are found within these malls.

Finally, the one block of **East Oak Street** between *North Michigan Avenue* and North Rush Street is home to an especially concentrated collection of upscale retail, most of it housed in historic row houses.

Flower baskets hanging from antique-style lamps make this narrow thoroughfare a delightful place to plunk down cash.

RITZY RETAIL:

North Michigan Avenue: Ann Taylor, Boss, Brooks Brothers, Bulgari, Cartier, Chanel, Coach, David Yurman, Fendi, Ferragamo, Gucci, Harley-Davidson (yes, you can pick up a new two-wheeled ride here on the Mag Mile), Henri Bendel, Louis Vuitton, Max Mara, Michael Kors, Montblanc, Neiman-Marcus, Ralph Lauren, Rolex, Swarovski, Tiffany, Tumi, Van Cleef & Arpels, Vera Bradley, Zegna.

East Oak Street: Armani, Carolina Herrera, Christian Louboutin, Christofle, Dolce & Gabbana, Escada, Harry Winston, Hermès, Ike Behar, Jil Sander, Jimmy Choo, Loro Piana, Moncler, Prada, St. John, Tom Ford.

MICHELIN-STARRED RESTAURANTS: Oriole ★★; Topolobampo ★; Spiaggia ★.

AAA FIVE-DIAMOND HOTELS: Trump International Hotel & Tower; the Peninsula Chicago.

EXPERIENCES: As we traverse the Mag Mile, we'll stop to check out the **Old Water Tower,** shaped like a castle, in **Byrne Plaza**. Later, we'll head to **360 Chicago**, the 94th-floor observation deck of the **John Hancock Center,** for amazing views of the Windy City and Lake Michigan.

8. **BAHNHOFSTRASSE** (Zurich): Switzerland is a small country, and Zurich is a relatively small city, but that doesn't stop it from having some of the highest retail rents on the planet.

These are found on the *Bahnhofstrasse*, the major north-south artery of the **Altstadt** (Zurich's historic old town) and one of the world's most prestigious shopping thoroughfares.

As you see, most of the *Bahnhofstrasse* can only be accessed by foot or by an electric tram system. I think you'll agree that this lack of cars, along with these trees and benches, results in one of the most strollable of all our exclusive retail districts.

The *Bahnhofstrasse,* which is about a mile long, runs from the **Bahnhofplatz**, or central railroad station, to **Lake Zurich**. Along the way we'll find a mixture of historic and modern architecture, as well as a blend of businesses, with banks and mass-market retailers like H&M sharing the avenue with more exclusive tenants.

As with some of our other luxury streets, the pricey shopping here overflows the principal avenue. Some of the retailers listed below are on side streets.

RITZY RETAIL: Bally, Bottega Veneta, Breguet, Brunello Cucinelli, Burberry, Chanel, Chopard, Dior, Dolce & Gabbana, Ferragamo, Giorgio Armani, Gucci, Hermès, Issey Miyake, Jimmy Choo, Longchamp, Loro Piana, Louis Vuitton, Massimo Dutti, Michael Kors, Montblanc, Omega, Piaget, Prada, Swarovski, Tiffany, Tod's, Van Cleef & Arpels, Victorinox, Zegna.

MICHELIN-STARRED RESTAURANT: Pavillon ★★.

FORBES FOUR-STAR HOTELS: (oddly, Zurich has no Forbes five-star hotels) Park Hyatt Zurich; Baur au Lac; Widder Hotel.

EXPERIENCE: Ready for a snack? Let's head to **Paradeplatz** for afternoon pastries at **Confiserie Sprüngli**, a favorite of Zurich's upper class since 1859. The hot chocolate is divine... don't you agree? And wait till you try the pralines and truffles!

9. **UNION SQUARE** (San Francisco, California): With its spectacular setting, major food scene, and well-preserved Victorian architecture, the city where millions have left their hearts doesn't need luxury shopping to make it appealing.

But luxury shopping it does have, most of which is concentrated around *Union Square*, the posh retail area directly southwest of **Chinatown** and the **Financial District**.

This attractively landscaped rectangle (as you'll notice, despite its name, *Union Square* is *not* square) and its charming side streets are home to dozens of luxury retailers. The square is also home to the historic **Westin St. Francis Hotel**, an ornate Beaux-Arts structure dating to 1913.

RITZY RETAIL: Alexander McQueen, BCBG Max Azria, Bloomingdale's, Bottega Veneta, Brooks Brothers, Brunello Cucinelli, Bulgari, Burberry, Carolina Herrera, Cartier, Chanel, Christian Louboutin, Coach, Dior, Emporio Armani, Ferragamo, Giorgio Armani, Gucci, Hermés, Jimmy Choo, John Varvatos, Loro Piana, Louis Vuitton, Macy's, Neiman-Marcus, Nordstrom, Prada, Rolex, Saint Laurent, Saks Fifth Avenue, Swarovski, Tiffany, Tory Burch, Tumi, Valentino, Vera Wang.

MICHELIN-STARRED RESTAURANTS: Benu ★★★; Saison ★★.

AAA FIVE-DIAMOND HOTEL: the Ritz-Carlton San Francisco.

EXPERIENCE: We just had pastries, but how about gelato? I know we're used to the real Italian variety by now, but **Emporio Rulli Caffè**, located rght here inside the square itself, measures up. I suggest the *cioccolato all'arancia* (chocolate orange) or the *frutti di bosco* ('fruits of the forest'). Or why not both?

10. **RODEO DRIVE** (Beverly Hills, California): The mother of all snobby shopping streets is appropriately set in the mother of all snobby cities: Beverly Hills.

While not officially part of Los Angeles, the area within the 90210 zip code is completely surrounded by the City of Angels, and actually functions as an exclusive *arrondissement* of La La Land.

The part of *Rodeo Drive* of interest to luxury shoppers runs between **Santa Monica** and **Wilshire** boulevards. All the international luxury brands are here, and that's *all* that's here—no banks or souvenir shops compete with the luxe boutiques. In fact, *Rodeo Drive* has more luxury shopping, in a more compact area, than any other street on our list.

That said, *Rodeo* does *not* take first place when it comes to pleasant meandering. Rows of palms do little to soften the predominantly modern architecture, consisting for the most part of stark boxes of glass and stone. The message: you're here to plunk down serious cash, not to enjoy yourself.

The street does, however, get points for the convenient parking terraces located at its intersection with Santa Monica Boulevard.

Whatever you do, don't refer to this street as *ROH'-dee-oh* Drive. There are no horses, cows, or cowboys here. It's *roh-DAY'-oh*.

RITZY RETAIL: (take a deep breath) Balenciaga, Bally, Barbara Bui, BCBG Max Azria, Boss, Bottega Veneta, Breguet, Brooks Brothers, Brunello Cucinelli, Bulgari, Burberry, Cartier, Chanel, Coach, David Yurman, Dior, Dolce & Gabbana, Emporio Armani, Fendi, Giorgio Armani, Gucci, Harry Winston, Hermès, Hervé Léger, IWC Schaffhausen, Jimmy Choo, Lalique, Lanvin, Louis Vuitton, Malo, Michael Kors, Miu Miu, Patek Philippe, Philipp Plein, Piaget, Prada, Ralph Lauren, Rimowa, Roberto Cavalli, Rolex, Saint Laurent, Stefano Ricci, Tod's, Tumi, Vacheron Constantin, Valentino, Van Cleef & Arpels, Vera Wang, Versace, Zadig & Voltaire, Zegna.

RESTAURANTS: Michelin doesn't rank restaurants in the Los Angeles area, but Zagat (zagat.com), another reliable guide, gives high marks to **Maude**, as well as to Wolfgang Puck's **Spago**.

AAA FIVE-DIAMOND HOTELS: the Beverly Hills Hotel & Bungalows; the Peninsula Beverly Hills.

EXPERIENCE: Let's end our shopping day with smoked-salmon pizza on the terrace of **The Blvd** restaurant, located on the ground floor of the **Beverly Wilshire Hotel**. This is luxury people-watching at its finest.

III. MATCHING

Wow! How was that for a whirlwind luxury shopping tour? I hope you paid attention. Now test yourself by matching each snobby shopping street with its city.

____ 1. Madison Avenue	a. Beverly Hills
____ 2. Bahnhofstrasse	b. New York
____ 3. Fifth Avenue	c. San Francisco
____ 4. Via Monte Napoleone	d. Rome
____ 5. Rodeo Drive	e. Zurich
____ 6. Union Square	f. Palm Beach
____ 7. Via dei Condotti	g. London
____ 8. Bond Street	h. Paris
____ 9. Avenue Montaigne	i. Milan
____ 10. North Michigan Avenue	j. Chicago
____ 11. Worth Avenue	

ANSWERS: (1) b; (2) e; (3) b; (4) i; (5) a (6) c; (7) d; (8) g; (9) h; (10) j; (11) f

IV. FILL IN THE BLANKS

Feeling confident now about where our ritzy retail is located? Fill each blank below with the name of the snob street that matches the given definition.

Madison Avenue	**Fifth Avenue**
Rodeo Drive	**Worth Avenue**
Union Square	**Avenue Montaigne**
Bahnhofstrasse	**North Michigan Avenue**
Via Monte Napoleone	**Via dei Condotti**
Bond Street	

1. _____ gritty street near Spanish Steps
2. _____ forms part of the Golden Triangle
3. _____ mainly pedestrian
4. _____ divided into old and new sections
5. _____ snob 'area' rather than snob street
6. _____ home to the bulk of Manhattan's snob shopping
7. _____ kinder, gentler version of New York's *Fifth Avenue*
8. _____ prime luxe shopping street on the U.S. West Coast
9. _____ located in the Quadrilatero della Moda
10. _____ luxury shopping begins at Rockefeller Center, ends at Plaza Hotel
11. _____ subtropical luxury street lined with Mediterranean-style architecture

ANSWERS: (1) Via dei Condotti; (2) Avenue Montaigne; (3) Bahnhofstrasse; (4) Bond Street; (5) Union Square; (6) Madison Avenue; (7) North Michigan Avenue; (8) Rodeo Drive; (9) Via Monte Napoleone; (10) Fifth Avenue; (11) Worth Avenue

V. TRUE OR FALSE

(T/F) 1. The section of *Madison Avenue* that offers luxury shopping is on Manhattan's Upper East Side.

(T/F) 2. *Bond Street* runs through the London district of Maytag.

(T/F) 3. Rome's *Via dei Condotti* looks freshly scrubbed.

(T/F) 4. You can easily drive to any uppity retail venue on the *Bahnhofstrasse*.

(T/F) 5. San Francisco's premier shopping area believes it's hip to be square.

(T/F) 6. *Rodeo Drive* has more luxury shopping outlets than any other luxury street featured in this lesson.

(T/F) 7. *Avenue Montaigne* is one of the loveliest and leafiest luxury shopping streets on the planet.

(T/F)   8. Milan's *Via dei Condotti* cuts through the city's Quadrilatero della Moda.

(T/F)   9. *Fifth Avenue,* while famous, does **not** provide the best pedestrian experience.

(T/F)   10. *Worth Avenue,* in Palm Beach, is often referred to as the Magnificent Mile.

ANSWERS: all true except (2), (3), (4), (8), and (10).

VI. WHERE IN THE RETAIL SNOB WORLD ARE YOU?

Fill the blanks below with snobby shopping streets and cities from the lists below.

Cities may be used more than once.

Madison Avenue	**San Francisco**
Fifth Avenue	**Rome**
Rodeo Drive	**New York City**
Union Square	**Zurich**
Bahnhofstrasse	**Chicago**
Via Monte Napoleone	**Paris**
Via dei Condotti	**Milan**
Bond Street	**London**
Avenue Montaigne	**Palm Beach**
North Michigan Avenue	**Beverly Hills**
Worth Avenue	

1. You take a public tram to get to this luxe thoroughfare, which is closed to automobiles. You are on the _____ in _____.

2. You watch as a famous actress hurriedly selects a pair of Jimmy Choos. Is she off to a red-carpet event? Then you step outside and lean against a palm tree as you take in the sunshine. You are on _____ in _____.

3. You stop to admire the architecture of the Ralph Lauren Manhattan men's flagship store, which is housed in a 19th-century mansion. You're on _____ in _____.

4. After a morning of shopping in Saks Fifth Avenue, you cross the street—taking in the salty sea breeze—and enter Neiman-Marcus. You're on _____ in _____.

5. The façades may be dilapidated, but the prices are not. After an afternoon of shopping on _____, in _____, you relax on the Spanish Steps.

6. After browsing the shops on the old section of this street, you move to the new section. You're on _____ in _____.

7. You're tired of high-end Christmas shopping, so you take a break to ice skate at Rockefeller Center. You're on _____ in _____.

8. The ghosts of 19th-century Italian aristocrats haunt this street, actually more of an alley. Careful—don't get hit by that Vespa! You're on _____ in _____.

9. This leafy street in the Golden Triangle is lined with elegant townhomes and apartment buildings that house boutiques of top designers on their ground floors. You're on _____ in _____.

10. Today you've been to Bloomingdale's, Nordstrom, and Macy's, each located in a separate mall on the same wide, landscaped boulevard. You're on _____ in _____.

11. You're in the middle of a palm-filled plaza, and by turning 360 degrees, you can see Macy's, Saks, Neiman-Marcus, Tiffany, and the historic Westin St. Francis Hotel. You're in _____ in _____.

ANSWERS: (1) Bahnhofstrasse/Zurich; (2) Rodeo Drive/Beverly Hills; (3) Madison Avenue/New York City; (4) Worth Avenue/Palm Beach; (5) Via dei Condotti/Rome; (6) Bond Street/London; (7) Fifth Avenue/New York City; (8) Via Monte Napoleone/Milan; (9) Avenue Montaigne/Paris; (10) North Michigan Avenue/Chicago; (11) Union Square/San Francisco

Exhausted from the walking?

From the sheer decadence of it all?

We hope you've enjoyed this frenetic foray into luxury retail. But remember, shops, hotels, and restaurants don't remain static. While the information in this lesson was accurate at the time of our visits, things may change by the time you stroll these elegant avenues again.

At any rate, get some shut-eye, because tomorrow we travel to a famous German spa town to learn snob words from miscellaneous languages.

Day 24

All Greek to Me
WORDS FROM VARIOUS LANGUAGES

LOCATION: **BADEN-BADEN, GERMANY**

Welcome to **Baden-Baden** (whose name means 'baths-baths' in archaic German), touted as Germany's smallest global town.

Nearly two millennia ago, the Romans discovered multiple hot springs here and built a bathing complex. But it wasn't until the 1850s that the city—perched at the northwest edge of the **Black Forest**—gained international fame and became the most fashionable spa in Europe.

It still holds that title, along with the distinction of being one of the most cosmopolitan cities in the world. That's why it's the perfect place for us to present today's lesson on snob words from German, Russian, Greek, and Spanish.

I know what you're thinking. We've had four lessons devoted to French snob words. Two devoted to Latin. One to Italian. Now we're going to cover snob words from four other languages in just one lesson?

Yes, that's correct. While today's featured languages certainly have worldwide importance, when it comes to creating uppity terminology that's been adopted by English, their native speakers just haven't done as much as the French, the ancient Romans, or the Italians. They have, however, given us a number of classic snob words, all of which will be embedded in your snobcabulary after today's lesson.

We'll begin our discussion here at my house (who am I kidding—it's a mansion, though the locals call it a *villa*) off **Lichtentaler Allee**, a strolling and cycling path that follows the **Oos River** through a magnificent park. The villa, built in the early 1800s for a French countess, has twenty-five rooms, all of which have fantastic views of the city and the surrounding countryside.

Let's unwind a few minutes with some bratwurst and sauerkraut as we take a look at today's first five words.

I. PRONOUNCE & DEFINE

1. **hoi polloi** (HOY'-puh-LOY')
2. **kudos** (KOO'-doze)
3. **intelligentsia** (in-tel'-uh-JENT'-see-uh)
4. **dacha** (DOTCH'-uh)
5. **mano a mano** (MAH'-no ah MAH'-no)

1. HOI POLLOI: ('the many' in Greek) used in English to denote the general populace or (gasp!) the masses, often in a pejorative sense (the rabble).

Since *hoi* is Greek for 'the,' it's redundant to write or say *the hoi polloi*. Don't do either of those things unless you want to look and sound like an uneducated member of *hoi polloi*.

2. KUDOS: this term's meaning is simple—glory, praise, or renown, generally in conjunction with a particular achievement or event.

- She gave me *kudos* for winning the wrestling match.

But be careful how you use the term. The difficulty comes from the word's Greek roots. *Kudos* is an English borrowing based on the singular noun *kydos*, meaning 'glory.'

Because *kudos* ends in *s*, some people assume it's plural, leading them to use an inexistent singular form: "She gave me a *kudo* for winning the wrestling match."

There's no such thing as a *kudo*.

It's always *kudos*.

3. **INTELLIGENTSIA**: (from the Russian *intelligentsiya*) well-educated thinkers, or intellectuals, who guide, or attempt to guide, the political, artistic, or social development of their society.

- President Barack Obama was the darling of the *intelligentsia.*

4. **DACHA**: originally 'land grant' in Russian, the term now means a Russian country house, especially one used during the summer. *Dachas* range in size from cottages to mansions.

5. **MANO A MANO**: (Spanish for 'hand to hand') direct competition or conflict, especially between two people.

While the term can refer to actual physical fights, it is often used in a figurative sense.

For example, Texas Senator Ted Cruz challenged Donald Trump (they were both presidential candidates at the time) to a *mano a mano* debate in 2016.

II. POP QUIZ!

As you ponder these definitions, let's take a short walk along Lichtentaler Allee to the **Frieder Burda Museum**, a striking glass and aluminum structure designed by American architect **Richard Meier** (b. 1934).

As we examine the **Abstract Expressionist** art inside, including works by Americans **Mark Rothko** (1903-70) and **Jackson Pollock** (1912-56), let's test you on our new words.

Fill each blank with one of the first five snob words from this lesson. Each word is used only once.

hoi polloi	**kudos**
dacha	**mano a mano**
intelligentsia	

1. The _____ seemed to be out of touch with everyone else in the country, especially the working-class people.
2. I just finished a novel in which a nasty Russian oligarch imprisons his wife in their _____ for five years.
3. The two candidates for the Kansas Senate seat really went _____ during the campaign.
4. Greta says I'm the best president the foundation has ever had, but I don't need her _____. Knowing the orphans are safe and well cared for is the only reward I need.
5. _____ go to movies. Serious students of cinema screen *films*.

ANSWERS: (1) intelligentsia; (2) dacha; (3) mano a mano; (4) kudos; (5) hoi polloi

III. PRONOUNCE & DEFINE

Let's continue down Lichtentaler Allee to the **Kurhaus**. This grand neoclassical structure was built in the 1820s to host receptions and other galas where aristocrats could see and be seen.

The complex houses a restaurant, boutiques, and the city's casino, believed to be the inspiration for *The Gambler*, the 1866 novel by **Fyodor Dostoyevsky** (1821-81).

The Kurhaus is surrounded by the **Kurgarten**, formally landscaped grounds that include an outdoor stage where the **Baden-Baden Philharmonic** performs. Listen, they're tuning up now!

Let's enjoy a concert as we meet today's second set of snob words. (Don't let the long German compounds frighten you. They don't bite!)

 6. **peccadillo** (peck-uh-DILL´-oh)
 7. **Schadenfreude** (SHAH´-dun-fwoy-duh)
 8. **Wunderkind** (VOON´-der-kint)
 9. **Weltschmerz** (VELT´-shmay´-ahts)
 10. **Gesamtkunstwerk** (guh-ZAHMT´-koonst-vay´-ahk)

6. PECCADILLO: misspelling of the Spanish *pecadillo*, meaning 'little sin.' Used in English to denote a slight offense.

NOTE: our final four snob words are capitalized in their native German. When used in English, however, they may be capitalized or left lower case, according to the user's preference. We say capitalize them—it's more snobby.

7. SCHADENFREUDE: a combination of the German words *schaden* (damage) and *freude* (joy), happiness obtained from the troubles and suffering of others.

If your mother-in-law falls in a manhole and has to be in a body cast for six months—and you're secretly elated—you're engaging in *Schadenfreude*.

8. WUNDERKIND: from the German *wunder* ('wonder') and *kind* ('child'), a prodigy, or person who succeeds in a difficult field at an early age.

PLURAL: *Wunderkinder* (VOON´-der-kin´-der)

9. WELTSCHMERZ: literally 'world pain' or 'world sorrow,' a fusion of *welt* ('world') and *schmerz* ('pain'). A state of sadness,

generally brought on by comparing the actual state of the world with an ideal state.

10. **GESAMTKUNSTWERK**: another German compound noun (they love inventing these things!) made up of *gesamt* ('whole'), *kunst* ('art'), and *werk* ('work'). A *Gesamtkunstwerk* is a complete or unified work of art produced through a synthesis of various art forms, such as music, drama, and set design.

The term is associated with composer **Richard Wagner** (1813-83), who used it in a long essay entitled *The Artwork of the Future* (1849). In the piece, Wagner employs *Gesamtkunstwerk* to refer to a type of opera (typified by his later works) in which poetry, drama, music, dance, and the visual arts are combined to form one completely unified performance.

Today, *Gesamtkunstwerk* is used to describe any work that fuses multiple art forms. Baroque palaces, for example, can be considered *Gesamtkunstwerks* (guh-ZAHMT'-koonst-vay'-ahks) because they combine architecture, sculpture, painting, and landscape design.

IV. POP QUIZ 2

Before we leave the Kurgarten, let's wander over to Baden-Baden's elaborate 19th-century pump room, the **Trinkhalle**. Here, behind a façade adorned with Corinthian columns and murals of the Black Forest, we'll get our first taste of the famous Baden-Baden spring water.

Not exactly your cup of tea?

Then let's head across the river to **Café König**, home to excellent cocoa and the best pastries between Paris and Vienna.

We'll sit on the terrace overlooking **Lichtentalerstrasse,** one of the city's best addresses, and sample the sumptuous **Linzer torte**, a crumbly hazelnut pastry topped with raspberry-currant jam. Meanwhile, I'll give you a second quiz to evaluate your progress on today's lesson.

Fill each blank with one of the snob words listed below. Each word is used only once.

Wunderkind	**Gesamtkunstwerk**
Weltschmerz	**Schadenfreude**
peccadillo	

1. When I heard that James Fox had been convicted of laundering money (he fired me from the bank, remember), I was filled with _____.
2. Ellen is overcome with _____. She just can't get over the pointless bombings in Syria.
3. I'm so jealous of Greta Davis, the _____ who joined the gymnastics team a month ago. She's five years younger than the rest of us, but she dominates every event.
4. For the opening ceremonies of the junior games, I plan to propose a _____, a fusion of music, dance, and drama that will blow the spectators away.
5. Yes, Janice used foundation money to buy caviar for her personal use, but I don't see that as a crime. It's more of a _____.

ANSWERS: (1) Schadenfreude; (2) Weltschmerz; (3) Wunderkind; (4) Gesamtkunstwerk; (5) peccadillo

V. TRUE OR FALSE

We've seen some greenery, checked out a museum, visited historic buildings, listened to music, and tried the pastries. Maybe some shopping is in order.

Baden-Baden's most fashionable retail street is **Sophienstrasse**, where we'll find luxury firms like Hermès, Escada, and MaxMara set in ornate 18th- and 19th-century buildings.

As we take in the extravagant window displays, let's play a true-or-false game.

(T/F) 1. *Schadenfreude* is the act of taking pleasure in someone else's pain.

(T/F) 2. Members of the *intelligentsia* are well educated people who often exert political influence.

(T/F) 3. A man who suddenly becomes a billionaire in his nineties could be called a *Wunderkind.*

(T/F) 4. A traditional production of *Romeo and Juliet* would be considered a *Gesamtkunstwerk.*

(T/F) 5. It's redundant to say "the *hoi polloi.*"

(T/F) 6. The term *dacha* originated in Greece.

(T/F) 7. *Weltschmerz* is a feeling of sorrow for things that are wrong with the world.

(T/F) 8. To go *mano a mano* means to take someone's hand in friendship.

(T/F) 9. You should give a person one *kudo* if he or she has done one good thing.

(T/F) 10. A *peccadillo* is a large sin or major mistake.

ANSWERS: all false except (1), (2), (5), and (7).

VI. PARTY TALK

We can't leave Baden-Baden without taking in a performance at the city's elegant **Festspielhaus**.

This complex consists of a modern auditorium attached to the back of the city's grand 19th-century railway station, which serves as the facility's entrance.

Tonight's presentation is ***Orpheus in the Underworld*** (1858), an **operetta** (similar to light opera, but with spoken dialogue and dance numbers), by **Jacques Offenbach** (1819-80). It will be followed by a VIP reception. (Of course we're invited!)

But if you're like me, you often find yourself at a loss for clever things to say at these formal social functions.

Never fear: there's nothing like a foreign term (especially a compound German noun) to spice up the conversation.

Fill the blanks below with the appropriate snob words from this lesson. Each word is used once.

hoi polloi	kudos
Wunderkind	Gesamtkunstwerk
intelligentsia	Weltschmerz
mano a mano	peccadillo
Schadenfreude	dacha

1. I just finished my latest _____, a rock-opera ballet with poetry readings and video clips.
2. It looks like I'll be going _____ with my ex-best friend over the rights to our future hit song.
3. We'll fly into Moscow and then drive two hours to my in-laws' _____.
4. Yes, my son Andres is a _____. He graduated from high school at twelve, and now—at sixteen—he's working on his doctorate in biochemistry.
5. To me, taking one's sister's inheritance and then accusing her of forgery is more than a _____.
6. Of course we've been to Dubrovnik, but we weren't impressed. The crowds were awful—we couldn't move for _____.
7. I've been meaning to give you _____ for your role in saving the school music program.
8. It's not exactly _____, but I do admit to having laughed when I heard Martha was in prison.
9. I think if people like us—the _____ — were to get behind the bill, it might have a chance.
10. It's difficult to avoid a feeling of _____ after watching the evening news.

ANSWERS: (1) Gesamtkunstwerk; (2) mano a mano; (3) dacha; (4) Wunderkind; (5) peccadillo; (6) hoi polloi; (7) kudos; (8) Schadenfreude; (9) intelligentsia; (10) Weltschmerz

VII. COMPLETE THE STORY

We'll finish off our visit to Baden-Baden with a late dinner at one of the city's most acclaimed restaurants: **Le Jardin de France**, which has one Michelin star. (No restaurant in Baden-Baden has more than one, despite the city's reputation as an international snob center.)

We enter the restaurant through a delightful courtyard off **Lichtentalerstrasse**, and then sit down under an enormous skylight in the main dining room. As we feast on roast pigeon breast with Espelette-pepper gravy, glazed beets, and warm elderberry soufflé, let's check in with Giselle and Marco.

Use this lesson's snob words to fill the blanks in the passage below. Each word is used once.

hoi polloi	**kudos**
Wunderkind	**Gesamtkunstwerk**
intelligentsia	**Weltschmerz**
mano a mano	**peccadillo**
Schadenfreude	**dacha**

The Expensive Escapades of

MARCO & GISELLE

Professional Beautiful People

Episode Fourteen: Surprised in St. Moritz

It is now November, and Marco and Giselle are having lunch in a restaurant overlooking *St. Moritz*, Switzerland (we'll explore it in depth on Day 27), that most fabulous of all winter resorts.

Since our last episode, in which Giselle accuses Marco of wanting to break her heart, our couple has reconciled, and the two are now officially dating.

Suddenly, a tall blonde woman appears at their table.

TALL WOMAN: Marco, is that you? I do not see you forever!

MARCO: Helga! What are you doing in St. Moritz?

HELGA: Ah, Marco, you may be cute, but you are not a member of the (1)_____. This is where I escape from (2)_____ in the winter. I own a chalet here, remember? Actually, it is more of a (3)_____, since I design it in Russian style.

MARCO: Ah, yes, of course I remember. *(He also remembers that Giselle is sitting across from him.)* Excuse me, Helga, may I present Giselle Van de Kamp, my girlfriend. Giselle, Helga von Hoch.

HELGA: Girlfriend? *(turning to Giselle)* How long you are his girlfriend?

GISELLE: Just over a month.

HELGA: *(looking at Giselle)* (4)_____, and my sincere condolences. Two years ago, I am Marco's girlfriend for two months—this is all I can handle. We fight all the time. We go (5)_____ over every little thing. Don't get me wrong. Marco never do anything especially bad…he just commit a few (6)_____, like refusing to return my calls and forgetting my birthday.

MARCO: *(changing the subject)* So, Helga, I assume you are still modeling?

HELGA: No—I am artist now, and I just finish my latest piece, a (7)_____. It is amazing mixture of painting, dance, song, architecture, and sculpture.

GISELLE: Sounds fascinating.

HELGA: It *is* fascinating. But my work is also sad…full of (8)_____, since this world is never the ideal place I wish it were.

On the other hand, my career is not sad. In fact, the press is calling me the (9)_____ of the Swiss art world (I am only twenty-one, you know). I am so successful, at such a young age, that I inspire (10)_____ in everyone!

ANSWERS: (1) intelligentsia; (2) hoi polloi; (3) dacha; (4) kudos; (5) mano a mano; (6) peccadillos; (7) Gesamtkunstwerk; (8) Weltschmerz; (9) Wunderkind; (10) Schadenfreude

Will the budding romance between Marco and Giselle survive the appearance of this *femme fatale?*

Stay tuned.

Meanwhile, our congratulations on finishing yet another lesson of *Snob Words.*

Rest up, and don't ruin your appetite, because tomorrow we travel to Italy to delve into uppity restaurant terms.

Day 25

Mangeons and *Mangiamo!*
DINING OUT IN FRENCH & ITALIAN

LOCATION: **NAPLES, ITALY**

French and Italian are two of the world's most popular cuisines, and we're all familiar with certain elements of both: baguettes, pizza, quiche, spaghetti, crêpes, and ravioli, to name just a few.

But you may not be familiar with the full *baterie* of foreign terms one must know in order to dine with poise and confidence in French and Italian eateries, whether in France and Italy themselves, or in other countries.

While these terms are not snobby in their original languages, they take on snob value when used in English because most Anglophones are only passingly familiar with them.

Today we'll be based in the area around Naples, birthplace of Italy's most famous culinary export: the pizza. We'll stay at my villa on the nearby (and very snooty) island of **Capri** (properly pronounced COP′-ree) and take my yacht to the city.

So dust off your taste buds and *mangeons* and *mangiamo!*
(That's French and Italian for 'let's eat!')

I. PRONOUNCE & DEFINE

First, welcome to the tiny island—directly across the bay
from Naples—that Elizabeth Taylor and Jacqueline Kennedy
made famous in the 1960s. Actually, Capri (a favorite with
Roman emperors) has been a popular resort for millennia, but
Liz and Jackie brought it to the gossip pages.

My villa, set on the sheer cliffs of the town of **Anacapri**, was
built in the late 1700s. As you can see, it's small compared to
the modern monstrosities around it, but it's an architectural
gem with a perfect little garden and an unobstructed view of
the bay.

My neighbors are all jealous of my *bijou,* or dainty little jewel
of a house, which makes them constantly aware that their own
villas are vulgar and overdressed.

That's exactly the response I hoped to provoke by buying
and restoring this place, which was about to be demolished
when I first saw it.

But I digress. Let's take our first look at today's group of
snob words:

1. **prix fixe** (pre´-feeks´)
2. **table d'hôte** (tah´-bluh DOAT´)
3. **maître d'hôtel** (may´-truh doh-TELL´)
4. **bistro** (BEE´-stroh)
5. **brasserie** (BRASS´-ree)
6. **trattoria** (trah-tuh-REE´-uh)
7. **osteria** (oh´-stuh-REE´-uh)
8. **amuse-bouche** (AM´-yooz-BOOSH´)
9. **antipasto** (ahn´-tee-POSS´-toh)
10. **plat du jour** (PLAH´ doo ZHOR´)

1. **PRIX FIXE:** ('fixed price' in French) refers to a multi-course meal served for a set price. Specific courses are often pre-selected by the restaurant; in some cases diners are allowed to make choices and substitutions.

Prix fixe is the opposite of **à la carte**, the system in which a diner chooses individually priced items from a menu and pays for them accordingly. Many restaurants offer both *prix fixe* and *à la carte* options.

NOTE: most U.S. publications do *not* use a hyphen when using *prix fixe* as an adjective: *prix fixe lunch*, *prix fixe menu*, etc.

2. **TABLE D'HÔTE:** (literal French, 'table of the host') a set meal served to all guests at a stated hour and fixed price, as is the practice at some inns, simple eateries, and bed and breakfast lodgings.

In other words, it's like eating at home: everyone eats *what* mom (or dad, cook, chef) puts on the table *when* she (or he) puts it on the table.

In France, the *table d'hôte* style of dining is often used in small vacation lodgings called *chambres d'hôte.*

At times, *table d'hôte* is used as a synonym for *prix fixe.*

3. **MAÎTRE D'HÔTEL:** (often shortened to **maître d'**, pronounced may'-truh DEE') the head waiter or host who manages the dining room, as opposed to the kitchen area, of a formal restaurant.

Being on good terms with the *maître d'hôtel* can, at times, help a patron get a reservation on a busy night or get access to the best tables.

Our last four terms are types of eating establishments in France and Italy. While Americans use 'restaurant' to refer to everything from burger joints to the most lavish dining rooms, that's not so in French or Italian. In these languages, a 'restaurant' (*restaurant* in French, *ristorante* in Italian), is a formal place with printed menus and tablecloths.

4. **BISTRO**: a small French neighborhood eatery that serves moderately priced, simple meals in a modest setting.

Bistros generally feature **cuisine de grand-mère**, or grandmother's cooking, which includes slow-cooked foods such as *cassoulet*, a home-style bean stew.

Service at *bistros* is generally quick, but limited to mealtime hours.

5. **BRASSERIE**: a small French eating establishment that's larger than a *bistro*, but smaller than a formal restaurant.

Brasseries, which serve traditional French dishes such as *coq au vin* and *steak tartare*, have larger menus than *bistros*, and serve food at all hours, often into the night.

6. **TRATTORIA**: a small and rustic Italian eatery, less formal than a *ristorante*, but more formal than an *osteria* (see below).

Trattorie (trah-tuh-REE'-ay, the proper plural), are found throughout Italy, and are usually owned by families. Food, which is fresh, simple, and local, may be eaten *in situ* or purchased in containers to take home.

7. **OSTERIA**: an Italian eatery, even less formal than a *trattoria*, that serves simple meals, often without a menu. Offerings change daily, according to the market. Two or three courses are generally offered for a fixed price *(prix fixe)*.

PLURAL: *osterie* (oh-stuh-REE'-ay)

Our final three snob words are terms you are likely to encounter in French and Italian eateries:

8. **PLAT DU JOUR**: (French, 'plate of the day') a dish featured at a French eatery on a particular day, generally offered at a dis-

count; similar to the "daily specials" of some American diners and other restaurants.

9. **AMUSE-BOUCHE**: (literal French, 'mouth-amuser') a small dish served as an appetizer before a meal or between courses, complimentary at some restaurants.

10. **ANTIPASTO**: (literal Italian, 'before food') a first course or appetizer in Italian cuisine. A variety of *antipasti* (the plural, ahn´-tee-POSS´-tee) may be offered in an *antipasto* course, including cold meats, olives, cheeses, fresh and pickled vegetables, fruits, breads, and breadsticks.

Along with these traditional appetizers, Italian restaurants often serve more elaborate *antipasti*, such as stuffed mushrooms and seafood salads.

NOTE: publications and websites in English often use *antipasto* and *antipasti* interchangeably, but that's incorrect. *Antipasto* refers to the course, as well as a single entry in the course; *antipasti* refers to multiple entries in the course.

II. SO MANY DINING OPTIONS....

So little time!

There's great food here on Capri, but we must get to Naples to try the pizza. It's thicker and more pliable than the *pizza tonda* (thin and crispy) we had in Rome, but not as thick as most pizza in the U.S.

Let's take my Aston Martin (if you'd like to drive, go ahead, it's insured!) down to the harbor, where we'll board my yacht. As we descend this route, which has amazing views—along with some dizzying hairpin turns—let's play a game.

You and your significant other are trying to decide where to dine on a Saturday night.

Fill the blanks below with snob words from this lesson. Each word is used once. Make words plural where appropriate.

table d'hôte	prix fixe
plat du jour	trattoria
brasserie	osteria
bistro	amuse-bouche
antipasto	maître d'hôtel

Saturday Night Flavor

YOU: I'm in the mood for French, but I'm so hungry that I'd like something fast. Maybe we could stop by that little (1)_____ on the corner, although we'd have to hurry, because they stop serving dinner at nine. I think Saturday's (2)_____ is *cassoulet*. Or, in keeeping with the French theme, we could try the new (3)_____ across the street, which should be open until midnight, at least.

SIGNIFICANT OTHER: Those options sound fine, but I know the (4)_____ at the Fleur de Lis, downtown. He should be able to get us a quick table. The chef there serves a wonderful (5)_____ of foie gras with caviar—and it's complimentary!

YOU: I'm a little tight on money right now. Could we try something a little more...basic? Maybe Italian? I know of a little (6)_____ with wonderful pasta dishes and an (7)_____ table to die for! I'm talking stuffed mushrooms, pickled artichokes, grilled eggplant.

Or, why don't we go extremely informal and head to the (8)_____ on Main Street. It doesn't even have a menu! It offers one (9)_____ option with three courses—much cheaper than ordering *à la carte* anywhere else.

SIGNIFICANT OTHER: If I'd known you were going to be such a tightwad, I would have made reservations at the Cheapskate Inn. It's inexpensive, and quite charming, but reservations are *de rigueur*. They only have one sitting—at 9 p.m.—and service is (10)_____, in other words, everyone eats the same thing, at the same time, for the same price.

ANSWERS: (1) bistro; (2) plat du jour; (3) brasserie; (4) maître d'hôtel; (5) amuse-bouche; (6) trattoria; (7) antipasto; (8) osteria; (9) prix fixe; (10) table d'hôte

III. MULTIPLE CHOICE

Here we are, Naples. A little more chaotic than you imagined? Well, get ready for the real Italy, laundry-hanging-on-lines-between-tenements and all, because we're heading for the **Centro Storico,** or historic city center. This is where pizza originated, and where they still make the most authentic version of the dish, which is always baked in a wood-fired oven.

Purist **pizzerias** offer only two types of pies: **Margherita,** topped with tomatoes, fresh basil, and *mozzarella di bufala* (produced in the area around Naples, as you'll remember), and **marinara,** topped with tomatoes, oregano, garlic, and olive oil.

As we enjoy our pizza (you *are* enjoying it, right?), let's play the following multiple-choice game:

1. The proper plural of *trattoria* is:
   a. *trattorias*
   b. *trattorie*
   c. *trattorii*
2. Which of the following items would **not** likely be served as *antipasti:*
   a. fried chicken
   b. pickled vegetables
   c. stuffed mushrooms
3. A *brasserie* is:
   a. less formal than an actual restaurant
   b. more formal than a *bistro*
   c. both of the above
4. *Cuisine de grand-mère* is likely to be served in a(n):
   a. *table d'hôte*
   b. *bistro*
   c. *osteria*

5. A type of Italian eatery that often lacks a formal menu is a(n):
   a. *antipasto*
   b. *trattoria*
   c. *osteria*

6. A *plat du jour* is similar to a(n):
   a. daily special
   b. *amuse-bouche*
   c. *maître d'hôtel*

7. In *table d'hôte* service:
   a. everyone eats the same thing
   b. everyone eats at the same time
   c. both of the above

8. A meal of several courses, offered at a set price, is:
   a. *maître d'hôtel*
   b. *prix fixe*
   c. *amuse-bouche*

9. The manager of a formal restaurant dining room is the:
   a. *maître d'hôtel*
   b. *plat du jour*
   c. *maître d'restaurant*

10. An *amuse-bouche* is a(n):
    a. daily special
    b. appetizer
    c. breath mint

ANSWERS: (1) b; (2) a; (3) c; (4) b; (5) c; (6) a; (7) c; (8) b; (9) a; (10) b

IV. MATCHING

I ate far too much pizza. How about you? But we must move on to our next stop, the **Royal Palace of Caserta**, which is the Italian equivalent of the Palace of Versailles.

Built between 1774 and 1847 by the Bourbon rulers of Naples, this Baroque behemoth, measuring in at more than two million square meters, is the world's largest royal palace.

And with a two-mile walking path on three hundred acres, its gardens are equally gargantuan.

As we explore (and walk off that pizza), match the snob words below with their descriptions.

____	1. *trattoria*	a. 'fixed price'
____	2. *osteria*	b. only open at mealtimes
____	3. *brasserie*	c. system under which everyone eats the same thing at the same time
____	4. *bistro*	d. usually open late into the night
____	5. *prix fixe*	e. smallest and simplest type of Italian eatery
____	6. *table d'hôte*	f. appetizer that is sometimes complimentary
____	7. *antipasto*	g. midsize and midrange italian eatery, usually family run
____	8. *plat du jour*	h. may include olives, cold vegetables, and sausages
____	9. *amuse-bouche*	i. good person to know for last-minute dinner reservations
____	10. *maître d'hôtel*	j. 'plate of the day'

ANSWERS: (1) g; (2) e; (3) d; (4) b; (5) a (6) c; (7) h; (8) j; (9) f; (10) i

V. TRUE OR FALSE

I can see you're tired—the tour of the palace and its gardens was exhausting. Let's head back to the island and go straight to the actual town of **Capri**, the island's largest settlement, where we'll have gelato in the **Piazzetta** (little plaza), the premier place to see and be seen.

Known as the world's most fashionable square, this tiny rectangle of real estate, perched high above the **Tyrrhenian Sea**, offers unobstructed views of the water, as well as in-your-face views of the island's dramatic, craggy cliffs.

As we rub shoulders with Italian actresses, American billionaires, and *nouveaux-pauvres* (newly poor) nobles from all over Europe (here to form alliances with the billionaires?), let's play one more game, this time of the true-or-false variety.

(T/F)   1. The *maître d'hôtel* does the majority of the cooking in a *bistro*.

(T/F)   2. Under the *table d'hôte* system, diners select their own menu items and pay for them accordingly.

(T/F)   3. *Antipasto* is anything other than pasta.

(T/F)   4. *Bistros* feature grandmother-style cooking.

(T/F)   5. A *prix fixe* menu has a set price.

(T/F)   6. *Brasseries* serve food at all hours, while *bistros* serve only at mealtimes.

(T/F)   7. A *trattoria* is usually larger and more formal than an *osteria*.

(T/F)   8. An *amuse-bouche* is meant to please the eyes.

(T/F)   9. The contents of a *plat du jour* change daily.

(T/F)   10. A *bistro* is a fancy place for special occasions.

ANSWERS: All true except (1), (2), (3), (8) and (10).

Isn't this delightful? There's nothing like practicing *il dolce far niente* in Capri's Piazzetta as the sun goes down.

But all good things must eventually come to an end.

Congratulations on your hard work during this lesson. You are now qualified to dine in any type of French or Italian eatery.

But we have many more snob words to learn. Make sure to get plenty of beauty sleep tonight—tomorrow we head to Hollywood for your screen test.

Day 26

Ready for Your Close-Up?
HIGHFALUTIN' FILM TERMS

LOCATION: **BEL AIR, CALIFORNIA**

You watch movies, of course. But do you *screen films?* There's a major difference. *Star Wars* is a movie. *Citizen Kane*—which, according to many cinema critics, is the best motion picture ever made—is a *film*, or an artsy motion picture that most normal people don't really *get*.

As a word snob, you must learn Filmspeak in order to at least *pretend* to understand films, and to hold your own against those black-beret-wearing types who discuss *mise en scène* (definition below) while throwing darts at pictures of George Lucas.

Today's words by no means constitute an exhaustive list of snob words of the silver screen. There are dozens. But this group of ten, which includes a few technical terms, some film genres, and the name of one famous film, should help you get through many a cinematic snob situation.

As for where we'll be based today, where else but on location in Tinseltown? Of course, we won't actually be *staying* in Hollywood, which is insufferably downscale.

Instead, we'll be based at my mansion in **Bel Air**, the superluxe community that, along with **Beverly Hills** and **Holmby Hills**, forms the posh district of metro Los Angeles known as the **Platinum Triangle**.

We'll begin today's class in one of the dozen or so (I've never bothered to count them) cabañas surrounding my pool. From here, on a clear day—perhaps once or twice a year—you can see the giant white Hollywood sign perched on the Santa Monica Mountains.

I. PRONOUNCE & DEFINE

As we sip free-range açai-quinoa Juliuses concocted by my personal trainer, Chad, let's take a first look at our new terms.

1. **cinéaste** (SIN´-ee-ust)
2. **cinephile** (SIN´-uh-file)
3. **mise-en-scène** (mee-zahn-SEN´)
4. **montage** (MAHN´-tazh)
5. **jump cut**
6. **film noir** (film NWAHR´)
7. **cinéma-vérité** (SIN´-uh-muh vehr´-uh-TAY´)
8. **nouvelle vague** (new´-vell VAHG´)
9. **auteur** (oh-TUR´)
10. *Citizen Kane*

1. CINÉASTE: this term means 'filmmaker' in French, but Anglophones use it to refer to those who *make* films as well as those who *enjoy* them—devotees of motion pictures, or movie buffs.

It's similar to the way the term *fashionista* can be applied to *designers,* as well as *followers,* of fashion.

When used in English, *cinéaste* is occasionally spelled without the accent *(cineaste)*, and even without the final *e (cineast)*, but why not be snobby and spell it the proper French way?

2. CINEPHILE: (French, 'one who loves films') a person who is enthusiastic about cinema as an art form, and who knows a great deal about the subject.

3. MISE-EN-SCÈNE: (French for 'put into the scene') refers to all the elements that ultimately appear onscreen in a film, including setting, lighting, costumes, and staging.

The director usually has final say over a film's *mise-en-scène,* which determines its overall look and mood.

Mise-en-scène is a pet term of cinema snobs, who relish the fact that most normal people don't understand it.

4. MONTAGE: (from the French *monter*, 'to assemble') in Europe, the process of editing individual shots into sequences that will eventually result in a finished film.

In the United States, however, *montage* is often used to describe any unusual editing technique used for effect.

For example, U.S. filmmakers often use the term *montage* to refer to a string of short shots used to portray action or to suggest the passage of time.

5. JUMP CUT: a sudden, often jarring, cut from one shot or scene to another in film or video, sometimes done in error, but often used for effect.

For example, if a film cuts from a wide shot of a woman walking on a beach to a similar wide shot of the same woman walking on the same beach (from only a slightly different camera position), the resulting sequence will look as though the woman is "jumping" across the screen.

To avoid this effect, film editors generally follow a wide shot with a medium shot or a close-up.

Artistic jump cuts were quite popular with directors of the French *nouvelle vague* (see below).

NOTE: *jump cut* can also be used as a verb—to *jump-cut.*

6. FILM NOIR: (French, 'black film') a type of crime film produced in Hollywood (not in France, as the name would suggest) between 1940 and 1960.

The *film noir* genre is characterized by the use of black-and-white cinematography in a *chiaroscuro* style (remember that term from Day 2?), morally ambiguous themes, and complex mystery plots.

Films noirs (the proper plural, pronounced the same as the singular) also make use of stock characters, such as the cynical detective and the *femme fatale*, a mysterious, attractive woman who lures men into dangerous situations.

Well known examples of *film noir* include **Sunset Boulevard** (1950), directed by **Billy Wilder** (1906-2002), and **The Maltese Falcon** (1941), directed by **John Huston** (1906-87).

7. CINÉMA-VÉRITÉ: (French for 'cinema truth') a style of documentary filmmaking that uses simple equipment, such as hand-held cameras, to ask ordinary people probing questions in their natural environments. Action sequences are often filmed separately and synchronized with dialogue during editing.

The *cinéma-vérité* style was first explained in the writings of Russian filmmaker **Dziga Vertov** (1896-1954), who coined the term *kino-pravda,* or 'cinema-truth,' in the 1920s.

American filmmaker **Robert Flaherty** (1884-1951) used the style in his *Nanook of the North* (1922), but what is now known as the **French School** brought the genre to full development in the 1960s.

Cinéma-vérité is not synonymous with **direct cinema**, a fly-on-the-wall documentary style in which filmmakers avoid asking questions and attempt to be as unobtrusive as possible while filming real-life events.

English dictionaries vary on the spelling of *cinéma-vérité*. The snobbiest form is the French one, which we've used here (three accents and a hyphen). Some dictionaries drop the hyphen, and some use only one or two accents.

8. NOUVELLE VAGUE: ('new wave,' in French) a realistic and spontaneous style of creating fictional feature films. The technique emerged in France during the 1960s as a reaction to the then-standard studio system of producing movies.

Filmmakers of the *nouvelle vague* developed the *auteur theory* (see below), which resulted in films that were personal visions of their directors.

The plots of *nouvelle vague* films were often improvised, and films were usually shot on location with natural light. Sound was recorded directly, rather than dubbed in a studio, which had been standard practice for feature films up to that time. Themes followed the social and political upheavals of the era.

The editing style of *nouvelle vague* films included the use of frequent *jump cuts* and extended sequences of rapid cuts.

Many films in the *nouvelle vague* genre have explicitly sexual and violent themes, such as ***Jules and Jim*** (1962), by **Francois Truffaut** (1932-84), and ***Breathless*** (1960), by **Jean-Luc Godard** (b. 1930).

The Butcher (1970), by **Claude Chabrol** (1930-2010), is a relatively mild example of the genre.

NOTES: *nouvelle vague* is also referred to as the French **New Wave**, but that doesn't sound as snobby.

While 'New Wave' is almost always capitalized, *nouvelle vague* may be capitalized or left in lower case.

9. AUTEUR: (French, 'author') the director of a film of supposed artistic merit.

Directors seen as serious artists, like Alfred Hitchcock and Orson Welles, are considered *auteurs;* the directors of most Hollywood and made-for-television movies are not.

Auteur theory, developed during the French *nouvelle vague* (see above), is the belief that a high-quality film is the product of a personal artistic vision. As such, according to the theory, a film should bear the stamp of its director, much like a great work of literature bears the stamp of its writer.

Under *auteur theory*, film directors, or *auteurs*, get credit for the final cinematic product, although many others, of course—including actors, writers, cinematographers, and designers—make substantial and vital contributions to a film.

10. *CITIZEN KANE:* the most critically-acclaimed movie of all time, directed by **Orson Welles** (1915-85) at the surprisingly young age of twenty-five. Welles also plays the title role.

Released in 1941, and especially admired two decades later by critics and directors of the French *nouvelle vague*, *Citizen Kane* is an encyclopedia of filmmaking techniques: deep focus, rear projection, extreme close-ups, overlapping dialogue, flashbacks, multiple narrators, and multiple perspectives.

Citizen Kane also spans various genres, including Gothic horror, farce, melodrama, documentary, and surrealism.

According to the British Film Institute's *Sight and Sound* magazine, *Citizen Kane* was considered the best film of all time during the fifty-year period between 1962 and 2012. (The publication polls prominent film critics and film directors once each decade.)

In the institute's 2012 poll, Welles' masterpiece lost its first-place spot by a narrow margin to *Vertigo* (1958), directed by **Alfred Hitchcock** (1899-1980). With half a century in the number-one position, however, *Citizen Kane* is still the world's most celebrated film.

II. SENTENCE PAIRS

Never been to Hollywood, you say? You'll be shocked at how seedy and unattractive it is, but we'll drive to **Hollywood**

Boulevard, just so you can say you've seen it. In fact, my driver is pulling up with the limo right now.

We'll begin our tour at the former **Grauman's Chinese Theater** (now TLC Chinese Theatres), an iconic venue that dates to 1927.

This famed Hollywood movie palace has hosted many important movie premieres through the decades, including that of *Star Wars* in 1977.

Here in the forecourt, immortalized in cement, are the handprints and footprints of dozens of famous actors and actresses. From where we're standing, we can see the prints of Marilyn Monroe...Joan Crawford...and Fred Astaire, to point out just a few. Oh, and there's Shirley Temple.

As you search for your favorite stars, fill each blank in the following snob statements with the most appropriate snob word from this lesson.

Each word is used once; make words plural as necessary.

cinéaste	film noir
cinephile	cinéma-vérité
mise-en-scène	nouvelle vague
montage	auteur
jump cut	*Citizen Kane*

1. Joe's edit made the star of the film look as if she were jumping from one side of the screen to the other. Joe made a _____.

2. Jean-Luc, the director, has complete artistic control of the film. Jean-Luc is the film's _____.

3. It lost its status as "best film ever made" in 2012. But _____ continues to be admired by critics and film students.

4. For his documentary entitled *Women on Wall Street*, Doug is using a hand-held camera to interview female stockbrokers in their offices. Doug is using the techniques of _____.

5. Gabriel has spent months approving locations, props, and costumes, as well as carefully blocking out the position of every actor in every scene. Gabriel is very particular about

_____.

6. Joseph loves movies, but does not make them. He can best be described as a _____.

7. In her film, Clarissa hopes to suggest the passage of two decades with a twenty-second sequence of quick shots. Clarissa is making use of a _____.

8. It was a crime film, extremely dark, and clearly made in Hollywood in the 1940s or 1950s. It was a perfect example of _____.

9. Josh has made thirty-four feature films and twenty-five documentaries. You could call him a 'filmmaker' or a

_____.

10. In the 1960s, a group of French film critics and filmmakers advocated a new style of film that featured amateur actors, spontaneous dialogue, and real locations. This movement is known as the _____.

ANSWERS: (1) jump cut; (2) auteur; (3) *Citizen Kane*; (4) cinéma-vérité; (5) mise-en-scène; (6) cinephile; (7) montage; (8) film noir; (9) cinéaste; (10) nouvelle vague

III. MULTIPLE CHOICE

In front of the Chinese Theater, running for more than three miles along Hollywood Boulevard and part of **Vine Street**, is the **Hollywood Walk of Fame**.

Here more than two thousand performing artists—mostly movie stars—are honored with brass stars embedded in the sidewalk.

There's Julie Andrews...and look, there's Burt Reynolds. You say you found John Travolta? Tom Cruise's star is right over there. We could look further, but the area's a little sketchy.

Okay, a lot sketchy. Let's hurry across the street before we get mugged.

Now we're standing in front of another 1920s movie venue, **El Capitan Theater**, which the Disney company renovated in the 1980s. It's now used frequently for Disney film premieres.

Wait—I almost forgot! In less than twenty minutes, I have my quarterly ultra-teeth-whitening treatment.

While I do that, why don't you get a spray tan at the **Beverly Hills Hotel** spa? (Don't take this personally, but you're a little pale for La La Land.)

While you're getting sprayed, play the following game:

1. Which of the following terms can mean 'filmmaker?'
    a. *cinephile*
    b. *cinéaste*
    c. either of the above
2. Which of the following is **not** part of *mise-en-scène?*
    a. placement of actors
    b. catering services
    c. location
3. Proponents of the *nouvelle vague* believed:
    a. the best films are made by *auteurs*
    b. all films should include seascapes
    c. films should be vague
4. In 2012, *Citizen Kane* lost its status as "best film ever made" to which film?
    a. François Truffaut's *Jules et Jim*
    b. Alfred Hitchcock's *Vertigo*
    c. George Lucas's *The Empire Strikes Back*
5. *Cinéma-vérité* is a style of filmmaking used for:
    a. very cinematic films
    b. low-budget foreign soap operas
    c. documentaries
6. *Montage,* in its European sense, means:
    a. horseback riding in films
    b. the process of editing a film
    c. making films in mountainous areas

7. The dark crime films produced in Hollywood in the 1940s and 1950s belong to the genre known as:
   a. *films noirs*
   b. *filme noire*
   c. *film noir*
8. *Jump cuts* occur:
   a. in error
   b. on purpose
   c. for both reasons
9. A person who loves films may be called a:
   a. *cinéaste*
   b. *cinephile*
   c. either of the above
10. In *auteur theory*, the director of a film is similar to:
    a. the framer of a painting
    b. the writer of a novel
    c. the engineer of a building

ANSWERS: (1) b; (2) b; (3) a; (4) b; (5) c; (6) b; (7) c; (8) c; (9) c; (10) b

IV. LIGHTS, CAMERA, ACTION!

I must say your tanning session was a big success—you now look like an *Angeleno*, which is what the residents of Los Angeles call themselves.

Time for lunch, which we'll have at **Spago Beverly Hills**, the SoCal culinary landmark that celebrity chef **Wolfgang Puck** opened in 1982.

I'm going to have one (at two hundred dollars each, *yes*, just one) first-of-the-season Italian white *truffle* and a basket of wood-oven-roasted wild field mushrooms.

In fact, we should probably share my order, or the other diners will take us for gluttons. (A dozen actresses have been known to share a single salad here. How else do you think everyone stays so thin in the Big Orange?) As we eat (or pretend to eat) please enjoy our next activity.

Backstory: you and a friend decide to make an indie movie. Below you'll find a snippet of your brainstorming session. Fill the blanks with snob words from today's lesson. Each word is used only once; make words plural where necessary.

cinéaste	**film noir**
cinephile	**cinéma-vérité**
mise-en-scène	**nouvelle vague**
montage	**auteur**
jump cut	***Citizen Kane***

FRIEND: I'm thinking of something dark, along the lines of (1)_____, but you're more of a (2)_____ than I am, and you'll be the (3)_____ of the piece, so *you* tell *me*.

YOU: Truly you overestimate my talents! Yes, I watch a lot of movies, but I'm certainly no (4)_____ in the sense of having actually *made* films.

But I like your "dark" idea. Since we have no budget, we'll have to do it (5)_____ style, you know, on location, with amateur actors, and with natural light.

And since we're not exactly writers, we'll have to improvise the script.

FRIEND: Whoa, I'm starting to realize this whole idea might be a little ambitious. Remember, we're just beginners, especially with editing. It's all I can do to avoid (6)_____, let alone put a nice (7)_____ together.

YOU: You're right. And I'm still learning how to direct, which includes overseeing a film's (8)_____. (I can't even pronounce it!) Let's start with something simple—there's no need to start out making (9)_____. Maybe a short documentary in the style of (10)_____ would be in order.

ANSWERS: (1) film noir; (2) cinephile; (3) auteur; (4) cinéaste; (5) nouvelle vague; (6) jump cuts; (7) montage; (8) mise-en-scène; (9) *Citizen Kane*; (10) cinéma-vérité

V. TRUE OR FALSE

Our time is running out here in the City of Angels, but I hope that by now you're well on your way to committing this lesson's cinematic snob words to your permanent memory.

Before we leave, however, let's take a drive up the coast through **Malibu**, that beachside home-to-the-stars nestled between the Pacific Ocean and the Santa Monica Mountains.

As you look out over multi-million-dollar homes to the hopelessly blue water, take the following true-or-false quiz to reinforce what you've learned.

(T/F)   1. In the U.S., *montage* can mean a series of quick cuts to suggest action or the passage of time.

(T/F)   2. *Mise-en-scène* refers to all the behind-the-scenes elements that go into a movie.

(T/F)   3. The terms *cinéaste* and *cinephile* can **both** mean 'movie buff.'

(T/F)   4. *Auteur* means 'author of the screenplay.'

(T/F)   5. *Film noir* refers to all black and white films.

(T/F)   6. Proponents of the *nouvelle vague* believed a film should be the artistic expression of an *auteur.*

(T/F)   7. A *jump cut* is an edit that can make a subject look as if he or she 'jumps' on the screen.

(T/F)   8. *Cinéaste* can mean 'filmmaker' as well as 'motion picture aficionado.'

(T/F)   9. *Cinéma-vérité* is 'fly-on-the-wall' filmmaking.

(T/F)   10. *Citizen Kane* uses a wide range of cinematic techniques.

ANSWERS: All true except (2), (4), (5), and (9). With regard to question (9), 'fly-on-the-wall' filmmaking is called *direct cinema*.

Well, how do you feel about these movie terms?

Did our tour of down-at-the-heels Hollywood put an end to your dream of being a film star? You say you never want to see a movie again?

Relax.

Tomorrow we'll visit ten amazingly snobby vacation spots that will completely cleanse your cultural palate of the tawdriness of Tinseltown. (That's a lot of unintentional alliteration, but I'm too tired to change it.)

Good night!

Day 27

Jet-Set Journeys
SNOBBY SEA & SKI VACATIONS

LOCATION: **SNOB SPOTS AROUND THE WORLD**

Sure, vacations are relaxing and rejuvenating and all that, but as we all know, the real reason we take trips is to brag about them—before and afterwards.

Therefore, we must choose destinations with snob cred.

Jet-setters are well aware that once a place is "discovered," and Holiday Inn and JetBlue move in (bringing with them *hoi polloi),* the party's over. When a location loses its cachet, it's time to find another, so the poor members of the *beau monde* are on a constant hunt for new exotic and fantastic locations they can have to themselves.

There are a few destinations, however, that have stood the test of time: these have become *jet-set* classics.

In this chapter, we explore several of these, as well as a few other destinations that are current favorites of the *beautiful people,* the *glitterati,* and the *carriage trade.*

We've already traveled extensively in this course, as you're aware, but as we near the end of our snobcabulary journey, you deserve a vacation from our regular peregrinations before completing the final two lessons and the final exam.

Let's get started on this sampler of snooty sojourns by visiting five exclusive destinations with beaches.

I. SEA VACATIONS

` 1. **Bora Bora** (BOR´-uh BOR´-uh), French Polynesia
  2. **Cartagena** (car´-tuh-HAY´-nuh), Colombia
  3. **Saint-Barthélemy** (SAN´-bahr-tell-uh-MEE´),
    French West Indies
  4. **the Hamptons**, New York
  5. **Martha's Vineyard**, Massachusetts

1. **BORA BORA**, French Polynesia: forget Hawaii and forget the Caribbean—when true *jet-setters* want a sun and beach vacation, the current destination of choice is *Bora Bora*, a tiny island (six miles long and two miles wide) northwest of Tahiti.

Here, for $1000-plus a night, we'll get the following: a bungalow set on stilts over aquamarine water; views of **Mount Otemanu**, the dormant volcano that dominates the island; and snorkeling access to a pristine coral reef.

Bora Bora also offers multiple five-star beaches and friendly, French-speaking locals. Bicycles are the preferred mode of transportation. Paradise, anyone?

2. **CARTAGENA**, Colombia: if *Bora Bora* isn't an option, and you must stick closer to home, check out the new darling of the Caribbean. It's not an island, but rather a 16th-century colonial city on Colombia's northern coast.

Jet-setters have been secretly enjoying the delights of *Cartagena* for years, strolling the perfectly preserved colonial streets, dining under jacaranda trees in the lovely plazas, and getting lost in the three massive forts that once protected the city from pirates. But now the secret's out, and it's only a matter of time before the place is overrun with day-trippers from cruise ships.

While *Cartagena's* new city, **Bocagrande**, is lovely, it's the walled, colonial **Ciudad Vieja** that steals the show.

We'll stay in one of the 17th-century convents that now function as luxury hotels. The nuns of yesteryear would blush at the current amenities.

3. **SAINT-BARTHÉLEMY**, West Indies: if you must visit an *island* in the Caribbean, make it *Saint-Barthélemy* (its French name, but it's also known as *St. Barthélemy, St. Barts, St. Bart's, St. Barth,* and *St. Barth's*), the queen of West Indian snobdom.

Shaped like an ill-formed croissant, *St. Barts,* which is how most Americans refer to the island, is seven miles long and five miles wide, with white-sand beaches (twenty-one of them, to be exact), some of the best cuisine in the Caribbean, and swank boutiques with the latest international fashions.

While the island does attract its share of *nouveaux riches,* old-money residents manage to keep them in check. The only time the island gets crazy with movie stars and tech moguls is between Christmas and New Year's Day.

St. Barts has plenty of hotels, but we'll stay in my own red-roofed villa overlooking the impossibly picturesque **Baie de Saint-Jean.**

4. **THE HAMPTONS,** New York: more than twenty villages on the **South Fork** (southeast tip) of Long Island, two hours from Manhattan by car, that collectively form one of the most exclusive seaside colonies in the United States.

A few of the better known villages are **Southampton** (old money—we'll stay here, of course), **East Hampton** (new money), **Water Mill** (rural with celebrities), **Bridgehampton** (home to the Hampton Classic horse show), **Montauk** (hipster hangout), and **Sag Harbor** (resembles a New England fishing village).

Some members of "East End society," as *Hamptons* habitués are called, live in *the Hamptons* year-round, but the majority stay just for the summer. Most are wealthy residents of New York City and other parts of the Northeastern U.S.

A spate of private golf and tennis clubs adds to *the Hamptons'* aura of exclusivity.

5. **MARTHA'S VINEYARD**, Massachusetts: transfer a piece of *the Hamptons* to New England, remove a *soupçon* of snobbery, and you have *Martha's Vineyard.*

(Don't get me wrong. *The Vineyard* is plenty snobby—just not as snobby as *the Hamptons.*)

An island twenty miles long and ten miles wide, *Martha's Vineyard* lies about six miles off the Massachusetts coast, just south of **Cape Cod.**

Formerly inhabited by whaling-ship captains and a Methodist community, the island is now a summer vacation spot for top CEOs, wealthy New Englanders. and well known politicos. The Kennedy clan has been on *the Vineyard* for decades, the Clintons are frequent visitors, and former President Obama spent most summers here while in office.

Despite playing host to the rich and powerful, however, *Martha's Vineyard* retains a down-home vibe. We haven't come to gawk at celebrities: we're here to explore quaint towns lined with 18th-century architecture, to feast on fresh seafood, and to relax on uncrowded beaches.

Now let's switch gears and look at some exclusive *winter* resorts:

II. SKI VACATIONS

6. **St. Moritz** (san´-muh-RITZ´), Switzerland
7. **Courchevel 1850** (COO´-shuh-VELL´ meel-wee-SAHN´-san-CAHNT´), France

8. **Aspen**, Colorado
9. **Vail**, Colorado
10. **San Martín de los Andes** (sahn mahr-TEEN' day lohs AHN'-days), Argentina

6. **St. Moritz**, Switzerland: the world's first winter resort and arguably its most persnickety.

Set in the **Engadin Valley**, near the Swiss borders with Italy and Austria, *St. Moritz* is known for its great weather (ironic for a winter resort), which produces an average of 320 sunny days a year.

Look! Those people in ultra-fashionable skiwear are actually sunbathing on *chaises longues* surrounded by snow.

While skiing is good in *St. Moritz,* less than half the town's winter visitors actually participate in that sport. Instead, many come to spend money at the town's shops, which include outlets from every purveyor of luxury goods on the planet.

Because the official language of *St. Moritz* is Romansch (one of Switzerland's four official languages), the town's true name is **San Murezzan**. (Just so you know, in German it's called **Sankt Moritz**, and in French it's **Saint-Moritz**.)

7. **Courchevel 1850**, France: set in the French Alps near the borders of Italy and Switzerland, one of the most exclusive and attractive ski towns on the planet.

Courchevel 1850 is the most posh of the four villages in the **Courchevel** ski area, which has around 200 runs covering more than ninety miles. This ski area, in turn, is part of **Les Trois Vallées**, one of the world's largest winter sports regions.

The '1850' attached to the town's name refers to its altitude in meters, a device originally used to name all four Courchevel burgs (there was also Courchevel 1300, Courchevel 1550, and Courchevel 1650.)

The other towns have since been renamed, and now *Courchevel 1850* is officially just *Courchevel,* but the '1850' has stuck.

Home to manicured slopes, multi-million-dollar chalets, five-star hotels, Michelin-starred restaurants, and pricey boutiques, *Courchevel 1850* is full of upper-class Parisians and *nouveaux-riches* Russians, the latter anxious to flash their cash.

Notice that strict architectural codes keep growth in check and require new construction to harmonize with the setting.

8. **ASPEN**, Colorado: one of the world's great ski towns, and the favorite U.S. ski area of the rich and famous.

Reputed to have the highest property values in the U.S., the glamorous and glitzy resort—known as "Hollywood East"—caters to movie stars, rock stars, and corporate executives.

Set in the **Sawatch Range** of the Rockies, 170 miles west of Denver, Aspen offers us the choice of three ski resorts: **Buttermilk Mountain**, **Snowmass**, and **Aspen Mountain**.

Aspen's historic downtown, which once served silver miners, is now an upscale shopping district, as you can see, with outlets for luxury retailers such as Dior, Louis Vuitton, and Prada. Posh restaurants and hotels complete the scene.

9. **VAIL,** Colorado: second only to Aspen in the competition for snootiest U.S. ski area, the less flashy "Wall Street West" is favored by rich residents of the American Northeast.

Don't expect historic buildings: the town of Vail was built from scratch in 1962 as part of **Vail Ski Resort**.

The town does have excellent skiing, however, and restaurants and shopping venues also account for its draw. You won't find a Dior boutique here, but you will find a wide selection of high-end clothing stores, art galleries, and antiques emporia.

While we're here in *Vail,* we'll complain—*loudly*—about those crass *arrivistes* in Aspen, two hours to the southwest.

10. **SAN MARTÍN DE LOS ANDES**, Argentina: there was a time when **Bariloche**, once known as the Switzerland of the Andes, was the *beau-monde* favorite for South American ski vacations.

But now that Argentina's most famous winter destination has become crowded and overbuilt, the *beautiful people* have started to move on to more pristine locales.

One of these is *San Martín de los Andes,* 125 miles north of Bariloche in the **Argentine Lake District.** Set within **Parque Nacional Lanín,** the town's strict architectural codes have allowed it to retain its Swiss Alpine look despite recent growth.

San Martín is more rustic than the other ski towns on this list—bring your own Chanel and Ferragamo—but the town's main plaza is home to upscale boutiques and chic cafés.

Cerro Chapelco, the nearby ski area, has a high-speed gondola that will carry us to runs with views of the 12,000-foot **Lanín Volcano.**

REMEMBER: Argentina's seasons are opposite those of North America and Europe. If you want to ski in *San Martín*, you'll have to do it between late June and early October.

III. MATCHING

I realize that was a whirlwind tour—pause to catch your breath. Now match each destination with its state or country.

___ 1. *San Martin de los Andes*	a. Switzerland
___ 2. *Cartagena*	b. Massachusetts
___ 3. *Aspen*	c. Long Island, New York
___ 4. *Courchevel 1850*	d. Colorado
___ 5. *St. Moritz*	e. French West Indies
___ 6. *the Hamptons*	f. Colombia
___ 7. *Saint-Barthélemy*	g. Argentina
___ 8. *Vail*	h. France
___ 9. *Martha's Vineyard*	i. French Polynesia
___10. *Bora Bora*	

ANSWERS: (1) g; (2) f; (3) d; (4) h; (5) a (6) c; (7) e; (8) d; (9) b; (10) i

IV. BIG DECISIONS

Now that you know the basics of these luxe locations, it's time for some practical applications.

Picture yourself standing around the water cooler at your Manhattan law firm, discussing your vacation plans for the year with your partners.

Fill the blanks below with destinations from this chapter. Each destination is used once.

Bora Bora	St. Moritz
Cartagena	Courchevel 1850
Saint-Barthélemy	Aspen
the Hamptons	Vail
Martha's Vineyard	San Martín de los Andes

NICE PARTNER: We've been wanting to ski Argentina for years, so we're heading off to (1)_____ this summer.

STUPID PARTNER: You mean this *winter*.

NICE PARTNER: No, Argentina's seasons are opposite ours. The ski season there runs from June to October.

SNOBBY PARTNER: Everyone knows that! We had a place in Bariloche when I was growing up, but my parents sold it because they wanted something closer to New York.

They ended up buying a chalet in (2)_____.
They considered (3)_____, but they were tired of crowds and glitz.

They wanted something elegant, yet understated.

YOU: Good thing they didn't choose (4)_____, then, with all those *nouveaux-riches* Russians invading France.

SNOBBY PARTNER: Yes, they would never have survived there. Even (5)_____ is too flashy for them. They went once, got sunburned, and have never gone back to Switzerland.

YOU: Yes, Europe has its pros and cons. We considered going this summer, but we've decided to stay closer to home. I think we'll just spend a couple of weeks in (6)_____.

STUPID PARTNER: Why not try (7)_____ instead? It's not that much farther, it's more family friendly, and you won't have to worry about running into the Kardashians.

NICE PARTNER: *(changing the subject)* What about Christmas? Is anyone heading to the Caribbean?

SNOBBY PARTNER: The Caribbean! Does anyone still go to the Caribbean? We're going to (8)_____ for the holidays.

Sure, it costs three times as much as (9)_____, but it's worth it to get away from the celebrities and dot-com moguls that invade that island at Christmas.

YOU: I agree that most of the Caribbean is passé, but we've started going to (10)_____. The beaches are average, but there's so much to see: colonial architecture, massive forts, lovely plazas. My kids love it.

ANSWERS: (1) San Martín de los Andes; (2) Vail; (3) Aspen; (4) Courchevel 1850; (5) St. Moritz; (6) the Hamptons; (7) Martha's Vineyard; (8) Bora Bora; (9) Saint-Barthélemy or one of its nicknames; (10) Cartagena

V. MULTIPLE CHOICE

Glad you don't work for a Manhattan law firm with stupid and snobby partners?

My condolences if you actually do.

In this next exercise, reinforce your knowledge of our snob locations by playing the following multiple-choice game.

Enjoy!

1. *San Martín de los Andes* is:
    a. a Caribbean island
    b. a city in Colombia
    c. an Argentine resort

2. The '1850' in *Courchevel 1850* stands for:
    a. the town's permanent population
    b. the town's snobby attitude
    c. the town's altitude in meters

3. Formerly home to the whaling industry, this snobby vacation spot retains a down-home vibe:
    a. *the Hamptons*
    b. *Martha's Vineyard*
    c. *Saint-Barthélemy*

4. *St. Moritz* is:
    a. the world's first winter resort
    b. the world's snobbiest winter resort
    c. both of the above

5. A colonial gem on Colombia's Caribbean coast:
    a. *St. Moritz*
    b. *Courchevel 1850*
    c. *Cartagena*

6. A Caribbean isle known for its food scene:
    a. *Saint-Barthélemy*
    b. *Cartagena*
    c. *Bora Bora*

7. *The Hamptons* is:
    a. a group of twenty villages on Long Island
    b. one of America's snootiest vacation spots
    c. both of the above

8. The glitziest U.S. ski area:
    a. *Vail*
    b. *Aspen*
    c. *Courchevel 1850*

9. *Vail* is sometimes referred to as:
    a. "Wall Street on Ice"
    b. "Wall Street West"
    c. "Stockbrokers on Skis"

10. A French Polynesian paradise:
    a. *Courchevel 1850*
    b. *Cartagena*
    c. *Bora Bora*

ANSWERS: (1) c; (2) c; (3) b; (4) c; (5) c; (6) a; (7) c; (8) b; (9) b; (10) c

VI. FILL IN THE BLANKS

Based on your water-cooler discussion, let's make a visit to your travel agent to formalize your vacation plans for the year.

We'll continue to assume that you live in the New York City metro area.

Fill the blanks below with snob locations from this lesson.

Bora Bora	St. Moritz
Cartagena	Courchevel 1850
Saint-Barthélemy	Aspen
the Hamptons	Vail
Martha's Vineyard	San Martín de los Andes

AGENT: For your summer beach vacation, the easiest, and most obvious choice would be (1)_____, since you could easily drive there from your home in Westchester County, and you wouldn't have to worry about getting your young children on a plane.

YOU: That would be fine, but one of my partners suggested I consider (2)_____. I think my kids would like the idea of an island vacation.

AGENT: Yes, I think that would work. You could still drive, although it would be farther. But are you completely married to a beach vacation? You know, (3)_____ is a great summer destination (prices are lower and the celebs are gone), and so is nearby (4)_____. Both have excellent non-winter activities for kids.

341

YOU: Speaking of winter, one of my partners is taking a ski trip to Argentina this summer...which will be Argentine winter, of course.

AGENT: I hope he or she is going to (5)_____, or some other alternative to Bariloche, because that place is a mess, to put it kindly.

YOU: Speaking of messes, if we want to avoid one, we should probably plan my family Christmas trip today as well.

AGENT: Great idea! Places are starting to book up fast—especially (6)_____. There are only so many hotel rooms on that tiny island, and we'd have to book now to get you something over the water.

YOU: I was actually thinking more along the lines of a beach with some history and some interesting architecture, since we've enjoyed (7)_____ so much the past few years. I'd also like to spend a little less money than we have in previous years.

AGENT: I guess that rules out any of the French Caribbean islands, especially (8)_____. Are you set on a Christmas beach trip? What about a European winter resort?

I suppose (9)_____ would be out if you want to keep costs down, but I could find you a nice hotel in the Courchevel area—not in (10)_____, but in one of the other villages—that wouldn't break the bank.

ANSWERS: (1) the Hamptons; (2) Martha's Vineyard; (3) Aspen; (4) Vail; (5) San Martín de los Andes; (6) Bora Bora; (7) Cartagena; (8) Saint-Barthélemy or one of its nicknames; (9) St. Moritz; (10) Courchevel 1850

VII. TRUE OR FALSE

Now let's play the following true-or-false game:

(T/F) 1. Residents of *Martha's Vineyard* are referred to as "East End society."

(T/F)   2. *St. Moritz* features a dormant volcano.

(T/F)   3. Some members of the *jet set* have abandoned Bariloche for *San Martín de los Andes*.

(T/F)   4. Rich Russians seem to like *Courchevel 1850*.

(T/F)   5. Those who vacation in *the Hamptons* tend to be from the Northeastern U.S.

(T/F)   6. The old money on *Saint-Barthélemy* keeps the island from becoming a *nouveau-riche* nightmare.

(T/F)   7. *Bora Bora* has been ruined by overdevelopment.

(T/F)   8. Those who dislike glitz and conspicuous spending generally prefer *Vail* to *Aspen*.

(T/F)   9. With a private plane, it's easy to ski *San Martín de los Andes* and *Aspen* in the same week.

(T/F) 10. *Cartagena* is a village in *the Hamptons*.

ANSWERS: All true except (1), (2), (7), (9) and (10). Number (9) is false because *Aspen* and *San Martín* don't have snow at the same time of year—they're on opposite sides of the equator.

VIII. COMPLETE THE STORY

Time to check in with Giselle and Marco.

Use the exclusive destinations from this chapter to fill the blanks in the following passage. Each destination is used once.

The Expensive Escapades of
MARCO & GISELLE
Professional Beautiful People

Episode Fifteen: Fireworks in French Ski Country

Bora Bora	**St. Moritz**
Cartagena	**Courchevel 1850**
Saint-Barthélemy	**Aspen**
the Hamptons	**Vail**
Martha's Vineyard	**San Martín de los Andes**

If you'll remember, in our last episode, Marco and Giselle run into a woman named Helga (one of Marco's ex-girlfriends) in *St. Moritz*. The encounter makes Giselle insanely jealous.

In this episode, our heroine decides to get back at Marco by hiring one of her ex-boyfriends to "show up" in a certain village of Les Trois Vallées ski area, where she and Marco have met for a romantic dinner.

Giselle's plan backfires, however, when another of Marco's ex-girlfriends appears out of nowhere.

Get ready for pyrotechnics!

MARCO: This is absolutely my favorite restaurant here in (1)_____. The Russian hordes are annoying, but the view of the snow-covered slopes is to die for.

GISELLE: Yes, it is lovely. And even lovelier knowing that a certain person is far away in a certain Swiss winter resort— namely, (2)_____—and will not, therefore, be dropping in on us tonight.

MARCO: Giselle, I have told you, I feel nothing for Helga. You have nothing to be jealous about.

(Just then, a tall, handsome young man walks past their table. Giselle turns away and covers her face with her napkin.)

MARCO: What is wrong, *mi amor?* Who is that young man?

GISELLE: No one. No one at all.

MARCO: Why, then, are you hiding from him?

GISELLE: Hiding? Who, *me?* I'm not hiding from anyone. Maybe we should leave. I've suddenly lost my appetite.

MARCO: But we just ordered dinner.

GISELLE: It doesn't matter. Let's get on your plane and go far away—how about Argentina? We could have this same dinner with the same snowy view in a restaurant overlooking the slopes outside (3)_____. I've heard it's lovely.

MARCO: It is, but it is summer there right now, so there is no snow.

(The mysterious young man returns and approaches Giselle.)

YOUNG MAN: *Giselle?* Could that possibly be your angelic face behind that napkin?

GISELLE: *(revealing only part of her lovely face)* Duncan, I don't know how much more clear I can be. When I broke off our engagement, I said I never wanted to see you again, and I meant it. I'm sure there's a nice girl out there for you on some ski slope *somewhere*—perhaps in Colorado? Maybe you could find a Hollywood starlet in (4)_____ or a stockbroker-on-skis in (5)_____. But please stop chasing me around the world. You're humiliating yourself! I'll never recover from the scene you made in (6)_____, where you crashed my sister's birthday party in Sag Harbor and caused such a disturbance.

DUNCAN: Giselle, my love—if I may still call you *my love*—I can't help it. Since you broke my heart, I've been nothing but a shell of my former self. I find no happiness in anything. I was just in (7)_____, which was once my favorite place on earth (as you know, my house there is set over the pristine water with a lovely view of the volcano), but the fact it was to be the location of our honeymoon has turned it into a dark and dreary wasteland for me.

GISELLE: Duncan, please sell that place and buy a villa on (8)_____! There's no volcano, but the climate is similar, they speak French, and I happen to know there are many eligible young women there just waiting for a handsome, rich, and intelligent young man like you to arrive. Be off with you—and no, you may not continue to call me *your love*.

DUNCAN: Though it kills me, your wish is my command. But before I go, tell me where to find this polo-playing perpetrator of grand theft heiress, who now calls you *his* love, and who has deprived me of all happiness in this life and the next. I challenge him to a duel, here and now!

MARCO: *(rising) I* am Marco, and I accept your challenge. But our duel will be fought on the polo field. *En garde!*

DUNCAN: *(feigning shock)* You? Marco? Forgive me, I took you for a bodyguard.

MARCO: A *bodyguard?*

(Suddenly, out of nowhere, a beautiful and exotic young woman approaches the table and throws her arms around Marco.)

BEAUTIFUL AND EXOTIC YOUNG WOMAN: Marco! I have not seen you since (9)_____, where we had an *alfresco* dinner in the delightful Plaza San Diego. Then you took me on a tour of the fort, with all those frightening tunnels, and you started talking like a pirate—

MARCO: I do not remember that...at least not the pirate part.

GISELLE: Marco, who *is* this?

BEAUTIFUL AND EXOTIC YOUNG WOMAN: I am Maria Luisa Mendoza, Marco's girlfriend until he dropped me—like a proverbial hot potato—for some American heiress he met in Italy. From what I hear, she's rather dull, and not even very pretty.

DUNCAN: My dear lady, I would beg you to take back the words you have just spoken! You have before you, with a napkin inexplicably hiding a visage of unequalled beauty, none other than the heiress herself, the incomparable Giselle Van de Kamp!

MARIA LUISA: *(with a look of disdain)* You? Giselle? I see the rumors were correct! From what I can see of your face, you are not exactly beauty queen material.

DUNCAN: Retract your cruel words at once, dear lady! They are as false as your eyelash extensions and your faux Louis Vuitton tote! I'll have you know that Giselle is well known for her beauty in the state of Massachussetts, where she was crowned Miss (10)_____ one summer by former President Barack Obama himself!

And there we must leave our story—for now. Hard to put down, isn't it? Go ahead and check your answers.

ANSWERS: (1) Courchevel 1850; (2) St. Moritz; (3) San Martín de los Andes; (4) Aspen; (5) Vail; (6) the Hamptons; (7) Bora Bora; (8) Saint-Barthélemy or one of its nicknames; (9) Cartagena; (10) Martha's Vineyard

All tuckered out from our journeys?

Just want to stay home for awhile, you say?

Not an option!

Rest up, because tomorrow we return to France for our very last installment of French snob words. (Phew!)

Day 28

My *Bête Noire* is an *Enfant Terrible*
FINAL FRENCH SNOB WORDS

LOCATION: **BIARRITZ, FRANCE**

You may think I'm running out of snobby places to hold our lessons, but worry not—I still have a few great locations up my sleeve.

Today we'll be in **Biarritz**, France, the former fishing village on the **Côte Basque** (Basque Coast) that transformed itself into one of the world's most exclusive resorts during the 19th century. In contrast to most of the other European seaside resorts we've visited, Biarritz became famous as a summer, not a winter, resort.

Eugénie de Montijo (1826-1920), the future empress of France, fell in love with Biarritz while vacationing here as a child. After she married **Emperor Napoleon III** (1808-73), she convinced him to visit her old summer stomping grounds. He was so smitten that he authorized the building of an immense summer palace directly on the turbulent and breathtaking **Bay of Biscay**.

The palace is now the **Hôtel du Palais**, and we'll have lunch here on a terrace overlooking the wide, sandy beach.

As we enjoy local specialties such as *la poitrine de pigeon, rôtie à la broche* (roast pigeon breast) and *le gigot d'agneau de lait des pyrénées à la rôtissoire* (roasted leg of suckling lamb from the nearby Pyrenees), we'll take a first look at this lesson's snob words.

Today we present an assortment—a *potpourri*, if you will—of Gallic words and phrases with no particular connection to each other except that they're useful and snobworthy.

I. PRONOUNCE & DEFINE

1. **mot juste** (moh ZHOOST´)
2. **bon mot** (bone MOH´)
3. **pièce de résistance** (pee-ESS´ duh ray-see-STAHNCE´)
4. **élan** (ay-LAHN´)
5. **éminence grise** (ay-mee-nahnce-GREEZ´)

PLURALS: *mots justes, bons mots, pièces de résistance,* and *éminences grises,* all pronounced the same as their singular forms. The term *élan* has no plural.

Now consider the words in sentences that hint at their definitions:

1. As he writes his novels, Barnaby searches for the *mot juste*, the perfect word to express exactly what he means.
2. Donald seemed to have a droll *bon mot* for every occasion, which led to his reputation as an excellent conversationalist.
3. The meal's *pièce de résistance* was a five-layer chocolate torte. It was covered in almonds and served with raspberry sauce.
4. Toby's *élan* is contagious. He can bring energy and enthusiasm to even the dullest projects.

5. Professor Harper, the *éminence grise* of World War II historians, has written twenty books on subjects that range from Hitler to Hirohito.

II. FILL IN THE BLANKS

Enjoying your meal? Save room for dessert, which will be **gâteau basque**, a regional treat consisting of buttery pastry filled with jam made from local black cherries.

These cherries come from nearby **Itxassou**, a charming and typical Pyrenees village of white-washed houses with contrasting oxblood doors and shutters.

As we finish our lunch, fill each blank below with the snob word that best matches the given definition.

mot juste	bon mot
pièce de résistance	élan
éminence grise	

1. _____ a respected authority
2. _____ energy; enthusiasm
3. _____ a clever or witty remark
4. _____ the perfect word or phrase
5. _____ the most outstanding item or event within a group or series

ANSWERS: (1) éminence grise; (2) élan; (3) bon mot; (4) mot juste; (5) pièce de résistance

NOTE: while *éminence grise* most often refers to a respected authority, it can also refer to those who have influence over decision-makers without holding official positions.

- Civil servants are the ones who really have the power—they are the *éminences grises* behind the government ministers.

III. PRONOUNCE & DEFINE

Now that we've gorged ourselves, let's take a little walk around town to work off some calories.

Biarritz is not as elegant today as it was when the Empress Eugénie was in residence. For one thing, surfers have taken over the **Grande Plage**, the city's principal beach, alongside which the Empress and her retinue used to promenade.

But the town retains a regal vibe. In addition to the stately presence of the Hôtel du Palais, which dominates the beach and the burg, the gilt domes of the **Eglise Orthodoxe**, built so the Russian nobles who once summered here would have a place to worship, still shine as they did at their 1892 debut.

And **Place Sainte-Eugénie**, surrounded by shops and cafés in Belle-Epoque buildings—with an iron bandstand at its center—still functions as the town's elegant living room.

As we continue our walk, here are five more French snob words to pronounce:

6. **soirée** (swah-RAY´)
7. **bête noire** (bet´ NWAHR´)
8. **enfant terrible** (own-fahn teh-REE´-bluh)
9. **louche** (loosh)
10. **frisson** (free-SOHN´)

PLURALS: *soirées, bêtes noires, enfants terribles, frissons,* all pronounced the same as the singular. *Louche,* being an adjective, has no plural form when used in English.

Again, try to guess at the definitions of these words from their use in the following sentences:

1. I thought the reception was an afternoon affair, rather than a *soirée.* Otherwise, I would have canceled my evening plans and gone with you.

2. Natasha fired me, turned all my friends against me, vilified me on Facebook, and lit my house on fire. She is truly my *bête noire.*

3. Juan is the *enfant terrible* of the theater department: he's one of the youngest actors, extremely talented, but prone to throw fits, to show up late, and to improvise during performances.

4. Before gentrification set in, this neighborhood was *louche,* full of all-night bars frequented by actors, dancers, and other theater types.

5. When the votes were tallied, and Jones came out on top, a *frisson* of excitement swept through his supporters, who hadn't expected him to win.

IV. FILL IN THE BLANKS

Let's continue to explore Biarritz by taking a walk to the **Rocher de la Vierge** (Rock of the Virgin), a stony islet off the coast topped by a statue of the Virgin Mary.

We'll reach the islet via a graceful footbridge designed by **Gustave Eiffel** (1832-1923), of Eiffel Tower fame.

As we walk, notice the rough surf crashing on both sides of the bridge.

These tempestuous waters are the reason Biarritz is the hub of French surf culture, and why this particular section of the Côte Basque is known as the **Côte d'Argent**, or Silver Coast. (All the water in the air from the breaking waves looks silver in the sunlight.)

While we rest a moment, and enjoy the view of the town from the rock, match the snob words below with their definitions on the following page:

soirée   louche
bête noire   frisson
enfant terrible

1. _____ disreputable, often in an alluring way
2. _____ literally, 'terrible child;' a successful
person (usually young) prone to
shocking remarks and outrageous
behavior
3. _____ literally, 'black beast;' something or
someone strongly feared or disliked
4. _____ a sudden strong feeling of emotion
5. _____ an event held in the evening, often
outdoors

ANSWERS: (1) louche; (2) enfant terrible; (3) bête noire; (4) frisson; (5) soirée

V. SENSE...OR NONSENSE?

While officially belonging to France, Biarritz is also part of what is known as **Basque Country**, an area a little smaller than Rhode Island that straddles the Franco-Spanish border from the Pyrenees to the Bay of Biscay.

The Basques, an ancient people whose language isn't related to any other European language, have been a distinct ethnic group for millennia, but they've often been dominated by other kingdoms, countries, and empires.

Today Basque Country is divided between France (whose portion is called **Pays Basque)** and Spain (**País Vasco**). Though the area does enjoy some degree of autonomy, some Basques would like to see a completely independent Basque nation.

Be that as it may, the Basques work hard to keep their cultural traditions alive, and many of these are culinary. I know we finished lunch not long ago, but could you use a snack?

Let's head to the **Port des Pêcheurs**, the old fishing port, where we'll sample Bayonne ham, the Pays Basque version of *prosciutto*, and **pipérade**, a typical French Basque relish made of sautéed tomatoes, green peppers, and onions. The relish is seasoned with **Espelette pepper**, a special red powder vital to

Basque cuisine. It's made from a midly hot member of the capsicum family grown in the nearby town of Espelette.

As we dine, place a check beside each sentence below that makes sense.

____ 1. Greta had an appropriate *bon mot* for every situation.

____ 2. John always goes against whatever the rest of our group wants to do. He's a real *pièce de resistance.*

____ 3. My mother-in-law is my *soirée*—she drives me crazy with her meddling and her sarcastic comments.

____ 4. Rodrigo has a reputation as an *enfant terrible.* He's a successful young entrepreneur, but he says and does incredibly shocking things.

____ 5. If you find yourself at a dull party, it's always a good idea to drop a *mot juste.*

____ 6. Roger is the *élan* of San Francisco chefs.

____ 7. The principal of my daughter's school is truly my *bête noire.*

____ 8. I was surprised at the high rents because the area was rather *louche.*

____ 9. As Emily delivered the commencement speech, a *frisson* of emotion passed through me. How did my little girl grow up so quickly?

____ 10. Jane is always happy, always lively, always full of *éminence grise.*

ANSWERS: numbers (1), (4), (7), (8), and (9) should be checked.

VI. PLANNING A PARTY

Did you enjoy the pipérade? I knew you would.

But back to our Biarritz history.

Once the summer palace was finished in 1855, the imperial family spent most summers here until 1870. During that time, Biarritz became an international social hotspot due to visits from members of many European royal families, including those of Spain, Portugal, Belgium, and Bavaria.

To entertain these visitors, Napoleon and Eugénie hosted a steady stream of lavish entertainments, including balls, receptions, and fireworks displays.

Speaking of elegant social events, it's time to plan your annual Christmas fête!

The following is a fragment of a conversation you have with a professional party planner to help you pull off your most important social event of the year.

Fill the blanks below with snob words from this lesson. Each word is used only once, so choose the **best** answer, although more than one word may apply.

Use plurals where appropriate.

soirée	pièce de résistance
bête noire	frisson
enfant terrible	louche
mot juste	bon mot
éminence grise	élan

PARTY PLANNER: What type of event do you have in mind?

YOU: Well, since we always have the party at night, and since I insist on using our very large terrace, it will obviously be a (1)_____. And I don't like my parties to be dull—my guests have come to expect a certain degree of (2)_____ over the years, and I can't let them down now.

PARTY PLANNER: Do you have a theme in mind?

YOU: Not a theme, per se, but the (3)_____ of the evening must be an elaborate dessert, a magical entertainment, or something else so amazing that it causes a collective (4)_____ when it's revealed.

PARTY PLANNER: Okay, I've got you. And what about the guest list? What type of people do you expect to invite?

YOU: All types. My in-laws, of course, although they tend to be a bit (5)_____. They're an interesting and attractive couple, but they often make the other guests uncomfortable with their vulgar comments.

Then there's our cardiologist, Dr. Harrison. He's the undisputed (6)_____ of the cardiology department at NYU—very serious in his work—but he's the life of the party, literally dripping with (7) _____.

And we can't forget our daughter's boyfriend, Alexandre, the (8)_____ of the piano program at Juilliard. He'll insist on sitting down at the Steinway for awhile, but there's no sense asking exactly *what* or *when* he'll play.

He'll do as he likes, and it will probably be outrageous, like the time he invited a friend in a Santa suit to dance while he played a medley of Hanukkah songs.

PARTY PLANNER: That's rather bizarre. Is your daughter serious about this young man?

YOU: Yes, very serious, but don't get me wrong. I do like Alexandre—he's certainly not my (9)_____. He's just a little bit...what's the (10)_____? *Original*, I guess you'd say.

ANSWERS: (1) soirée; (2) élan; (3) pièce de résistance; (4) frisson; (5) louche; (6) éminence grise; (7) bons mots; (8) enfant terrible; (9) bête noire; (10) mot juste

VII. REALITY CHECK

We've been so busy that we haven't yet checked into my house, a three-story, Basque-style *aerie* on a cliff overlooking the surf at **Guéthary**, a village seven miles down the coast from Biarritz.

The beaches around Guéthary have some of the roughest waves in France, so, like Biarritz, the village is popular with the surf crowd. Shall we put on our wetsuits and join them?

Another time, you say?

All right, we'll watch the surf action from my terrace as we sample **p'tit basque**, a local artisanal cheese with a nutty, earthy flavor. Made from the milk of sheep that graze the highland pastures here in French Basque country, it's wonderful with a loaf of crusty bread and grilled vegetables, which Geneviève, my housekeeper, is preparing right now.

As we snack, let's look at how our snob words are used in the media. The following passages and headlines are taken from national and international publications and websites. Fill each blank with a word from this lesson. Each word is used once; alter words as necessary to fit context.

soirée	pièce de résistance
bête noire	frisson
enfant terrible	louche
mot juste	bon mot
éminence grise	élan

1. *GQ,* "Replace All Your Ugly Tech Accessories with These Beautiful Cords and Chargers," Oct. 2017:

   And the _____ are Native Union's marble charger docks that turn your desk into something more like a miniature MOMA exhibit and less like a Staples clearance table.

2. *New York Times,* "Remainder Night at the Convention," July 2016:

   The violent incidents at his rallies, he told me once, didn't worry him. He felt it added a _____ of excitement to the proceedings.

3. *New York Times,* "What to Expect on the Last Day of New York Fashion Week," Feb. 2015:

Ralph Lauren, New York's _____ in sneakers, shows his women's collection first, at 10 a.m.

4. *Wall Street Journal,* headline, July 2016:

   Casual Summer _____ Stand Out
   Often the most memorable Hamptons parties
   are casual and slightly impromptu

5. *Boston Globe*, "Johnny Depp is scary good as 'Whitey' in 'Black Mass,'" Sept. 2015:

   …but his performance here is contained and focused, lacking in the _____ decadence of recent parts.

6. *New York Times*, "Germany, Caught Between Two Violent Extremes," July 2016:

   …the fear of terrorism isn't limited to the possible attacks themselves; it is about what our _____, the German far right, will do with it.

7. *London Times*, "John Cleese is now about as witty as a dead parrot," Oct. 2016:

   Cleese posted a message on Twitter that must have seemed like a piercing _____ at the time: "Why do we let half-educated tenement Scots run our English press?"

8. *Los Angeles Times,* "Click here for actual journalism," Mar. 2016:

   Facebook uses small gray print to say, ambiguously, "sponsored." Twitter's _____ is "promoted."

9. *Vanityfair.com,* headline, Mar. 2016:

**Famous _____ Peter Brant Jr. Arrested
After Alleged Drunken Airport Tantrum**

> The fashionable heir was arrested at the
> airport for being drunk and belligerent.

10. *New York Times,* headline, June 2016:

Youthful _____ Mixed With Veteran Savvy

ANSWERS: (1) pièces de résistance; (2) frisson; (3) éminence grise; (4) soirées; (5) louche; (6) bête noire; (7) bon mot; (8) mot juste; (9) enfant terrible; (10) élan

How did you do with these real-life uses of our snob words? I keep telling you they're practical.

Enjoying your grilled vegetables? How about this view?

We must soon bid *adieu* to the Biarritz area, but before we go, let's review some plurals.

VIII. FUN WITH PLURALS

Fill each blank below with the appropriate plural of one of today's words.

Since two of our words don't have plurals, you will only use eight words total.

soirée	pièce de résistance
bête noire	frisson
enfant terrible	louche
mot juste	bon mot
éminence grise	élan

1. Sure, it's quite easy to dash off a quick Twitter tirade, but it's much more difficult to craft an op-ed with all the
_____.

2. The room was chock-full of witty, intelligent people, which meant the _____ were flowing nonstop.

3. Over the years, the shows at Jean-Claude's gallery have featured some amazing _____: one included a full-size monster truck as part of an installation; another featured live goats with trays of soft drinks strapped to their backs.

4. It was a rather dry conference. The _____ of global warming presented papers on decreasing rainfall rates.

5. I've been to some spectacular _____ in my day, but my niece's wedding reception, held on a giant raft off the island of *Saint-Barthélemy*, takes the cake.

6. We've all experienced _____ of joy, love, patriotism—unforgettable moments when we feel very strongly about something.

7. We never get much accomplished at our group therapy sessions. We simply go around the table and complain about our _____.

8. I'm acquainted with two _____. They're both young, brilliant, and outrageous, and they happen to be my brothers.

ANSWERS: (1) mots justes; (2) bons mots; (3) pièces de résistance; (4) éminences grises (5) soirées; (6) frissons; (7) bêtes noires; (8) enfants terribles

How about those plurals? A little tricky? Go back and study any you may have missed.

Then it's time to get to bed. Tomorrow we cross the Atlantic to review for our final exam.

Day 29

Final Snob Words Review
READY FOR THE DAY OF RECKONING?

LOCATION: **THE ADIRONDACKS, NEW YORK STATE**

Has a month actually passed since we began this journey together? Time truly does fly when you're having fun, but judgment day has arrived. You'll take your final snobcabulary exam tomorrow, and it will cover every snob word in this volume—all 250 of them (plus a few bonus words).

But we won't abandon you in your time of need. We've prepared a series of review games designed to reinforce the learning you've done over the past twenty-eight days. These consist of one invigorating exercise lifted from each past lesson that presented new words. (Don't be alarmed that Day 1, Day 10, and Day 20 are missing—these were days devoted to the course introduction and the two midterms.)

At any rate, please take the review seriously.

To help you concentrate, I'm going to give you free reign of my compound in the **Adirondacks**, that hoity-toity mountain range in upstate New York where the Northeastern upper classes go to get back to nature (albeit in multi-million-dollar "camps").

My place, a heavily wooded area on **Lower Saranac Lake**, dates to the 1920s. It was designed to accommodate more than a hundred guests in a great lodge surrounded by more than a dozen cabins, but you'll have it all to yourself. You'll find a private lake, tennis courts, a swimming pool, a private chef, and my favorite amenity...a croquet lawn. Enjoy!

After you finish and score the exercises, review any words you may have missed by going back to the appropriate lessons.

Day 2
PAINTING & DRAWING TERMS
MULTIPLE CHOICE

1. Monet's *atelier* in Giverny would have contained:
   (a) olive oil; (b) oil paint; (c) motor oil

2. Who used the *screen print* technique?
   (a) Pop artists (b) Impressionists (c) Byzantine monks

3. The *etching* process involves placing a metal plate in:
   (a) an offset press; (b) etching solution; (c) acid

4. If you're not sure of your painting's composition, and plan to experiment, you'd be wise to use:
   (a) *sfumato;* (b) *atelier;* (c) *gouache*

5. The *chiaroscuro* technique uses contrasting areas of:
   (a) light/shadow; (b) red/green; (c) matte/gloss

6. Artists who paint *en plein air* complete all, or at least most, of a painting:
   (a) on the plains; (b) outdoors; (c) in a helicopter

7. A painting executed between 1350 and 1800 (A.D.) is called a(n):
   (a) *chiaroscuro;* (b) *Old Master;* (c) *triptych*

8. Limestone was originally used to transfer an image in:
   (a) *lithography*; (b) *etching*; (c) *screen printing*

9. *Sfumato* comes from the Italian word for:
   (a) fumes; (b) smoke; (c) tomato

10. A painting consisting of three separate panels is a:
    (a) *triptych*; (b) *polyptych*; (c) *diptych*

ANSWERS: (1) b; (2) a; (3) c; (4) c; (5) a; (6) b; (7) b; (8) a; (9) b; (10) a

Day 3
FRANCOPHONE ADJECTIVES
TRUE OR FALSE

(T/F) 1. A *gauche* person shows a lack of concern for social norms.

(T/F) 2. A *chic* woman is stylish and confident.

(T/F) 3. Paying one's income tax is *de rigueur*.

(T/F) 4. If something is *de trop*, you want more of it.

(T/F) 5. A person who is *au courant* has his or her head in the sand.

(T/F) 6. In order to look *soigné*, a man should be neatly groomed and appropriately dressed.

(T/F) 7. A restaurant that tries too hard to be elegant runs the risk of becoming *chichi*.

(T/F) 8. If something is *comme il faut*, it is probably unethical and possibly illegal.

(T/F) 9. An *outré* idea is appropriate and conventional.

(T/F) 10. Restaurants with three Michelin stars likely employ chefs *par excellence*.

ANSWERS: all true except (4), (5), (8), and (9).

Day 4
DESIGN FRENCH

MATCHING

____ 1. *boiserie*   a. small object with artistic merit
____ 2. *étagère*   b. light armchair with open arms
____ 3. *objet d'art*   c. wide armchair with closed arms
____ 4. *bergère*   d. fine wood paneling
____ 5. *fauteuil*   e. set of open shelves
____ 6. *chaise longue*   f. long chair
____ 7. *chinoiserie*   g. 'old rule'
____ 8. *passementerie*   h. decorative fringe and tassels
____ 9. *trompe l'oeil*   i. furniture and other decoration
                                in the Chinese style
____ 10. *ancien régime*   j. 'trick the eye'

ANSWERS: (1) d; (2) e; (3) a; (4) c; (5) b (6) f; (7) i; (8) h; (9) j (10) g

Day 5
THE LOWDOWN ON HIGH FASHION

MULTIPLE CHOICE

1. *Women's Wear Daily* is:
   a. issued in print weekly, with daily online updates
   b. the most influential publication in women's fashion
   c. both of the above
2. A *couturier* is a(n):
   a. *haute couture* sample used for photo shoots
   b. male dressmaker or designer of women's clothing
   c. expert on the history of *haute couture*
3. *Prêt-à-porter* clothing is:
   a. made to order
   b. ready to wear
   c. ready to order

4. *Coco Chanel* was:
    a. a famous style icon
    b. a famous *couturière*
    c. both of the above

5. Which of the following cities is **not** a member of *fashion's Big Four*?
    a. Milan
    b. Berlin
    c. London

6. The term *fashionista* refers to:
    a. fascists who like fashion
    b. designers, promoters, journalists, and anyone else who is really into fashion
    c. Latin American fashion designers

7. Another term for 'latest fashion' is:
    a. *dernier cri*
    b. *demi crie*
    c. *haute couture*

8. High-priced women's clothing made to order by top designers is called:
    a. *haute cuisine*
    b. *haute couture*
    c. *haute couturier*

9. The best way to describe an ensemble that is stylish, yet classic and understated is:
    a. *prêt-à-porter*
    b. *bon chic, bon genre*
    c. *dernier cri*

10. *Fashion week* is not just one week, but rather:
    a. at least ten official "Fashion Weeks" held each year in *Big Four* cities
    b. two weeks: one in New York and one in Paris
    c. five weeks: one each in New York, Paris, London, Milan, and Tokyo

ANSWERS: (1) c; (2) b; (3) b; (4) c; (5) b; (6) b; (7) a; (8) b; (9) b; (10) a

Day 6
FOODIE UNIVERSITY

SENSE...OR NONSENSE?

Check each sentence that makes sense.

____ 1. As an exchange student in Paris, my host family always wished me *"bon appétit!"* before going to bed.

____ 2. As an *epicure*, I take great pleasure in quality food.

____ 3. My mother's a *locavore*, since she'll only eat food produced in the United States and Canada.

____ 4. I truly dislike *cuisine classique*. With my lactose intolerance, I can't handle the cream.

____ 5. I consider myself a *gastronome:* I'll eat anything.

____ 6. Some days, when I have no food in the house, I *forage* in the botanical gardens down the street.

____ 7. Some adherents of *nouvelle cuisine* have a fear of overcooking vegetables.

____ 8. I enjoy various types of *haute cuisine,* including fast food.

____ 9. I'm thinking of opening a *gourmand* restaurant for people with highly discriminating palates.

____ 10. Joan is a true *gourmet:* she loves to cook, loves to eat, and knows a lot about food and its preparation.

____ 11. I love pasta, but it has to be cooked *al dente*.

ANSWERS: numbers (2), (4), (6), (7), (10) and (11) should be checked.

Day 7
THE SOUNDS OF CLASSICAL MUSIC

FILL IN THE BLANKS

Fill each blank with one of the following words:

opus	chamber music
tessitura	aria
staccato	sonata
oratorio	cantata
pizzicato	concerto

1. _____ range of a piece of music or musical role, from lowest to highest note

2. _____ composition performed by one or more solo instruments accompanied by full orchestra

3. _____ Latin term used to number musical compositions

4. _____ music meant to be performed in private rooms by a small number of musicians

5. _____ musical direction to play a note in a detached, choppy manner

6. _____ long narrative musical work for soloists, chorus, and orchestra, usually based on the Bible

7. _____ composition with three or four distinct sections, written for one or more musical instruments

8. _____ sacred or secular multi-movement work for one or more voices and accompaniment

9. _____ melodic composition for single voice, with or without accompaniment

10. _____ technique of plucking a stringed instrument

ANSWERS: (1) tessitura; (2) concerto; (3) opus; (4) chamber music; (5) staccato (6) oratorio; (7) sonata; (8) cantata; (9) aria; (10) pizzicato

Day 8
ARCHITECTURAL SNOB TERMS
SENSE...OR NONSENSE?

Check each sentence that makes sense.

___ 1. This morning I had breakfast on the *colonnade* while admiring the sunrise.

___ 2. My architect told me I can't remove the *pilasters* because they're structural.

___ 3. The only thing I dislike about our *portico* is its lack of a roof.

___ 4. I refuse to go ahead with the *entablature* until I've had time to study some authentic Greek models.

___ 5. When I heard the gunman was loose, I quickly locked the *porte-cochère*.

___ 6. Having dinner on the *loggia* was a nice idea, but the cold November rain made it a miserable experience.

___ 7. We need a small, inconspicuous opening to let some light into the bathroom—maybe a *Palladian window* would do the trick.

___ 8. I wish you'd stop calling the *veranda* a 'lanai.' You do realize we're living in Siberia.

___ 9. The effect of the *enfilade* was ruined because Andrew refused to leave the doors open.

___10. I'd like to put some hanging ferns on my *veranda*, but it would be too much trouble to take them to the second floor.

ANSWERS: numbers (2), (4), (5), (6), (8), and (9) should be checked—the other sentences are nonsense.

Day 9
TERMS FOR WEALTH & RENOWN

TRUE OR FALSE

(T/F) 1. A person who is rich, fashionable, and of high social pedigree belongs to the *beau monde.*

(T/F) 2. A *nouveau riche* generally comes from generations of family money.

(T/F) 3. Members of the *glitterati* always wear shiny, showy clothing.

(T/F) 4. An *arriviste* is someone who has 'arrived,' or made it to the top.

(T/F) 5. Members of the *haute bourgeoisie* are just below the upper class on the social scale.

(T/F) 6. Businesses that cater to the *carriage trade* sell wheels, axles, hay, and oats.

(T/F) 7. You can find the *jet set* at the world's most exclusive resorts.

(T/F) 8. To be counted among the *beautiful people*, one must be a movie star or a fashion model.

(T/F) 9. The daughter of a village baker could be described as a *scion.*

(T/F) 10. A duke could demonstrate *noblesse oblige* by donating his estate gardens to the city for use as a public park.

ANSWERS: all false except (1), (5), (7), and (10).

Day II
GALLICISMS FOR MANNERS & BEHAVIOR

MATCHING

___ 1. *flâneur*	a. 'between the two of us'
___ 2. *entre nous*	b. person of refined taste who enjoys parties and good food
___ 3. *bon vivant*	c. zest for life
___ 4. *joie de vivre*	d. brief, but embarrassing situation
___ 5. *mauvais quart d'heure*	e. man who wanders about town
___ 6. *bonhomie*	f. false step; social mistake
___ 7. *savoir faire*	g. exchange of good-natured insults
___ 8. *repartee*	h. clever conversation
___ 9. *badinage*	i. knowledge of what to do in any social situation
___10. *faux pas*	j. easy friendliness; geniality

ANSWERS: (1) e; (2) a; (3) b; (4) c; (5) d; (6) j; (7) i; (8) h; (9) g; (10) f

Day 12
HELLO HAUTE HORTICULTURE

SENSE...OR NONSENSE?

Put a check beside each sentence that makes sense.

____ 1. We plan to hold the receiving line in the *treillage*.

____ 2. I picked lemons from the *espaliers* this morning.

____ 3. The *pergola* has a great view of the stars.

____ 4. Ellen keeps her orchid collection in the *orangerie*.

____ 5. Of course it was a *folly!* That ruined temple cost a fortune!

____ 6. I love the *grotto*—it's full of light and fresh air.

_____ 7. The *tapis vert* needs water. It's looking dry.
_____ 8. I like to sit and admire the flowers on the *allée*.
_____ 9. You can't call it a *belvedere*. There's no view!
_____ 10. The boys often played soccer on the *parterre*.

ANSWERS: numbers (2), (4), (5), (7), and (9) should be checked.

Day 13
EXCLUSIVE REAL ESTATE

MULTIPLE CHOICE

1. A large, symmetrical home in Tuscany with spacious rooms and high ceilings is a:
   a. *casa colonica*
   b. *Tuscan villa*
   c. *Tuscan farmhouse*

2. A Provençal house originally built for aristocrats is a:
   a. *mas*
   b. *bastide*
   c. *Provençal farmhouse*

3. An apartment made up of two stories is a:
   a. *bipartment*
   b. *double-decker*
   c. *duplex*

4. A *loft*-style apartment in a **new** building is called a:
   a. *hard loft*
   b. *soft loft*
   c. *loft for softies*

5. A *prewar apartment* has:
   a. generous rooms
   b. high ceilings
   c. both of the above

6. The most sought-after *brownstones* have:
    a. ornate 19th-century details
    b. ground-floor kitchens
    c. garden ornaments
7. The literal meaning of *pied-à-terre* is:
    a. 'foot in the air'
    b. 'foot to the ground'
    c. 'house on potato farm'
8. *Co-ops* are known to:
    a. have elaborate roof gardens
    b. be picky in admitting new members
    c. shun non-Bohemian types
9. You would **not** find an *hôtel particulier* in:
    a. Paris
    b. Madrid
    c. Bordeaux
10. Which is **not** an example of an *aerie?*
    a. a garden apartment in New Jersey
    b. a mansion in the hills overlooking Los Angeles
    c. a Manhattan penthouse

ANSWERS: (1) b; (2) b; (3) c; (4) b; (5) c; (6) a; (7) b; (8) b; (9) b; (10) a

Day 14
SNOB SPORTS & LEISURE ACTIVITIES

MULTIPLE CHOICE

1. Skiing *off-piste* means skiing:
    a. in the backcountry
    b. off-kilter
    c. off a runway
2. In *dressage,* a horse and rider must show off:
    a. fancy wardrobes
    b. elaborate and difficult movements
    c. quick costume-change skills

3. The term *ski-in, ski-out:*
   - a. always means you can ski directly to your door
   - b. has several meanings
   - c. always means a valet service will drop off your ski equipment at the lift
4. *Piste* is a fancy French word for:
   - a. a post-skiing party
   - b. high-quality snow
   - c. a ski slope, run, or trail
5. *Badminton* was originally:
   - a. played in bad parts of London
   - b. played on a tennis court
   - c. an indoor game
6. *Après-ski* does **not** usually include:
   - a. dining
   - b. scrapbooking
   - c. shopping
7. *Polo* ponies are:
   - a. full-sized horses
   - b. always Thoroughbreds
   - c. Shetland ponies
8. The metal hoops in *croquet* are called:
   - a. crickets
   - b. briquettes
   - c. wickets
9. To win a *cricket* match, a team must:
   - a. knock the bail off the wicket
   - b. score more runs than the opposing team
   - c. stump the pitch
10. A *steeplechase:*
   - a. is held in a churchyard
   - b. requires horse and rider to jump obstacles
   - c. is so named because horses and riders were originally required to jump over steeples

ANSWERS: (1) a; (2) b; (3) b; (4) c; (5) c; (6) b; (7) a; (8) c; (9) b; (10) b

Day 15
PERFORMING ARTS TERMS

MULTIPLE CHOICE

1. A dance by two performers is a(n):
   a. *en pointe*
   b. *pas de deux*
   c. *intermezzo*
2. The *West End* is:
   a. home to London's theater district
   b. Milan's fashion district
   c. Manhattan's high-end shopping district
3. *Bel canto* is:
   a. a type of Italian cheese
   b. a bell choir
   c. a sweet style of singing
4. When ballet dancers perform on the tips of their toes, they are said to be:
   a. *bel canto*
   b. *en pointe*
   c. *en garde*
5. The correct form of *bravo* to use when showing appreciation for the efforts of a group of females is:
   a. *bravi*
   b. *brava*
   c. *brave*
6. The *Stanislavsky method* encourages actors to:
   a. use past emotions to make their acting more believable
   b. forget the past and focus on the present
   c. live in the moment
7. A performer with extreme technical skill is a:
   a. *bravo*
   b. *bel canto*
   c. *virtuoso*

8. *Opera buffa* is opera that is:
   a. boring
   b. light and humorous
   c. serious and tragic

9. The term *libretto* refers to:
   a. comic opera
   b. a short entertainment between the acts of a play or an opera
   c. the text of an opera or other musical production

10. The correct plural of *intermezzo* is:
   a. *intermezzos*
   b. *intermezzi*
   c. *intermezzoes*

ANSWERS: (1) b; (2) a; (3) c; (4) b; (5) c; (6) a; (7) c; (8) b; (9) c; (10) b

Day 16
LATIN WORDS & PHRASES

MATCHING

____ 1. *ad nauseam*   a. in place

____ 2. *gravitas*   b. excessive to the point of nausea

____ 3. *pro bono*   c. something in exchange for something else

____ 4. *in situ*   d. in reality; actually

____ 5. *quid pro quo*   e. without limit or end

____ 6. *ad infinitum*   f. a rarity

____ 7. *ad hoc*   g. an unwelcome person

____ 8. *de facto*   h. for a particular purpose

____ 9. *rara avis*   i. for the public good; without charge

____ 10. *persona non grata*   j. seriousness in bearing and manner

ANSWERS: (1) b; (2) j; (3) i; (4) a; (5) c; (6) e; (7) h; (8) d; (9) f; (10) g

377

Day 17
ESTEEMED EDIBLES

MATCHING

___ 1. *haricots verts*	a.	strawberries from the woods
___ 2. *Wagyu*	b.	top-quality Spanish ham
___ 3. *petits pois*	c.	world's most expensive food
___ 4. *truffles*	d.	cheese made of buffalo milk
___ 5. *fraises des bois*	e.	tiny and tender green beans
___ 6. *prosciutto*	f.	livers of force-fed ducks and geese
___ 7. *jamón ibérico*	g.	meat from Japanese cows
___ 8. *crème fraîche*	h.	fermented, thickened French cream
___ 9. *mozzarella di bufala*	i.	small peas
___ 10. *foie gras*	j.	Italian dry-cured ham

ANSWERS: (1) e; (2) g; (3) i; (4) c; (5) a; (6) j; (7) b; (8) h; (9) d; (10) f

Day 18
MORE INTERIOR DESIGN

MATCHING

___ 1. *parquet de Versailles*	a.	process in which glass is painted on its reverse side
___ 2. *marquetry*	b.	elegant wall treatment obtained through the application of multiple coats of plaster
___ 3. *verre églomisé*	c.	printed cotton fabric used for upholstery and draperies

___	4. *chintz*	d.	wooden flooring with a distinct diagonal pattern
___	5. *shagreen*	e.	non-geometric mosaic veneer of different woods or other materials
___	6. *boulle*	f.	green material made of horse, mule, shark, or ray skin
___	7. *faux marbre*	g.	gilt bronze
___	8. *Venetian plaster*	h.	type of marquetry, usually executed in brass and tortoiseshell
___	9. *ormolu*	i.	rare and expensive wallpaper
___	10. *papier peint*	j.	painted to resemble marble

ANSWERS: (1) d; (2) e; (3) a; (4) c; (5) f; (6) h; (7) j; (8) b; (9) g; (10) i

Day 19
ITALIAN WORDS & PHRASES

TRUE OR FALSE

(T/F)   1. A person who seems to put a great deal of effort into his or her dress, and succeeds in always looking elegant, exhibits *sprezzatura*.

(T/F)   2. A man may use *bravado* to attempt to impress women.

(T/F)   3. An *imbroglio* is a minor problem.

(T/F)   4. Jessica is living *la dolce vita:* her husband left her with three kids, she can't find a job, and she has a serious heart problem.

(T/F)   5. If you're eating *alfresco,* you're eating outside.

(T/F)   6. *Cognoscenti* are experts in a particular field.

(T/F)   7. If one speaks at all during an opera, one should do so *sotto voce*.

(T/F)   8. People show *gusto* toward things they don't like.

(T/F)   9. Professional athletes are generally **not** members of the *literati.*

(T/F) 10. Manhattan's Wall Street is a good place to practice *il dolce far niente.*

ANSWERS: all false except (2), (5), (6), (7), and (9).

Day 21
MORE LATIN

FILL IN THE BLANKS

Fill each blank below with one of the following snob words. Each word is used only once.

terra firma	ipso facto
carpe diem	ex post facto
i.e.	deus ex machina
e.g.	mea culpa
modus operandi	ne plus ultra

1. After the ten-hour flight, it was quite a relief to set foot on _____.

2. The _____ of fashionable winter resorts is Switzerland's swank St. Moritz.

3. Europe is also home to many other stylish winter resorts, _____, Courchevel, Megève, and Cortina.

4. Since the 1960s, the Swiss resort of Gstaad has been popular with the *jet set*, _____, people with time and money to travel the world in search of pleasure.

5. After falling and breaking her leg, Brigitte confessed to us, _____, that she'd never learned to ski.

6. She then performed a tearful _____, begging everyone's forgiveness for ruining the trip.

7. The poor girl assumed—quite wrongly—that her broken leg would _____ end the ski trip for everyone in the party.

8. "_____!" I said to the group. "We're wasting precious slope time by worrying about Brigitte's leg."

9. Then came the _____: a renowned orthopedic surgeon, who happened to be staying at our hotel, performed a revolutionary surgical technique, and Brigitte returned to the slopes immediately.

10. This time she had a ski instructor, with whom she flirted unceasingly. That's her _____, of course.

ANSWERS: (1) terra firma; (2) ne plus ultra; (3) e.g.; (4) i.e.; (5) ex post facto; (6) mea culpa; (7) ipso facto; (8) carpe diem; (9) deus ex machina; (10) modus operandi

Day 22
USEFUL FRENCH PHRASES

SENSE...OR NONSENSE?

Place a check beside each sentence that makes sense.

____ 1. I really like Claire's wedding dress—it has a certain *au contraire.*

____ 2. The desk was decorated with *carte blanche* executed in ivory and pewter.

____ 3. Jan's kitchen has a certain *je ne sais quoi.* It really speaks to me.

____ 4. The exterior of my husband's new car is done in *fait accompli.*

____ 5. We thought we'd be invited to Joe's bar mitzvah, but in the end, he celebrated *en famille.*

____ 6. Aunt Mabel took Jeremy on a *tour de force:* she made him see Germany, Switzerland, and Luxembourg in just three days.

____ 7. When bad things happen, it's best to sigh and murmur, *"C'est la vie."*

____ 8. It was the happiest day of my life, so when Marc asked how I was, I said, *"Comme ci, comme ça."*

____ 9. Francine suggested a neighborhood *tête-à-tête* to discuss the matter.

____ 10. The practice of separating children from their families at the Mexican border became a *cause célèbre.*

ANSWERS: numbers (3), (5), (7), and (10) should be checked.

Day 23
EXCLUSIVE SHOPPING

MATCHING

Match each snobby shopping street with its city.

____ 1. Madison Avenue   a. Beverly Hills

____ 2. Bahnhofstrasse   b. New York

____ 3. Fifth Avenue   c. San Francisco

____ 4. Via Monte Napoleone   d. Rome

____ 5. Rodeo Drive   e. Zurich

____ 6. Union Square   f. Palm Beach

____ 7. Via dei Condotti   g. London

____ 8. Bond Street   h. Paris

____ 9. Avenue Montaigne   i. Milan

____ 10. North Michigan Avenue j. Chicago

____ 11. Worth Avenue

ANSWERS: (1) b; (2) e; (3) b; (4) i; (5) a (6) c; (7) d; (8) g; (9) h; (10) j; (11) f

Day 24

WORDS FROM VARIOUS LANGUAGES

TRUE OR FALSE

(T/F) 1. *Schadenfreude* is the act of taking pleasure in some-one else's pain.

(T/F) 2. Members of the *intelligentsia* are well educated people who often exert political influence.

(T/F) 3. A man who suddenly becomes a billionaire in his nineties could be called a *Wunderkind*.

(T/F) 4. A traditional production of Shakespeare's *Romeo and Juliet* is a *Gesamtkunstwerk*.

(T/F) 5. It's redundant to say "the *hoi polloi*."

(T/F) 6. A *dacha* is a country house anywhere in Europe.

(T/F) 7. *Weltschmerz* is a feeling of sorrow for things that are wrong with the world.

(T/F) 8. To go *mano a mano* means to take someone's hand in friendship.

(T/F) 9. You should give someone one *kudo* if they've done one good thing, and several *kudos* if they've done multiple good things.

(T/F) 10. A *peccadillo* is a large sin or major mistake.

ANSWERS: all false except (1), (2), (5), and (7).

Day 25

DINING OUT IN FRENCH & ITALIAN

MATCHING

____ 1. *trattoria*   a. 'fixed price'

____ 2. *osteria*   b. only open at mealtimes

____ 3. *brasserie*   c. everyone eats the same thing at the same time

383

___	4. *bistro*	d. usually open late into the night
___	5. *prix fixe*	e. smallest and simplest type of Italian eatery
___	6. *table d'hôte*	f. appetizer that is sometimes complimentary
___	7. *antipasto*	g. italian eatery, usually family run
___	8. *plat du jour*	h. may include olives, cold vegetables, and sausages
___	9. *amuse-bouche*	i. good person to know for a last-minute dinner reservation
___	10. *maître d'hôtel*	j. 'plate of the day'

ANSWERS: (1) g; (2) e; (3) d; (4) b; (5) a (6) c; (7) h; (8) j; (9) f; (10) i

Day 26
HIGHFALUTIN' FILM TERMS

MULTIPLE CHOICE

1. Which of the following terms can mean 'filmmaker'?
    a. *cinephile*
    b. *cinéaste*
    c. either of the above
2. Which of the following is **not** part of *mise-en-scène?*
    a. placement of actors
    b. catering services
    c. location
3. Proponents of the *nouvelle vague* believed:
    a. the best films are made by *auteurs*
    b. all films should include seascapes
    c. films should be vague
4. *Citizen Kane* lost its status as "best film ever made" to which of the following films in 2012?
    a. François Truffaut's *Jules et Jim*
    b. Alfred Hitchcock's *Vertigo*
    c. George Lucas's *The Empire Strikes Back*

5. *Cinéma-vérité* is a style of filmmaking used for:
   a. very cinematic films
   b. low-budget foreign soap operas
   c. documentaries

6. *Montage,* in its European sense, means:
   a. horseback riding in films
   b. the process of editing a film
   c. making films in mountainous areas

7. The genre of dark Hollywood crime films is called:
   a. *films noirs*
   b. *filme noire*
   c. *film noir*

8. *Jump cuts* occur:
   a. in error
   b. on purpose
   c. for both reasons

9. A person who loves films may be called a:
   a. *cinéaste*
   b. *cinephile*
   c. either of the above

10. In *auteur theory*, the director of a film is similar to:
   a. the framer of a painting
   b. the writer of a novel
   c. the engineer of a building

ANSWERS: (1) b; (2) b; (3) a; (4) b; (5) c; (6) b; (7) c; (8) c; (9) c; (10) b

Day 27
SEA & SKI VACATIONS

MULTIPLE CHOICE

1. *San Martín de los Andes* is:
   a. a Caribbean island
   b. a city in Colombia
   c. an Argentine resort

2. The "1850" in *Courchevel 1850* stands for:
    a. the town's permanent population
    b. the town's snobby attitude
    c. the town's altitude in meters

3. Formerly home to the whaling industry, this snobby vacation spot retains a down-home vibe:
    a. *the Hamptons*
    b. *Martha's Vineyard*
    c. *Saint-Barthélemy*

4. *St. Moritz* is:
    a. the world's first winter resort
    b. the world's snobbiest winter resort
    c. both of the above

5. A colonial gem on Colombia's Caribbean coast:
    a. *St. Moritz*
    b. *Courchevel 1850*
    c. *Cartagena*

6. One of the Caribbean's best food scenes is in/on:
    a. *Saint-Barthélemy*
    b. *Cartagena*
    c. *Bora Bora*

7. *The Hamptons* is:
    a. a group of twenty villages on Long Island
    b. one of America's snootiest vacation spots
    c. both of the above

8. The glitziest U.S. ski area is:
    a. *Vail*
    b. *Aspen*
    c. *Courchevel 1850*

9. *Vail* is sometimes referred to as:
    a. "Wall Street on Ice"
    b. "Wall Street West"
    c. "Stockbrokers on Skis"

10. A South Pacific paradise in French Polynesia is:
    a. *Courchevel 1850*
    b. *Cartagena*
    c. *Bora Bora*

ANSWERS: (1) c; (2) c; (3) b; (4) c; (5) c; (6) a; (7) c; (8) b; (9) b; (10) c

Day 28
FINAL FRENCH SNOB WORDS

FILL IN THE BLANKS

Fill each blank with one of the following snob words. Each word is used once.

élan	**bon mot**
mot juste	**soirée**
pièce de résistance	**louche**
éminence grise	**bête noire**
enfant terrible	**frisson**

1. _____ a respected authority
2. _____ energy; enthusiasm
3. _____ a clever or witty remark
4. _____ the perfect word or phrase
5. _____ the most outstanding item or event within a group or series
6. _____ disreputable, often in an alluring way
7. _____ a successful person (usually young) prone to shocking remarks and outrageous behavior
8. _____ something or someone highly disliked

9. _____ a sudden strong feeling of emotion
10. _____ an evening event, often held outdoors

ANSWERS: (1) éminence grise; (2) élan; (3) bon mot; (4) mot juste; (5) pièce de résistance; (6) louche; (7) enfant terrible; (8) bête noire; (9) frisson; (10) soirée

I realize that was a long review, but I think it'll pay off in the end. If you're still having trouble with any of the words, please go back to the appropriate lessons and study them.

Meanwhile, I hope you enjoyed your time here at my camp. You're welcome back any time.

Remember, tomorrow you take the final exam, so get a good night's sleep.

Day 30

Final Snob Words Exam
SHOW US YOUR SNOB SIDE!

LOCATION: **BOSTON, MASSACHUSETTS**

No place in the United States is more intellectually snobby than the Boston metro area, home to **Harvard University** and the **Massachusetts Institute of Technology.**

And no address in Boston is more snobby than **Beacon Hill.** I happen to own a townhouse here on **Acorn Street**, a cobbled lane lined with brick sidewalks and antique gas lamps. The house absolutely *oozes* New England elitism, with its red-brick façade, black shutters, iron balconies, and window boxes filled with asparagus ferns.

Here you'll take your final exam, which covers all 250 snob words (and some bonus words) featured in this course. If you pass the test, you'll receive your Ph.D. in snobcabulary.

It's been a joy to guide you through the pleasures and perils of learning these vitally important and practical terms. We're going to miss you.

But don't forget about us! Please come back and visit often so we can help you maintain these snob words in your permanent vocabulary.

The best way to retain these words, however (as we've stated *ad nauseam*) is to *use* them—at every possible opportunity.

But back to the exam, or final game, rather. It's probably not what you expected. There are no multiple-choice, true-or-false, or any other typical exam questions. Surprise! The entire test is devoted to the final installment of *The Expensive Escapades of Marco and Giselle, Professional Beautiful People.*

Why? Because the best way to find out whether you truly know a word is to see if you can use it properly in context.

So, here we go! Show us your stuff! Fill the blanks in the following passages with snob words from the accompanying lists. Each word in a list is used just once in the subsequent passage. (For extra practice, however, we've included certain snob words in more than one list.)

You may need to make some words plural, and you may need to modify some words to make them comply with the gender and number indicated. Remember to use accent marks and to capitalize when appropriate.

Viel Glück, bonne chance, buena suerte, and good luck!

The Expensive Escapades of
MARCO & GISELLE
Professional Beautiful People

Episode Sixteen: Happily Ever After?

When we last left Giselle and Marco, they were in a restaurant in *Courchevel 1850,* France, where Giselle had paid an ex-boyfriend, Duncan, to show up and attempt to make Marco jealous. The plan worked.

In the first section of our final episode, we find Marco and Giselle in Colombia, where Marco plans to propose marriage.

Section 1: **Committing in Colombia**

Cartagena	bon vivant
entre nous	pied-à-terre
en plein air	faux pas
repartee	scion
hôtel particulier	parterre
nouveau riche	carriage trade
haute bourgeoisie	savoir faire
tapis vert	bon mot
beau monde	arriviste
mauvais quart	espalier
d'heure	

GISELLE: I absolutely *adore* colonial South American cities! Thank you so much for inviting me to meet your charming grandmother here in (1)_____. Since you referred to her place as a(n) (2)_____, I expected something smaller, but I'd have to describe this house—with its large front entrance court and this lovely garden in back—as sort of a Colombian (3)_____.

In fact, the garden reinforces the French motif, with these lovely (4)_____ of shrubs and flowers, as well as that large green (5)_____. And I adore those (6)_____ growing against the walls. Oh, how wonderful to be (7)_____ in the most romantic garden I've ever visited!

MARCO: I am happy you feel that way, but I must confess that my purpose in inviting you here was not to meet my grandmother, or to see her garden, charming as they both may be.

GISELLE: Then why *did* you invite me here?

MARCO: Giselle, this whole thing may have been a colossal (8)_____ on my part, since I am not sure how you feel about me, but to avoid putting either of us through a(n) (9)_____, I am going to dispense with the clever (10)_____ (although I know I am not much of a conversationalist) and the (11)_____ (though I realize I rarely come up with them) and get straight to the point. *(He gets down on one knee.)* Will you marry me?

GISELLE: *(unsurprised)* Of course I'll marry you.

MARCO: *(shocked)* You are giving me your answer...just like that? You do not want to think about it?

GISELLE: I've been thinking about it ever since I met you on that fateful day in Milan.

MARCO: Do you really mean it? I was so afraid that you— the (12)_____ of such a powerful American family—would find *my* family so inferior that you would not consider marrying into it.

As you are aware, while my mother is from the French (13)_____ (you know, fashionable society), my father behaves like a(n) (14)_____, or an insecure new arrival.

As I have told you, he was actually born into the Argentine (15)_____, and raised in Buenos Aires with a good education and the finer things in life. He should, therefore, conduct himself as a polished (16)_____.

But as you have witnessed, after spending his adult life out on the Pampas, he acts like a(n) (17)_____, throwing a great deal of money about with a complete lack of (18)_____.

GISELLE: I can't believe you were worried that I thought *your* family was inferior!

You know where *our* money comes from? Frozen seafood! (19)_____, my great-grandfather was a fisherman. Not exactly (20)_____ material.

ANSWERS: (1) Cartagena; (2) pied-à-terre; (3) hôtel particulier; (4) parterres; (5) tapis vert; (6) espaliers; (7) en plein air; (8) faux pas; (9) mauvais quart d'heure; (10) repartee; (11) bons mots; (12) scion; (13) beau monde; (14) arriviste; (15) haute bourgeoisie; (16) bon vivant; (17) nouveau riche; (18) savoir faire; (19) entre nous; (20) carriage trade

Section 2: **Fashion Forward**

In which Marco and Giselle continue their fascinating conversation in the garden of Marco's grandmother's house.

chic	haute couture
couturier	beautiful people
jet set	Coco Chanel
polo	fashion's Big Four
hoi polloi	fashionista
ne plus ultra	bon chic, bon genre
dernier cri	fashion week
bonhomie	*Women's Wear Daily*
glitterati	prêt-à-porter
flâneur	gauche
i.e.	

MARCO: Well, I guess it does not matter whether we descend from the (1)_____, that international group of well-heeled people who travel frequently to exclusive resorts, or (2)_____, as long as there exists a degree of (3)_____ between our families...and as long as we are madly in love.

GISELLE: I couldn't agree more. But will your mother accept the fact that I'm not a(n) (4)_____? I mean, she reads (5)_____ religiously, quotes the late (6)_____ constantly, and is always jetting off to one (7)_____ or another in one of (8)_____. I suppose she'd love to have a daughter-in-law who paid attention to the (9)_____.

MARCO: My dear, you worry too much.

GISELLE: Don't get me wrong. I absolutely love your mother, but we could not be more different. She always looks so (10)_____ in her (11)_____, with the personal number of every (12)_____ in Paris in her contacts. She's the (13)_____ of poise and refinement. I, on the other hand, am the exact opposite of (14)_____—that coveted upper-class French quality—in my bohemian (15)_____. I feel so (16)_____ when I'm around her.

MARCO: Not to worry, my dear—she loves and accepts you the way you are.

I am the one who has need to be concerned about acceptance. Your father gives me the idea that he sees me as a(n) (17)_____ of the world, aimlessly traveling the globe in search of adventure, wasting my life hobnobbing with the (18)_____, those people from glamorous fields like art and fashion, and the (19)_____ (who, as we all know, do not actually have to be physically attractive).

He does not seem to recognize the fact that playing professional (20)_____, (21)_____, riding a horse around a large field with a stick in one's hand, is an actual job.

ANSWERS: (1) jet set; (2) hoi polloi; (3) bonhomie; (4) fashionista; (5) *Women's Wear Daily;* (6) Coco Chanel; (7) fashion week; (8) fashion's Big Four; (9) dernier cri; (10) chic; (11) haute couture; (12) couturier; (13) ne plus ultra; (14) bon chic, bon genre; (15) prêt-à-porter; (16) gauche; (17) flâneur; (18) glitterati; (19) beautiful people; (20) polo; (21) i.e.

Section 3: Fear of Father-in-Law

In which the scintillating conversation continues.

joie de vivre	**de rigueur**
bravado	**carpe diem**
badinage	**il dolce far niente**
sprezzatura	**cricket**
la dolce vita	**off-piste**
badminton	**persona non grata**

croquet   c'est la vie
the Hamptons   gravitas
modus operandi   au contraire
gusto   tête-à-tête
rara avis

GISELLE: I know my father gives you a hard time about your lifestyle, but it's just good-natured (1)_____. In some ways, I think he's jealous of your (2)_____. With workaholism as his (3)_____, he's never enjoyed life himself.

As for your "job" as a polo player, I think he's also a little jealous of that, since the most strenuous thing he ever does is count his money. Oh, and put on his whites and play (4)_____ at our club in (5)_____.

He'd be better off playing (6)_____, where he'd have to vigorously swing a bat, or (7)_____, where he'd be forced to hit a birdie over a net. Or taking up (8)_____ skiing—that would get his heart beating.

MARCO: Yes, your father could do with some exercise. But despite your kind comments to the contrary, I know he thinks I lack (9)_____, and he gives me the distinct feeling I am (10)_____.

GISELLE: (11)_____, my love. My father actually thinks a great deal of you. For one thing, he admires your (12)_____. That confident (if not slightly arrogant), competitive spirit seems to come naturally to you Latins, but it's difficult for "Gringos" to pull off. Your (13)_____ is another quality he admires. You make everything look so easy. You have a(n) (14)_____ for life, a(n) (15)_____ attitude, or desire to 'seize the day,' that he lacks.

MARCO: Thank you, my dear, you have made me feel better, but I still think your father sees me as a lazy weirdo, if you will

excuse the colloquialism—a(n) (16)_____ with
the "less work is more" philosophy of (17)_____.
But, (18)_____! I cannot please everyone.

    GISELLE: You please me, and that's what matters.

    MARCO: I am so glad we had this (19)_____.
Let us prepare to share (20)_____! I think a little kiss is now (21)_____.

ANSWERS: (1) badinage; (2) joie de vivre; (3) modus operandi; (4) croquet;
(5) the Hamptons; (6) cricket; (7) badminton; (8) off-piste; (9) gravitas;
(10) persona non grata; (11) au contraire; (12) bravado; (13) sprezzatura;
(14) gusto; (15) carpe diem; (16) rara avis; (17) il dolce far niente; (18) c'est
la vie; (19) tête-à-tête; (20) la dolce vita; (21) de rigueur

Section 4:

Mapping out Matrimony in Manhattan

In which the Van de Kamps host Marco and his parents
(Ignacio and Alessandra Grimaldi) in New York to discuss different wedding options.

foie gras	truffle
kudos	soirée
en famille	comme ci, comme ça
terra firma	cognoscente
al dente	prosciutto
fraises des bois	haricots verts
antipasto	bon appétit
cuisine classique	mozzarella di bufala
Wagyu	jamón ibérico
bête noire	petits pois
crème fraîche	

MRS. VAN DE KAMP: Welcome to New York, all of you! *(She
air-kisses each guest three times toward alternating cheeks.)* Thank
you for flying all the way from Argentina. We could have held

our conversations via telephone, of course, but I much prefer doing it here, (1)_____. How was your flight?

MRS. GRIMALDI: To be honest, (2)_____.We came in Marco's plane, which is on the smaller side, so we had a great deal of turbulence—truly my (3)_____. It's so good to be back on (4)_____.

MRS. VAN DE KAMP: You poor dear! I'm sorry for all of you! Please, come warm yourselves by the fire. Giorgio, our chef, has prepared a(n) (5)_____ table. Please help yourselves to olives, meats, and marinated vegetables. (6)_____! Or, in Italian, *buon appetito!*

MR. GRIMALDI: Ah, my favorite, (7)_____ with cantaloupe! A match made in heaven. I adore Italian ham!

MR. VAN DE KAMP: Yes, Italian ham is wonderful, but I'm sure you agree that (8)_____, from Spain, is the best ham in the world.

MARCO: Oh, yes, and the (9)_____ would agree with you.

MRS. GRIMALDI: This (10)_____—obviously made from the milk of real water buffalo—is *divino* with these vine-ripened tomatoes and fresh basil!

GISELLE: Speaking of wonderful edibles, I have the most fantastic idea for the reception buffet: (11)_____ fillets—only the world's best beef will do, of course—topped with (12)_____ (I hope no one objects to that on moral grounds...you know, the *gavage,* or force feeding) and white (13)_____, served with buttered (14)_____ (just the tiniest ones) and (15)_____ (just the most thin and tender specimens), perfectly steamed (16)_____.

MRS. VAN DE KAMP: I suppose this makes me a devotee of (17)_____, but I think vegetables should be fully cooked.

GISELLE: Oh, mother!

MRS. VAN DE KAMP: Julia Child agreed with me! But let's not

argue in front of our guests. Alessandra, what do you think of Giselle's menu?

MRS. GRIMALDI: I find it *absolutely fabulous!* Are you thinking of an afternoon or an evening event?

GISELLE: I was thinking of a(n) (18)_____, since I find afternoon weddings tiresome. Don't you?

MRS. GRIMALDI: Abominably so! But might I suggest a dessert to go with the delightful menu you have just described? I think you'll love it: (19)_____ with sweetened (20)_____ and candied violets.

MRS. VAN DE KAMP: *Eureka!* It's so simple, yet so elegant! I must give you (21)_____ on such a perfect idea!

GISELLE: Yes, it *is* a wonderful idea. And Mother, while you, Daddy, and the Grimaldis continue to discuss wedding plans, I think Marco and I will retire to the dining room to discuss where we plan to live once we're married.

MRS. VAN DE KAMP: That is a *fantastic* idea, my dear. You can leave the wedding plans to us.

(Giselle and Marco depart for the dining room, leaving the four parents together.)

ANSWERS: (1) en famille; (2) comme ci, comme ça; (3) bête noire; (4) terra firma; (5) antipasto; (6) bon appétit; (7) prosciutto; (8) jamón ibérico; (9) cognoscenti; (10) mozzarella di bufala; (11) Wagyu; (12) foie gras; (13) truffles; (14) petits pois; (15) haricots verts; (16) al dente; (17) cuisine classique; (18) soirée; (19) fraises des bois; (20) crème fraîche; (21) kudos

Section 5: **Hot-Diggity Digs**

In which the parents continue their conversation.

Venetian plaster	prewar apartment
ad nauseam	co-op
faux marbre	fait accompli
de trop	shagreen
boiserie	au courant

verre églomisé	boulle
hôtel particulier	persona non grata
duplex	brownstone
trompe l'oeil	ormolu
pied-à-terre	ancien régime
ad infinitum	marquetry
parquet de Versailles	sotto voce

MRS. GRIMALDI: Well, here we are—the happy parents of the happy couple. But before we delve deeper into wedding plans, let me say that your home is *lovely*. There's nothing like a(n) (1)_____, of course. These large rooms! These high ceilings!

We've tried for years to obtain a two-story apartment like this—in other words, a(n) (2)_____—for use as a(n) (3)_____, but the (4)_____ boards always reject us.

MR. GRIMALDI: Yes, I'm not sure why, but we are definitely (5)_____ when it comes to Manhattan real estate.

MR. VAN DE KAMP: My condolences! The boards can be notoriously difficult. We stayed in our (6)_____ in the Village for several years after we bought this place until the board finally agreed to let us combine the two floors.

MRS. GRIMALDI: Well, I must say it turned out beautifully. The (7)_____ on these living room walls is absolutely yummy! Is it antique?

MRS. VAN DE KAMP: Yes! It's solid oak, taken from a Paris (8)_____ dating to the (9)_____. It was a shame the old place had to be demolished, but it was a(n) (10)_____ by the time we heard about it. The house was gone, and everything they salvaged was in a warehouse. The (11)_____ on these floors (which is actually in need of waxing) came from the same demolished dwelling.

MRS. GRIMALDI: Well, everything looks *fabulous,* especially this exquisite marble fireplace.

MRS. VAN DE KAMP: Oh, that's just (12)_____. There's actually a lot of (13)_____ going on in this apartment.

MRS. GRIMALDI: I would never have guessed! I assume the (14)_____ on the foyer walls is real. It would be difficult to fake the translucent effect of all those layers.

MRS. VAN DE KAMP: Oh yes, of course, that *is* real. But the (15)_____ design on that table, for example— in what seems to be (16)_____ work in tortoise-shell and brass—is simply painted.

MRS. GRIMALDI: Really? Well, I could go on making compliments (17)_____—truly, I could go on forever— but I pronounce the design *perfect.* Everything is significant, nothing is (18)_____. *J'adore* the way the green color and rough texture of this (19)_____ banquette contrasts with the perfect smoothness of that golden, gleaming panel of (20)_____. Inspired! And the entire scheme is a perfect backdrop for that Louis XV commode and its shiny (21)_____ mounts. Such a classic piece used in a contemporary, (22)_____ manner. I love it!

MR. VAN DE KAMP: *(turning to Mr. Grimaldi and speaking* (23)_____ *)* Our wives will go on about furniture (24)_____. Why don't we go to the library, where we can discuss more interesting matters?

MRS. VAN DE KAMP: I heard that, Myron! All right, you and Ignacio may go to the library, but I'll give you an assignment— come up with some options for the honeymoon. Giselle is considering a commune in Nicaragua! Please think of some more traditional ideas, for Marco's sake.

(The fathers leave for the library.)

ANSWERS: (1) prewar apartment; (2) duplex; (3) pied-à-terre; (4) co-op; (5) personae non gratae; (6) brownstone; (7) boiserie; (8) hôtel particulier; (9) ancien régime; (10) fait accompli; (11) parquet de Versailles; (12) faux marbre; (13) trompe l'oeil; (14) Venetian plaster; (15) marquetry; (16) boulle; (17) ad infinitum; (18) de trop; (19) shagreen; (20) verre églomisé; (21) ormolu; (22) au courant; (23) sotto voce; (24) ad nauseam

Section 6: **Fastidious Fashionistas**

In which the two mothers continue their conversation.

Wunderkind	Worth Avenue
Bora Bora	Fifth Avenue
Bahnhofstrasse	Union Square
lanai	belvedere
alfresco	enfant terrible
comme il faut	soigné
Madison Avenue	Via Monte Napoleone
bravo	treillage
Via dei Condotti	allée
pergola	Avenue Montaigne
veranda	orangerie
folly	chichi
grotto	North Michigan Avenue
Bond Street	tour de force
Rodeo Drive	West End

MRS. VAN DE KAMP: Well, here we are—alone. Now maybe we can get some work done.

MRS. GRIMALDI: Yes—exactly. But before we begin, might I say that you look *très* (1)_____ in that ensemble.

MRS. VAN DE KAMP: Oh, this? Thank you, but it's just a little thing I picked up on (2)_____ when I was in Rome last month. *I'd* like to know who *you* are wearing.

MRS. GRIMALDI: None other than the (3)_____ of Los Angeles fashion! Of course, he's young, he throws fits, he pulls ridiculous stunts, and he has the largest ego on (4)_____. But he's an *absolute genius.*

MRS. VAN DE KAMP: You mean Gianfranco Armucci, the greatest designer in California?

MRS. GRIMALDI: Who else? After wearing Gianfranco, it's painful to wear any other designer.

MRS. VAN DE KAMP: That would certainly appear to be so, although I just discovered an *amazing* up-and-coming designer in London—on (5)_____ in the (6)_____. His name is Robert Smith, and he is the very definition of a(n) (7)_____. So young, yet already so successful in such a difficult field.

MRS. GRIMALDI: I think I've heard of him. Did he, by chance, just open a Manhattan outlet on (8)_____? Or is it on (7)_____, just down from Ralph Lauren's store in the Rhinelander Mansion?

MRS. VAN DE KAMP: I must admit that I wasn't aware that Bobby had a New York shop at all. I've been to his boutique on (8)_____, in Paris, of course, and on (9)_____, in Milan. Oh, and I've been to his shop in Zurich, directly on the (10)_____.

MRS. GRIMALDI: Based on your comments, and many other things I've heard about this young man, we'll soon see him on (11)_____, in Chicago, on (12)_____, in Palm Beach, and in San Francisco's (13)_____.

MRS. VAN DE KAMP: One can only hope! But back to the wedding. Giselle and I have been toying with the idea of having it at our villa on (14)_____.

Obviously, it would not be a traditional Christmas wedding, since the island is so green and tropical—not exactly (15)_____, I know—but Giselle says she's bored with traditional Christmas weddings.

We've discussed holding the majority of the nuptial festivities (16)_____, with hors d'oeuvre served on the first-floor (17)_____, as well as on the second-story (18)_____.

MRS. GRIMALDI: You two have come up with a *fabulous* idea. *Bravo!* Or technically, I should say, (19)_____!

MRS. VAN DE KAMP: Thank you. We thought we'd have the actual ceremony in the charming secret garden, which is surrounded by (20)_____ covered in pink bougainvillea. Guests would walk from the house to the garden via a(n) (21)_____ of jacaranda trees. Then they'd pass through the (22)_____, which is covered in the sweetest-smelling jasmine, before joining the ceremony.

MRS. GRIMALDI: How divine!

MRS. VAN DE KAMP: But we can't decide whether to display the cake in the (23)_____, with its amazing views of the bay, or in the (24)_____, a divine little building in the form of a miniature Greek temple.

What do you think?

MRS. GRIMALDI: Why not have two cakes?

MRS. VAN DE KAMP: *Fabulous* idea! And because December nights can get quite warm on the island, I thought we'd put some tables in the (25)_____, so guests could escape the heat.

MRS. GRIMALDI: *D'accord!*

MRS. VAN DE KAMP: And in case of rain, we'd have the ceremony in the (26)_____. (I know, they're not common in tropical climates, but we have one there for my orchids.)

I thought we'd move all the plants up against the windows, and then decorate the interior with tulle, antique chandeliers, lilies, gardenias, and candles. Or would all that decoration cross the line from stylish into (27)_____ territory?

MRS. GRIMALDI: Certainly not! The entire event will be a complete (28)_____!

ANSWERS:(1) soignée; (2) Via dei Condotti; (3) enfant terrible; (4) Rodeo Drive; (5) Bond Street; (6) West End; (7) Wunderkind; (8) Avenue Montaigne; (9) Via Monte Napoleone; (10) Bahnhofstrasse; (11) North Michigan Avenue; (12) Worth Avenue; (13) Union Square; (14) Bora Bora; (15) comme il faut; (16) al fresco; (17) veranda; (18) lanai; (19) brave; (20) treillage; (21) allée; (22) pergola; (23) belvedere; (24) folly; (25) grotto; (26) orangerie; (27) chi-chi; (28) tour de force

Section 7: **A Little Night Music**

In which the conversation turns musical.

literati	tessitura
cantata	oratorio
intelligentsia	aria
staccato	sonata
Gesamtkunstwerk	virtuoso
opus	concerto
pizzicato	noblesse oblige
chamber music	

MRS. VAN DE KAMP: The only thing Giselle and I have *not* yet discussed is music for the reception. She, no doubt, will want something strange and nontraditional. I, however, will fight for (1)_____—I'd love to have several string quartets stationed around the property. One piece I will insist upon is the fourth movement of Bartók's *String Quartet No. 4.* It's all (2)_____. No bows allowed!

MRS. GRIMALDI: And what about the flute? There's nothing more wonderful than solo flute accompanied by a full orchestra. Molique's (3)_____ *69,* known as the *Flute* (4)_____ *in D Minor*, would be a wonderful addition to the evening. And I know a gentleman who is a(n) (5)_____ flautist!

MRS. VAN DE KAMP: Please do invite him! I'll invite the orchestra! And why not some solo piano? Beethoven's *Moonlight*

(6)_____ would be absolutely and completely *fantastic!* Not the first movement, of course, which is funereal, but the second, with its detached, (7)_____ passages, as well as the very fast-moving third movement.

I'd also love to have some vocal music. A few of Mozart's (8)_____ (you know, those sweet melodies from his operas) would be nice, as well as some nice Christmas (9)_____ and selections from the world's most famous (10)_____, Handel's *Messiah.* Pure heaven! Some of the soprano parts have a murderously high (11)_____, but I have an acquaintance (she's a soprano with the Met) who can pull them off exquisitely.

MRS. GRIMALDI: This whole event is going to be *absolutely fabulous!* Everything will be so completely integrated and harmonious—the food, the music, the décor. It will be a true (12)_____!

MRS. VAN DE KAMP: I certainly hope so. But let's not forget the guest list. *We* plan to invite around five hundred people, including friends, relatives, and some members of the (13)_____, whom my husband counts as acquaintances. Imagine, Myron fancies himself an "intellectual!" Now, how about *your* guest list?

MRS. GRIMALDI: Well, ours will be much smaller than yours, of course—just family and a few close friends.

Since we live on the Pampas, we rarely interact with other people, and certainly not with the (14)_____. (I love that word—doesn't it come from Russian?)

But with your permission, we *would* like to invite all the members of the household staff at our *estancia.* Not out of a sense of (15)_____, but because they have been with us for decades and are truly family to us.

ANSWERS: (1) chamber music; (2) pizzicato; (3) opus; (4) concerto; (5) virtuoso; (6) sonata; (7) staccato; (8) arias; (9) cantatas; (10) oratorio; (11) tessitura; (12) Gesamtkunstwerk; (13) literati; (14) intelligentsia; (15) noblesse oblige

Section 8: **Fathers Know Best**

In which we head to the library, where we check in with the fathers.

Courchevel 1850	**bistro**
brasserie	**prix fixe**
ski-in, ski-out	**entre nous**
St. Moritz	**osteria**
plat du jour	**piste**
table d'hôte	**dacha**
nouveau riche	**trattoria**
gastronome	**gourmand**
nouvelle cuisine	**al dente**
forage	**amuse-bouche**
gourmet	**epicure**
haute cuisine	**ad hoc**
mano a mano	**antipasto**
locavore	**cuisine classique**

MR. VAN DE KAMP: Welcome to my humble library! First things first—you *must* be hungry. My wife has lunch planned, of course, but at the rate she talks, who knows when that will happen. Let's find something to eat.

MR. GRIMALDI: Thank you, but I quite filled up on all the different and delicious (1)_____ your dear wife just served. *(He burps.)*

MR. VAN DE KAMP: Oh, please! That was nothing but a(n) (2)_____! Let's get some *real* food. I'd make a request of our chef, but he'd certainly tell my wife, who has me on an extremely strict diet. Trust me, you don't want to go (3)_____ with that woman!

MR. GRIMALDI: I understand completely.

MR. VAN DE KAMP: So, if we want to eat, we can sneak into the kitchen and make a(n) (4)_____ meal of whatever we find, or we can order something. Actually, let's just order! What suits your fancy?

MR. GRIMALDI: Obviously, from the size of my stomach, you can see I like almost everything, but I tend to favor French (5)_____. Within that category, however, I gravitate more to (6)_____, with its butter, rich sauces, and *foie gras,* than to the lower-fat and healthier (7)_____, with all its crisp vegetables.

MR. VAN DE KAMP: I'll go ahead and assume you're not a (8)_____, then, since I doubt you produce your own *foie gras* on the Pampas.

MR. GRIMALDI: Are you kidding? I'm an *omnivore!*

MR. VAN DE KAMP: Then I'll also assume you don't go out and (9)_____ for exotic mushrooms and rare berries.

MR. GRIMALDI: Ha! While I am a(n) (10)_____ in some respects (I *do* appreciate the pleasures of good food), I am more of a(n) (11)_____ than a(n) (12)_____. In other words, the end goal is to fill my stomach, as quickly and easily as I can.

MR. VAN DE KAMP: A man after my own heart, although I *do* fancy myself something of a(n) (13)_____. I don't cook, but I understand the basics of selecting and preparing good food, and I know a great deal of culinary history.

Be all that as it may, however, we need to find food, and we need to find it *now.* I don't know where to get *cuisine classique* at this hour, but if you'd be okay with Italian, I know a(n) (14)_____—less formal than a *ristorante,* of course—that makes the most divine pastas, perfectly cooked (15)_____. And they deliver.

Or, if you're in favor of taking a short walk, there's a(n) (16)_____ (an even *less* formal Italian place, as you know), two blocks away. No menu, of course, but the talented cook always serves a wonderful three-course, (17)_____ lunch. It's (18)_____, so everyone is served exactly the same thing at exactly the same time, which is 1 p.m. sharp. Oh, look, it's already ten after. We missed it!

MR. GRIMALDI: That is unfortunate.

MR. VAN DE KAMP: Yes, but we have several other options. If you happen to be in the mood for *home-style* French, there's a(n) (19)_____ down the street with a *cassoulet* to die for. I think they're still serving lunch. If not, our neighborhood (20)_____ serves meals at all hours. It also delivers. It's Tuesday, so the (21)_____ should be *steak tartare*. Could I interest you?

MR. GRIMALDI: Certainly!

MR. VAN DE KAMP: I'll have my butler order it immediately. While we wait, we can discuss...what was it?

MR. GRIMALDI: The honeymoon.

MR. VAN DE KAMP: Ah, yes! The honeymoon. Now, strictly (22)_____, this wedding will cost us both a fortune, so I suggest we go cheap on the honeymoon. I say let the kids stay in Bora Bora as long as they like, and then we send them to (23)_____, which, as you know, is in the Swiss Alps. I have a chalet there set directly *en* (24)_____, which makes it (25)_____. (Who wants the hassle of toting skis around?)

What European winter resort could be more glamorous, with the possible exception of (26)_____? But there you have to deal with all those (27)_____ Russians and their tasteless and arrogant chalets built to resemble (28)_____.

MR. GRIMALDI: Quite true.

ANSWERS: (1) antipasti; (2) amuse-bouche; (3) mano a mano; (4) ad hoc; (5) haute cuisine; (6) cuisine classique; (7) nouvelle cuisine; (8) locavore; (9) forage; (10) epicure; (11) gourmand; (12) gourmet; (13) gastronome; (14) trattoria; (15) al dente; (16) osteria; (17) prix fixe; (18) table d'hôte; (19) bistro; (20) brasserie; (21) plat du jour; (22) entre nous; (23) St. Moritz; (24) piste; (25) ski-in, ski-out; (26) Courchevel 1850; (27) nouveaux-riches; (28) dachas

Section 9:
Honeymoons and High Culture

In which the fathers continue their conversation.

frisson	après-ski
Weltschmerz	cinephile
film noir	pas de deux
nouvelle vague	intermezzo
opera seria	ipso facto
Citizen Kane	steeplechase
San Martín	jump cut
de los Andes	libretto
en pointe	cinéaste
bel canto	bravo
Vail	dressage
mea culpa	mot juste
peccadillo	auteur
opera buffa	Aspen
mise-en-scene	montage
cinéma-vérité	

MR. VAN DE KAMP: On the other hand, if Marco and Giselle want to honeymoon here in the States, I have a lovely chalet in (1)_____ (which is far too full of movie stars for my taste) with (2)_____ opportunities galore, such as shopping, dining, and even snow polo. I also own an amazing spread in (3)_____—another popular U.S. winter destination, as you know—but I never go there because all those Wall Street types drive me crazy.

MR. GRIMALDI: Good options, but I have one more: the newlyweds are welcome to use my chalet in (4)_____, although it will be summer there in December.

MR. VAN DE KAMP: Summer is good! And we wouldn't have to tell Giselle that you own the place! Slightly dishonest? Maybe, but not a sin—a mere (5)_____. If she finds out the truth, we simply offer a quick (6)_____.

At any rate, enough of wedding plans. My wife tells me you have quite an impressive *estancia*—I think that's how you say it—in Argentina.

MR. GRIMALDI: Yes, and you are welcome any time. I would love to show you the place, which is so large, and so remote, that it is best done on horseback.

MR. VAN DE KAMP: Thank you! I'd love to visit, and I'm actually something of an experienced rider. When I was younger, I competed in (7)_____—you know, you have to get your horse to do all kinds of difficult movements—and in (8)_____, which is, of course, a race with obstacles in the form of ditches and fences.

But tell me about *your* interests, other than painting cattle, which, I understand, you do frequently.

MR. GRIMALDI: Yes, I absolutely love to paint cattle. But I also love opera—especially the lighter, comic variety known as (9)_____.

MR. VAN DE KAMP: Opera! That's the only one of the performing arts that I don't understand at all. I must confess that I've always considered it (10)_____ *boring.* I know a little about ballet—what it means for dancers to be (11)_____, for example, or on their toes—and I can recognize a(n) (12)_____, a dance by two performers. But opera? I just don't get it.

MR. GRIMALDI: I think the problem is that you have only been exposed to (13)_____—serious opera— which is, in truth, *quite* insufferable.

During works in that category, I pray that there will be a(n) (14)_____ (a musical interlude that marks the halfway point in some operas), so I can gracefully escape.

Opera is also difficult to understand because of the language barrier, since the (15)_____ are in Italian, of course.

MR. VAN DE KAMP: That all may be so, but the other thing I dislike about opera is the singing style. So harsh, so heavy!

MR. GRIMALDI: That may also have to do with the particular operas you have seen. While many operas *do* require a rather strong vocal style, there is a sweeter style, called (16)_____, that many consider more pleasing.

Do not worry, I will take you to some great opera. Soon we will have you shouting, (17) "_____!"

MR. VAN DE KAMP: I hope so! I'm always willing to explore a new artistic genre.

I tried writing a novel once, but I had a very hard time finding the (18)_____, or coming up with exactly the right words to express what I wanted to say.

So now I've decided to pursue cinema. You could call me a(n) (19)_____, since I love film as an art form. You could also call me a(n) (20)_____ in the sense that I'm a devotee of motion pictures, but not in the sense that I actually make films.

I would *like* to make a movie, though—someday—either a dark, brooding (21)_____, full of pessimism and (22)_____, or a documentary in the (23)_____ style, in which I would ask interesting people probing questions about their lives using a hand-held camera.

Or maybe I'll toy with the (24)_____ genre, with an improvised script, amateur actors, natural lighting, and innovative editing techniques. I'd include plenty of jarring (25)_____ and (26)_____ (you know, those series of quick cuts that suggest the passage of time or add zest to action sequences).

I'd be the (27)_____, obviously, with complete control over the (28)_____, or costumes, settings, placement of actors...everything you see onscreen.

Of course, I'll never be able to produce anything approaching (29)_____—that film will never be equaled, let

411

alone surpassed—but I get a(n) (30)_____ of creative delight just thinking about the possibilities!

MR. GRIMALDI: Please, tell me more!

ANSWERS: (1) Aspen; (2) après-ski; (3) Vail; (4) San Martín de los Andes; (5) peccadillo; (6) mea culpa; (7) dressage; (8) steeplechase; (9) opera buffa; (10) ipso facto; (11) en pointe; (12) pas de deux; (13) opera seria; (14) intermezzo; (15) libretti; (16) bel canto; (17) bravo; (18) mots justes; (19) cinephile; (20) cinéaste; (21) film noir; (22) Weltschmerz; (23) cinéma-vérité; (24) nouvelle vague; (25) jump cut; (26) montage; (27) auteur; (28) mise-en-scène; (29) *Citizen Kane;* (30) frisson

Section 10: Hooray for Hollywood

In which Mr. Van de Kamp explains his screenplay.

Schadenfreude	pro bono
éminence grise	maître d'hôtel
cause célèbre	louche
Stanislavsky method	ex post facto
deus ex machina	quid pro quo

MR. VAN DE KAMP: I have a tentative screenplay for the dark and brooding feature film I mentioned. It's the story of a(n) (1)_____ named Franco Frizzelli, who runs the dining room of a top L.A. restaurant.

He's in love with an actress, Starletta, who frequents the place. But she has a boyfriend, Strong Powers, who's a rather (2)_____, yet powerful, Hollywood producer.

MR. GRIMALDI: Sounds good so far.

MR. VAN DE KAMP: It gets better. One night, Powers is found dead in his Beverly Hills pool. Frizzelli hears the news while working at the restaurant, and he's overcome with a bout of (3)_____. He stupidly announces that he's happy the producer died. "The jerk had it coming," he says.

Unfortunately for Frizzelli, the Los Angeles chief of police, whom many consider the (4)_____ of Southern California law enforcement, is dining in the restaurant at the time. He has Frizzelli arrested as a suspect.

Meanwhile, Starletta knows Frizzelli is innocent because it was *she* who killed Powers.

MR. GRIMALDI: How did she do it?

MR. VAN DE KAMP: She poisoned his drink, he went for a swim, and that was that.

Frizzelli suspects that Starletta is the culprit and confronts her. But since he's in love with her, the two reach a (5)_____: if Frizelli will stand trial, Starletta will be his girlfriend. And, since she happens to have a law degree, she will represent him (6)_____.

MR. GRIMALDI: That's the least she should do!

MR. VAN DE KAMP: Certainly! And the trial turns into a(n) (7)_____ bigger than the O.J. Simpson case.

MR. GRIMALDI: And how does it end?

MR. VAN DE KAMP: I'm not exactly sure. I was planning to have a massive earthquake strike right before the verdict, destroying the courtroom and everyone in it except Frizzelli and Starletta. But then I realized that would be too much of a(n) (8)_____.

My other idea was to have the California legislature pass a law, (9)_____, that statements made in restaurants *cannot* be used as evidence in criminal trials. Hence, Frizzelli would go free, and he and Starletta would live happily ever after.

MR. GRIMALDI: That would be a good ending.

MR. VAN DE KAMP: You think so? The whole thing will be very realistic. I'll insist, of course, that my actors follow the (10)_____, which means they'll have to re-live past experiences—mostly nasty, miserable ones—in order to bring true emotion to the set.

ANSWERS: (1) maître d'hôtel; (2) louche; (3) Schadenfreude; (4) éminence grise; (5) quid pro quo; (6) pro bono; (7) cause célèbre; (8) deus ex machina; (9) ex post facto; (10) Stanislavsky method

Section 11: Debate over Dwellings

In which we return to Giselle and Marco.

aerie	entablature
Tuscan villa	alfresco
pilaster	colonnade
portico	je ne sais quoi
passementerie	loggia
chinoiserie	loft
objet d'art	bergère
fauteuil	Palladian window
e.g.	étagère
élan	enfilade
pièce de résistance	screen print
de facto	

MARCO: Well, my dear, now that we are going to be husband and wife, we must decide where we are going to live. I was thinking of a(n) (1)_____ at the top of a nice high-rise building in Buenos Aires, with the principal rooms arranged in a(n) (2)_____ so that sunlight penetrates the whole apartment. I can also picture some Doric (3)_____, or square columns, in the living and dining areas to add a certain classical (4)_____.

GISELLE: You think we're going to live in Argentina? I assumed we'd get a nice (5)_____ in an old industrial building in Soho. And I thought we'd decorate it with pieces of (6)_____, (7)_____, lacquered screens, end tables shaped like pagodas, and Ming vases.

To add a bit of (8)_____, I'd throw in some assorted French pieces. Perhaps a couple of Louis XV (9)_____ (wide enough to accommodate women in poofy ball gowns—not that I'd ever wear one, but some women do), as well as, perhaps, an Empire-style (10) _____, you know, with the open arms.

I'd also get a nice (11)_____ to use to display my (12)_____, including my miniature paintings and my Fabergé eggs. But no curtains, and absolutely no (13) _____! I loathe all that froufrou.

MARCO: Decorate as you wish, my dear, and we can have as many dwellings as you'd like—in New York, Buenos Aires, Paris—and wherever else you please. I would like a weekend place in Italy, a(n) (14)_____ with a long and impressive (15)_____ across the front topped with a noble (16)_____.

The entrance would be through a grand and impressive (17) _____, of course, and there would be several large (18)_____ to let in the light. I would also like a second-story (19)_____, where we could dine (20)_____ but still have a roof over our heads.

And an office! I really do need a place to keep my files, pay my bills, and do my taxes, which I only have time for on weekends. Currently, my (21) _____ office is my plane, but that's not working out so well.

But I digress. The (22)_____ of this Italian retreat would be my Andy Warhol (23)_____ of a Campbell's Soup can, which I would display in a special alcove in the foyer.

ANSWERS: (1) aerie; (2) enfilade; (3) pilasters; (4) je ne sais quoi; (5) loft; (6) chinoiserie; (7) e.g.; (8) élan; (9) bergère; (10) fauteuil; (11) étagère; (12) objets d'art; (13) passementerie; (14) Tuscan villa; (15) colonnade; (16) entablature; (17) portico; (18) Palladian windows; (19) loggia; (20) alfresco; (21) de facto; (22) pièce de résistance; (23) screen print

Section 12: **the Final Stretch**

In which our story comes to a touching conclusion.

bastide	chiaroscuro
papier peint	in situ
Old Masters	sfumato
Martha's Vineyard	outré
lithograph	tour de force
ad nauseam	Saint-Barthélemy
imbroglio	triptych
etching	chaise longue
atelier	carte blanche
gouache	chintz
porte-cochère	par excellence

GISELLE: Frankly, I think placing a Warhol soup can in a traditional Italian setting is a little (1)_____, but I don't want to cause a(n) (2)_____. Have it your way.

But speaking of weekend places, *I* would really like a(n) (3)_____ in Provence with an elaborate wrought iron (4)_____ giving vehicles access to a front courtyard.

Behind the house, I'd install a large swimming pool, built (5)_____, of course, not prefabricated, and surrounded by half a dozen (6)_____ covered in bright floral (7)_____. Inside, I'd like some antique, hand-painted (8)_____ to brighten up the walls. It would be a complete (9)_____.

MARCO: No doubt. And while we obviously have very different tastes when it comes to living spaces, you'll always have (10)_____ to decorate however you wish.

GISELLE: Thank you. I suppose we could continue to discuss decorating schemes (11)_____, but let's talk a little more about your taste in art. Do you like any artists other than Andy Warhol?

MARCO: Of course! I own several (12)_____, for example. I am fascinated by the techniques those artists used, including (13)_____, which, as you probably know, is a blurring of outlines, and (14)_____, which is the use of extreme contrast between light and dark.

GISELLE: Yes, I'm very familiar with those terms! Two summers ago, my mother sent me to Paris to be an apprentice in the (15)_____ of Jean-Claude van Manoir, an artist (16)_____.

In addition to paintings, he does (17)_____, prints made through a process that makes use of a wax-coated metal plate. He also does (18)_____, which are prints made through a process that originally used a piece of stone.

Before I left Paris, Jean-Claude gave me an absolutely gorgeous (19)_____ of a banana grove done in (20)_____ (a medium similar to watercolor, but opaque enough to allow for corrections).

All three panels of the work are now hanging in my parents' villa on (21)_____. We had it, for a time, at our place on (22)_____, but the piece's tropical vibe clashed with the New England Puritan thing. It goes much better in the Caribbean.

MARCO: I am sure it is a lovely piece, my dear, but nothing can compare to *your* loveliness.

GISELLE: Thank you, Marco. You know, I honestly don't care where we live, or how we decorate, as long as we're together. Forever.

ANSWERS: (1) outré; (2) imbroglio; (3) bastide; (4) porte-cochère (5) in situ; (6) chaises longues; (7) chintz; (8) papier peint; (9) tour de force; (10) carte blanche; (11) ad nauseam; (12) Old Masters; (13) sfumato; (14) chiaroscuro; (15) atelier; (16) par excellence; (17) etchings; (18) lithographs; (19) triptych; (20) gouache; (21) Saint-Barthélemy; (22) Martha's Vineyard

Take a moment to dry your eyes. Don't worry—you haven't seen the last of Marco or Giselle. They'll be back with us in the next course in this series, *Snob Words, Part Deux: 30 Days to an Even More Sophisticated Vocabulary*.

Now add up your scores from all twelve sections of the exam. Then consult the following table to see where you stand:

245-265	We hereby present you with your **Ph.D. in snobcabulary**. Congratulations!
200-245	**Go back and study** the review on Day 29; then take the final exam again.
0-200	**What happened?** Take the course again, and then we'll talk.

No matter how you did on the exam (we assume you did well), we thank you for joining us on this journey, and we look forward to seeing you on the next one. We also hope to see you frequently at snobwords.com.

Meanwhile, use the 250 snob words you've just mastered at every opportunity!

WORD LIST

Page numbers refer to the most complete definition of each word.